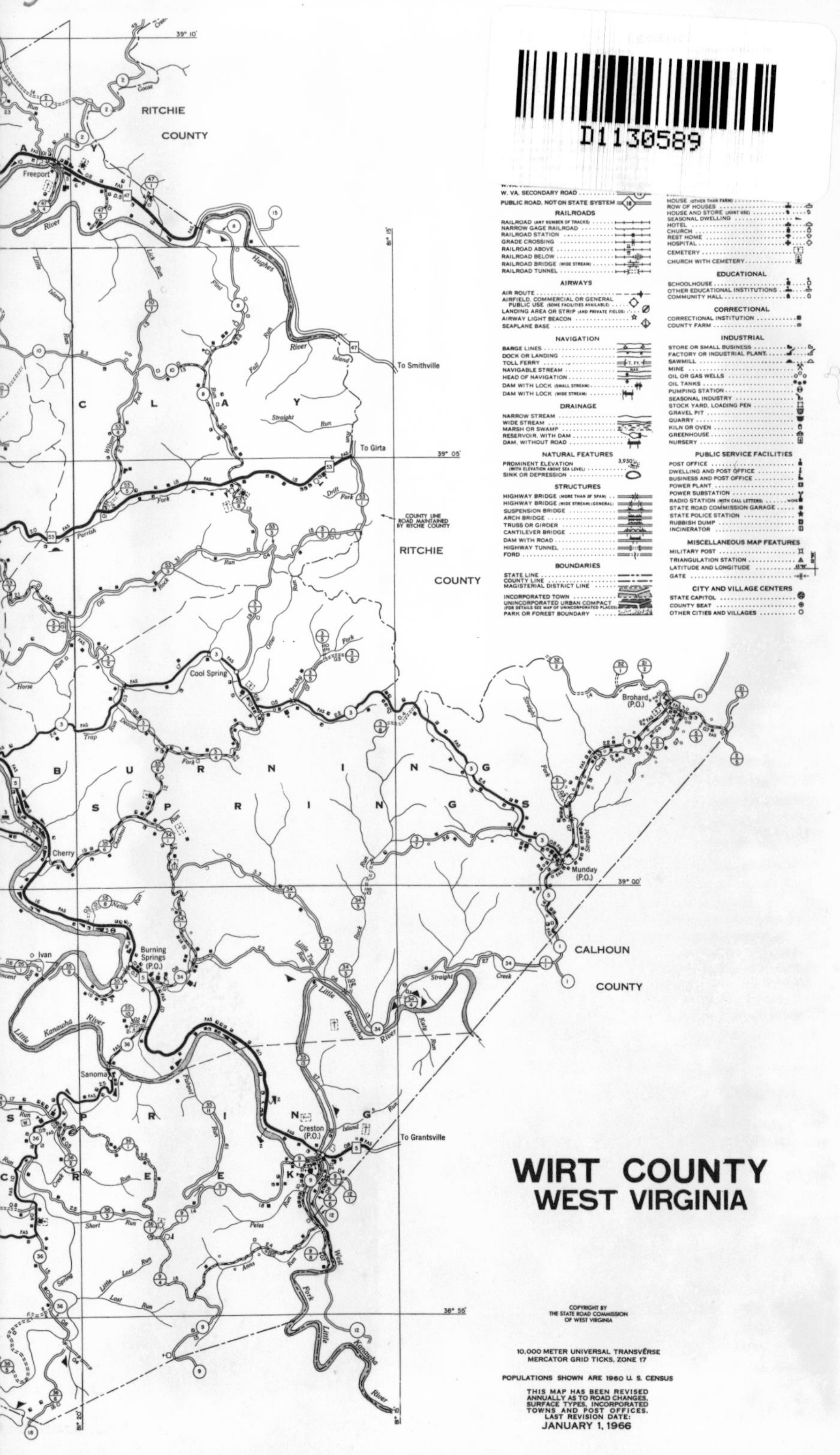

D1130589
RITCHIE
COUNTY
Freeport
To Smithville
C L A Y
To Girta
39° 10'
39° 05'
81° 15'
COUNTY LINE ROAD MAINTAINED BY RITCHIE COUNTY
RITCHIE
COUNTY
Cool Spring
B U R N I N G S
S P R I N G S
Brohard (P.O.)
Munday (P.O.)
39° 00'
Cherry
Ivan
Burning Springs (P.O.)
CALHOUN
COUNTY
Sanoma
S P R I N G
C R E E K
Creston (P.O.)
To Grantsville
38° 55'
81° 20'
81° 10'
Little Kanawha River
Hughes River
W. VA. SECONDARY ROAD
PUBLIC ROAD, NOT ON STATE SYSTEM
RAILROADS
RAILROAD (ANY NUMBER OF TRACKS)
NARROW GAGE RAILROAD
RAILROAD STATION
GRADE CROSSING
RAILROAD ABOVE
RAILROAD BELOW
RAILROAD BRIDGE (WIDE STREAM)
RAILROAD TUNNEL
AIRWAYS
AIR ROUTE
AIRFIELD, COMMERCIAL OR GENERAL PUBLIC USE (SOME FACILITIES AVAILABLE)
LANDING AREA OR STRIP (AND PRIVATE FIELDS)
AIRWAY LIGHT BEACON
SEAPLANE BASE
NAVIGATION
BARGE LINES
DOCK OR LANDING
TOLL FERRY
NAVIGABLE STREAM
HEAD OF NAVIGATION
DAM WITH LOCK (SMALL STREAM)
DAM WITH LOCK (WIDE STREAM)
DRAINAGE
NARROW STREAM
WIDE STREAM
MARSH OR SWAMP
RESERVOIR, WITH DAM
DAM, WITHOUT ROAD
NATURAL FEATURES
PROMINENT ELEVATION (WITH ELEVATION ABOVE SEA LEVEL)
SINK OR DEPRESSION
STRUCTURES
HIGHWAY BRIDGE (MORE THAN 20' SPAN)
HIGHWAY BRIDGE (WIDE STREAM) (GENERAL)
SUSPENSION BRIDGE
ARCH BRIDGE
TRUSS OR GIRDER
CANTILEVER BRIDGE
DAM WITH ROAD
HIGHWAY TUNNEL
FORD
BOUNDARIES
STATE LINE
COUNTY LINE
MAGISTERIAL DISTRICT LINE
INCORPORATED TOWN
UNINCORPORATED URBAN COMPACT (FOR DETAILS SEE MAP OF UNINCORPORATED PLACES)
PARK OR FOREST BOUNDARY
HOUSE (OTHER THAN FARM)
ROW OF HOUSES
HOUSE AND STORE (JOINT USE)
SEASONAL DWELLING
HOTEL
CHURCH
REST HOME
HOSPITAL
CEMETERY
CHURCH WITH CEMETERY
EDUCATIONAL
SCHOOLHOUSE
OTHER EDUCATIONAL INSTITUTIONS
COMMUNITY HALL
CORRECTIONAL
CORRECTIONAL INSTITUTION
COUNTY FARM
INDUSTRIAL
STORE OR SMALL BUSINESS
FACTORY OR INDUSTRIAL PLANT
SAWMILL
MINE
OIL OR GAS WELLS
OIL TANKS
PUMPING STATION
SEASONAL INDUSTRY
STOCK YARD, LOADING PEN
GRAVEL PIT
QUARRY
KILN OR OVEN
GREENHOUSE
NURSERY
PUBLIC SERVICE FACILITIES
POST OFFICE
DWELLING AND POST OFFICE
BUSINESS AND POST OFFICE
POWER PLANT
POWER SUBSTATION
RADIO STATION (WITH CALL LETTERS)
STATE ROAD COMMISSION GARAGE
STATE POLICE STATION
RUBBISH DUMP
INCINERATOR
MISCELLANEOUS MAP FEATURES
MILITARY POST
TRIANGULATION STATION
LATITUDE AND LONGITUDE
GATE
CITY AND VILLAGE CENTERS
STATE CAPITOL
COUNTY SEAT
OTHER CITIES AND VILLAGES
WIRT COUNTY
WEST VIRGINIA
COPYRIGHT BY THE STATE ROAD COMMISSION OF WEST VIRGINIA
10,000 METER UNIVERSAL TRANSVERSE MERCATOR GRID TICKS, ZONE 17
POPULATIONS SHOWN ARE 1960 U. S. CENSUS
THIS MAP HAS BEEN REVISED ANNUALLY AS TO ROAD CHANGES, SURFACE TYPES, INCORPORATED TOWNS AND POST OFFICES.
LAST REVISION DATE:
JANUARY 1, 1966

The
William Edward Reis
Library

Allegheny College

Warning in Appalachia

LOUIS REED

917.54
R251w

Warning in Appalachia

A STUDY OF WIRT COUNTY,
WEST VIRGINIA

by

Louis Reed

WEST VIRGINIA UNIVERSITY LIBRARY
MORGANTOWN
1967

Copyright © 1967
LOUIS REED
ELIZABETH, W. VA.

Library of Congress Catalog Card No. 67-16503

McClain Printing Company
Parsons, West Virginia

To Mildred, my wife.

CAT Nov 19'74

210284

9-27-74 B&T 7.00 HEW

Introduction

The subject of this study is Wirt County, West Virginia, where I was born and where some of my great-grandparents are buried, about which at the outset the following particulars are furnished:

WIRT COUNTY, WEST VIRGINIA

FORMATION: Formed by act of the General Assembly as Wirt County, Virginia, in 1848 from older adjoining counties. Became Wirt County, West Virginia, June 20, 1863. Named in the Act creating the county in honor of William Wirt, Special Prosecutor for the Government in the treason trial of Aaron Burr and Harman Blennerhassett, and Attorney General of the United States during the administrations of James Monroe and John Quincy Adams. William Wirt served as Attorney General longer than any other man (twelve years). He was candidate for President of the United States against Andrew Jackson in 1832, and received the seven votes of the state of Vermont in the Electoral College. So far as is known he never set foot in the county which bears his name.

AREA: 234.41 square miles.

LOCATION: Little Kanawha River near Ohio Valley.

COUNTY SEAT: Elizabeth. Named in honor of Elizabeth Beauchamp, the wife of a man who owned a plantation there and built a red brick house which still stands. The house, now a museum, was built about 1830, and was formerly owned by my uncle, Edward V. Black. The population of Elizabeth in 1960 was 767.

POPULATION: Wirt County in 1960, 4,391.

VOTING PRECINCTS: 16.

TOTAL ASSESSED VALUATION: $9,269,165.00 (1964).

The population of 4,391, according to census of 1960, gives Wirt County the distinction of having the fewest inhabitants of the fifty-five counties of the State. Compare 4,391 with 252,925, the 1960 population of Kanawha County, West Virginia, and it becomes apparent that the practice of establishing a county court house within easy travel distance of every citizen, which prevailed in the early days of this republic, did not envision the age of the automobile, the jet airplane, and the space rocket. Remember that each county is a political unit of the State electing its own law making and law enforcement officers, supporting and supervising its own free schools with State aid, maintaining the roads within its borders, though the State Road Commission pays road employees, and, above all, levying taxes on its citizens to defray the ever increasing costs of government. Consider that Wirt County was and is a marginal agricultural county, and that, in these days of automated work, marginal agricultural areas everywhere are losing population to industrial areas. In this context lies the real image of the people who live here, and, to lesser extent, the image of Appalachia.

In choosing my native county for this study, I am aware of many advantages and some disadvantages. All the advantages occur in the area of mythology, legend, and tradition. For instance, in my boyhood my grandfather Reed told me the story of Mrs. Thomas Cunningham, who was captured by marauding Indians, after seeing her four children murdered, in 1785, remained three years with the savages, and was finally ransomed by the notorious renegade Simon Girty in 1788. (See Withers' *Chronicles of Border Warfare*, pp. 367-372.) My grandfather often talked to Mrs. Cunningham when he was a boy. (She lived until 1852.) I think it worthy of note that I have talked to a man who in turn had talked to a woman who was captured by the Indians before the Constitution of the United States was written and adopted.

The disadvantages are those that occur naturally when one human being undertakes observations of other human beings. In such situations the ideal of detachment, so necessary to scientific research, is often impossible of attainment. This is particularly true when one endeavors to study his own relatives, friends, and neighbors, a combination that in former times would have been called a tribe. The tribal influence indeed is so strong that I am inserting here some essential autobiography.

Wirt County today is an insignificant portion of real estate on the western edge of the Appalachian plateau. Time and erosion have converted the plateau into a chain of low-lying mountains. Geologically, the land is very old and has often been inundated by the sea. Many years ago, I saw a core specimen of rock, containing the fossilized remains of trilobites, which had been brought up from 5,800 feet beneath the surface.

The first inhabitants of Wirt County, whose memorials are known to us, were the legendary Mound Builders. A small prehistoric mound stands within a mile of my home. At one time it was believed that the Mound Builders were a separate race of men antedating the American Indian, but modern scholarship makes them ancestors of the Indian tribes found in North America by the Spanish, French and English explorers. They were a Stone-Age people. They left behind a large assortment of flint arrowheads, stone axes, spear points, bone awls, and stone vessels in addition to their earthen mounds. The mounds themselves appear to have been places of burial and sacrifice.

The descendants of the Mound Builders were the tribal Indian nations known to history. They, too, were a Stone-Age people, though for some reason they discontinued the practice of building mounds. Upon the arrival of the white man in America, the Indians were either dispossessed, expelled, or exterminated. The white men appropriated their lands. In the process there was a great deal of fraternizing, so that the descendants of frontiersmen today have much Indian blood in their veins. Since I am part Indian myself, I have sometimes wondered if that Indian mound near my home could possibly be the final resting place of one of my own ancestors.

Such speculation is less fantastic than it seems if one considers the question of ancestors mathematically. Each of us has two parents and each of our parents had two parents. Allowing thirty years to a generation and assuming that none of the ancestors were related by blood, (which is preposterous), a child born in 1965 would have had 536,870,912 living ancestors in 1065 A.D. The year 1065 corresponds roughly to the date of the Norman Conquest of England. If the calculations are carried back to the time of Christ, the figures become astronomical. Since each human being certainly has two parents, the mathematical table seems to prove that representatives of the Europeanized white race are all related by blood within the past two thousand years, through a multiplicity of common ancestors, and the same probability may be urged with respect to other races of men long separated from the white race by geography. If it were possible to trace a family tree back far enough, a common ancestor could undoubtedly be found with the Chinese in Peking and with the Negroes in the Congo.

This brief discourse on ancestors is relevant because I spent a great deal of time trying to establish the national origins of the present inhabitants of Wirt County, the results of which are presented in a later chapter. What I could not determine was what was back of the national origin. If the national origin is French, what is a Frenchman? A German? An Englishman? Are not all hybrids of numberless tribes stretching back to prehistory, scattered and regrouped by wars, invasions, rapine, and slavery? If America is indeed the melting pot of the nations, there is nothing new in the process. The loss of identity on the part of countless tribes, languages, and religions, the perpetual modification and blending of cultures, and the centralization of political power in the upward progress of mankind, all testify that the melting of the nations is an attribute of civilization.

Here is my own autobiography: Louis Eckert Reed, born in Wirt County, 1899; attended one room school in Wirt County, 1905; lived and attended school in East Liverpool, Ohio, 1906-1908; lived and attended school in Wirt County, 1908-1912; lived and attended school in Boone County, West Virginia, 1912-1915; attended Davis and Elkins Academy, Elkins, West Virginia, 1915-1918; served in France and Germany in United States Army, 1918-1919; student at Cornell University, 1919-1923; married Ruth Baldwin in Norwich, New York, July 3, 1923; lived and worked in Kansas City and New York, 1923-1924; son William Baldwin Reed, born August 18, 1924; high school football coach in West Virginia, 1924-1925; student in Law school, 1925-1928; practiced law in Winfield, West Virginia, 1928-1934; wife contracted tuberculosis, 1929; free lance writer, 1931; short story republished in O'Briens, *Best Short Stories of 1933;* practiced law in Grantsville, West Virginia, 1934-1942; listed in America's Young Men 1935; listed in *Who's Who in the East,* 1936; served as Chief Investigator, Office of Price Administration, Charleston, West Virginia, 1942-1944; served as Administrative Assistant to U. S. Senator Chapman Revercomb, Washington, D. C., 1944-1949; wife died of tuberculosis in Washington, 1945; practiced law in Elizabeth, Wirt County, West Virginia, 1949 to 1965; married Mildred B. Johnston in Arlington, Virginia, 1961; Republican nominee for Secretary of State of West Virginia, defeated in General Election, 1964.

When I came back to Wirt County from Washington more than fifteen years ago, I did not foresee that I would ultimately write this book, even though an opportunity for writing was one of my reasons for returning. In sober truth my return, after an absence of thirty-eight years, contained some disappointments. On Capitol Hill an Administrative Assistant to a Senator is a person of considerable, though anonymous, importance. The Administrative Assistant is recognized everywhere as the Number One man in his Senator's life. As the head of my Senator's office staff, I spent my working hours in the luxurious surroundings of the Capitol and the Senate Office Building. Sometimes, I spent the evenings at cocktail parties, receptions, and other social affairs. THE PEOPLE was a phrase often heard in Senate debates, but THE PEOPLE were notably absent on the Washington cocktail circuit. To heighten the contrast, I was transported suddenly from the place where THE PEOPLE are talked about to the place where THE PEOPLE really are.

In this book I relate how I established a law practice in my native village and thereupon observed for the first time that many of my neighbors bore French names. Having been reared on the Scotch-Irish myth, I embarked on a project to determine the national origins of all the families in the county from their own family legends. Aside from plain curiosity, I thought at the outset that the information could be useful to an anthropologist. Then, I discovered that many of the family names appeared in the oldest documents of the colonies, that practically all the inhabitants of Wirt County claim to have American Indian blood, and that the people are unquestionably an amalgam of English, Scotch-Irish, French, German, and American Indian nationalities, with a trace of other nationalities. They are nominally Protestant in religion, though I was surprised when I compiled the statistics on church affiliation.

In the 1950's the after effects of automation of the coal mines had become apparent and Appalachia had acquired notoriety as a pocket of poverty. Such notoriety was not wholly deserved. As an officer of the local bank where the problem was not starvation but too many savings accounts, I had occasion to reflect on the role of radio and television in modern life. Radio and television reporters undoubtedly perform a useful function in disseminating news, but the nature of their work and their competitive impulse urges them toward sensationalism. They are masters of the one-day visit and they create public images that are stereotyped and overdrawn. Even in Appalachia a man does not bite a dog every day.

Gradually, I began to understand that a quantitative study of Wirt County, by a native, could be a useful contribution to knowledge. Is there a natural inference to be drawn from a community in which the average age is above forty-four years and in which one person in four is above sixty? With birth control established as a policy of the national government and with the span of life increasing each decade, it may be instructive to look at a fringe area which already bears the scars of aging and birth control.

LOUIS REED

Elizabeth, West Virginia
December 7, 1965

1. Recollections of 1910

WIRT COUNTY was not always the smallest county in the State in population. As a matter of fact, a century ago when Los Angeles, California, was a sleepy village and Phoenix, Arizona, was not even a post office, Wirt County had more people living within its borders than it has today. The following population figures for Wirt County are taken from the West Virginia Blue Book, an annual publication of the State Senate:

Census	*Wirt County Population*
1870	4,804
1880	7,104
1890	9,411
1900	10,284
1910	9,047
1920	7,536
1930	6,358
1940	6,475
1950	5,119
1960	4,391

The population curve of Wirt County shows that there was a steady if unspectacular growth in population from 1870 to 1900. Those were the days of big families, and the West was still open to exploitation and settlement. No one will ever know how many young men and women of Wirt County "went West" in the Nineteenth Century, but the total must have been considerable. I remember meeting about 1905 a man, named John Virtue, whose father and my own great-great-uncle had been killed by Indians in Kansas in the 1860's. As late as 1915 my grandfather, Amaziah Reed, was still corresponding with some of his cousins in Colorado. (Whatever happened to them?) Nevertheless, the population of Wirt County continued to grow until 1900 and began to decline in the decade 1900 and 1910.

In 1910 I was myself ten years of age, and I therefore

have personal knowledge of conditions in my own farm community and in the County generally at that time. The following information is taken from books, where books supply the answer, and from memories imprinted on the mind of a curious ten-year-old boy.

The population of Wirt County in 1910 was 9,047.

There was but one municipal corporation in the County, Elizabeth, the County Seat, though there had formerly been another municipality at Burning Springs, an oil town. More about Burning Springs later. Elizabeth was a village of about one thousand inhabitants, including the County officials, three doctors of medicine, four or five lawyers, two dentists, two druggists, and an undertaker. The village also supported three general stores, a hardware store, two shoe repair shops, two blacksmith shops, two hotels, one livery stable, and one commercial bank. (Forty-five years later I became a member of the Board of Directors of this bank.) Prior to this time there had been three saloons, but these had been voted out by local option.

Elizabeth boasted a fairly new (1897) red brick, two-story elementary school, which held winter sessions lasting six months for children and summer sessions called Institutes and lasting six weeks for teachers. There was no high school. The highest education obtainable in the County was an intimate knowledge of the Five Readers (by 1910 these were the Elson Readers instead of McGuffey's), Writing, Spelling, Arithmetic which included a special course called Mental Arithmetic, Geography, Physiology, American History, primary and advanced, State History, Civil Government (Civics), and Bookkeeping, single and double entry. Teachers were certified not by taking advanced courses elsewhere but by taking a written examination on the subjects they had studied in school and were expected to teach. (I passed this Uniform Examination, as it was called, when I was fourteen years old.) Certificates were graded One, Two, and Three, and salaries were adjusted accordingly. A person who held a Number One Certificate was generally credited with knowing everything worth knowing in books, with the sole exception of the Bible.

Elizabeth, in common with villages all over America, had its secret societies called lodges. As a boy I never saw the inside of these places, but I remember their names and their colorful funerals. There were the Masons, the Odd Fellows, the Knights of Pythias, and the Junior Order of United American Mechanics. There may have been others which escaped my attention. The local organization that delighted a boy the most was the Major Joe Steele Post of the Grand Army of the Republic. (Major Joe Steele was the son of Reverend Jonathan Steele, a Methodist minister, who lost four sons in the Civil War. Steele Magisterial District in adjoining Wood County is said to have been renamed in his honor.) The Grand Army had a band, and on special occasions, such as Memorial Day and the Fourth of July, the old veterans stuck out their chests, pulled in their stomachs, and marched through the streets. Because there were still a number of Confederate veterans in the area the band was under orders not to play "Marching Through Georgia"—a precaution stemming less from magnanimity than from the conviction that, if the band played it, war would erupt again.

There were five churches in Elizabeth, all Protestant. They were the Methodist Episcopal, the Methodist Protestant, since merged with the Methodist Episcopal, the Baptist, the Presbyterian, and the Church of Christ, commonly called Campbellites. Of the ministers in these churches only the Presbyterian was college and seminary trained. Throughout the remainder of the County were many other country churches of the same denominations as those in Elizabeth, the Methodists and Baptists predominating. In spite of the surprisingly large incidence of Irish and French names among the inhabitants, there was not, to my knowledge, a single Roman Catholic in the County. This is true today with one exception. In the 1930's a Catholic family named Earle bought a farm in Wirt County. I am told that they attend Mass in Parkersburg, twenty miles distant from Elizabeth.

Outside Elizabeth there were a few scattered sawmills, but the virginal forests that originally blanketed the hills and the valleys had already been chopped down. There was also a dwindling and depleted oil industry for Wirt County was the site of the second producing oil field in the United States. This was the Burning Springs Oil Field opened in 1860, and the site of an early oil rush. In 1861 Burning Springs, which had been a farm the year before, had 6,000 inhabitants. The town was destroyed by Confederate Cavalry under General William E. Jones in 1863, thereby becoming the first military oil objective in the history of warfare. In 1910 some of the oil wells were still pumping and a few optimistic entrepreneurs were still boring holes in the earth, but the impressive oil strikes were being made in such faraway places as Texas, California, Mexico, South America, and Southeast Asia. (Today the old Burning Springs oil field is practically a jungle. What will happen to Iran and Saudi Arabia when the wells run dry?) There were no coal mines because the workable bituminous coal seams in Wirt County are buried hundreds of feet beneath the surface.

The mass of the population was comprised of small farmers, though the word farmer in 1910 had a different meaning than it has today. Most of Wirt County, as is true of the whole of Appalachia, is unsuited topographically for farming on a large scale. Nearly all the land stands on edge between narrow valleys and steep hillsides, but the soil, nevertheless, is rich and the rainfall abundant. In a society isolated by distance from markets, farm families tend to become self-sufficient. Self-sufficiency was compelling to the earliest pioneers, and it was compelling to a lesser degree to the farmers of Wirt County in 1910. When I was a boy, farmers had discarded the spinning wheel, the carding machine, and the practice of making moccasins from animal hides. Clothes and shoes were bought at stores and so were such articles of food and comfort as coffee, sugar, and tobacco. The stores also furnished luxuries in the form of canned sardines, vienna sausage, oranges, bananas, soda crackers, and oysters in season. Yet, by and large, the food consumed by the farmer's family was produced on the farm.

In Wirt County and throughout Appalachia there were few, if any, tenant farmers. The farms tended to be small, but they were nearly all individually owned. Recently, I saw a television program about Appalachia in which it was stated that the natives were not farmers but displaced industrial workers, meaning coal miners. These people were farmers for more than a hundred years before the coal mines were opened. The typical farmhouse was located on a creek with some level land around it, and the farm included the adjoining hillsides for pasture and woodlots. The physical aspect of farmhouses varied according to the taste and the financial circumstance of the owner. The more affluent farmers built two-story frame houses, often in the shape of a T, surrounded by porches. A few lived in log cabins, relics of a bygone day. Some lived in mere shacks. Regardless of the appearance of the farmhouse itself, there were necessarily a number of outbuildings and enclosures—a barn for the livestock, a chicken house, a corn crib, a cellar house, a covered water well, a hog lot with feeding troughs, and fenced pastures. By 1910 worm rail fences had largely been replaced with barbed wire. Since there was no electricity and no running water, each farmhouse inevitably sprouted its outdoor privy plentifully supplied with newspapers and Sears and Roebuck catalogs.

The farmhouse with its outbuildings and enclosures was designed primarily for the raising and preservation of food. Each farm had some level land for a garden and corn field and corn was often raised on steep hillsides. A farmer owned or could borrow from his neighbor a limited assortment of plows. There was a fine steel plow drawn by a team of horses that was suitable for the level land in the valleys. A bull-tongued plow, often called a root jumper and drawn by one horse, was used on the hillsides. After the crops were planted, a double shovel plow was used to flush out the weeds between the rows. Other farm tools included mowing machines, cradles, hay rakes, disks, pitchforks, harrows, hoes, sledge hammers, carpenter hammers, shovels, pole axes, double bitted axes, adzes, crosscut saws, handsaws, scythes, sickles, posthole diggers, crowbars, cornplanters (not the modern type but a hand drill), cider mills, sorghum vats, buckets, shoe lasts for home repairing, steel traps, shotguns, rifles, hunting knives, paring knives, pocket knives, harness, saddles, sleds, wagons, and buggies. A farm also displayed a large assortment of earthen jars, churns, crocks, and jugs, all of which were useful in storing milk, making butter, and preserving food. The kitchen required an even larger assortment of pans, pots, jars, kettles, dishes, griddles, knives, forks, and spoons, and it was a poor family indeed that did not have a set of chinaware, at least for company.

To the self-sufficient farmer of those days, horses, cows, hogs, and chickens were an absolute necessity. The quality of his land and the numbers of his livestock established a man's place and that of his family in the social hierarchy. There were glaring inequalities in ownership, as there are today, but there was no real consciousness of class. Ever since the Declaration of Independence Americans have interpreted the word equality to mean equality of opportunity, and the most striking aspect of our republican system is the swift change which takes place constantly in the social maelstrom. In Wirt County, as elsewhere, the *haves* were generally the ones with brains, energy, and enterprise while the *have nots* were often lazy, shiftless, or stupid. (I am not discussing the deeper implications of this statement. A man, after all, is born with or without brains. I am merely reporting what I believe to be facts.) There was one man in the county who began as a farmer, acquired a store, bought other farms, and gained control of the bank. He remodeled a 22-room house in Elizabeth, was elected sheriff, and owned hundreds of horses and cattle. But he was the exception rather than the rule.

The ordinary farmer had at least two horses, two or more cows, half a dozen hogs, and a flock of chickens. With such a nucleus, even on a hillside farm, no one ever went hungry. The horses did the heavy work and also served as saddle horses. (What has happened to the millions of work horses that lived in rural America a mere half century ago? In 1963 only eleven horses were listed for taxation in Wirt

County, and the eleven included one mule.) The cows furnished milk and butter. The chickens not only provided eggs but also added zest to Sunday dinners. The hogs were butchered in the barnyard each fall, after which the hams and shoulders were smoked and cured, the side meat was salted, and the remainder was ground into sausage or rendered into lard.

Throughout the summer months the farmer, his wife, and his children worked steadily in preparation for the winter. The children picked scores of gallons of wild blackberries and raspberries, and the wife canned all not used immediately in stone and glass jars, sealing the jars tight with sealing wax. Every farm had its orchard—apple trees, peach trees, pear trees, plum trees, quince trees and grapevines, and the surplus fruit was likewise canned for winter use. An enjoyable family sport was making apple butter over an open fire in a twenty-gallon copper kettle. Sometimes, the making of apple butter continued for weeks and literally hundreds of gallons would be stored away.

The vegetables commonly raised on Wirt County farms were lettuce, sweet corn, beans, cabbages, potatoes, rhubarb, tomatoes, onions, beets, turnips, peppers, cucumbers, pumpkins, squashes, gourds, watermelons, and muskmelons. The vegetables were raised in the vegetable garden, which often contained clumps of gooseberry and currant bushes. For canning purposes sweet corn was ordinarily cut off the cob and cooked with green beans, cabbages were either sliced and tamped in the sauerkraut jar or were buried whole with the potatoes. At the potato harvest the farmer dug a large circular hole in his garden, and filled it with potatoes, cabbages, apples, and sometimes turnips. He covered the vegetables with a high, conical mound of earth, using a white oak board at the base of the mound for a convenient entry way, and there they stayed without freezing or rotting until needed. One of the less pleasing memories of my childhood is scraping potatoes out of the potato hole on a rainy winter night. Onions were dried in the cellar house. Pumpkins were kept in the cellar house also, but since pumpkins rot quickly they were often canned and so were beets. Watermelons and muskmelons were primarily summer foods, though watermelon rinds were used to make a table delicacy called watermelon preserves. Cucumbers of all shapes and sizes were converted into sweet and sour pickles. Field corn was carried on horseback to the mill to be ground into meal.

With all the food stored up for the winter, the Wirt County farmer could live comfortably on what today would be considered an infinitesimal sum of money. Hard money, in fact, was not easy to come by. The farmer could exchange eggs, chickens, hams, and other produce at a general store, but he had to earn money for taxes. Sometimes, he worked for more prosperous farmers at a wage of $1.00 for a ten-hour day; sometimes he got a job at a comparable wage at a sawmill or an oil rig. Sometimes he could sell a cow or a horse for cash. The price varied from ten to twenty-five dollars.

The horse and buggy days in Wirt County were more often horse and wagon days, since a buggy was a luxury. The roads were dusty in summer and often impassable for wheeled vehicles in winter. Mud and wet feet were common. During the fall, winter, and spring men, women, and children usually wore arctics (galoshes) or felt boots which were removed on entering a dwelling. Baths in the urban sense were unknown. Some farm families bathed only in the creeks and rivers in the summertime. Others used zinc wash tubs weekly. Houses were heated by wood fires, either open fireplaces or cast iron heating stoves. Cookstoves were called ranges and often burned coal in addition to wood. By 1910, the kitchen was always the warmest room in the house in winter and the hottest in summer.

The life was hard, though by no means unbearable. Infant mortality was high, but those who survived were tough and resourceful. Social life centered about the churches and the one-room schools. The winter season was the time for religious revivals and literary societies. The former were largely exercises in emotion in which the preacher expounded the dire consequences of hell and eternal damnation, and called on sinners to repent. The quality of the latter established the intellectual climate of each separate community.

Without discussing literary societies in detail, since the practice was widespread and the subject has been adequately treated by others, it should be noted that literary societies were essentially debating societies, that they operated under adopted rules of order, and that the right to debate was open to all who wanted to get up and speak, irrespective of age or sex. In those days women did not have the right to vote nor to serve on juries, but any woman could get up in a literary society and speak her mind on the subject under discussion. Many of them did. A favorite subject for debate was: Resolved that women should have the right to vote as well as men. The arguments used in favor of Woman Suffrage at that time sound utterly ridiculous today. Under Victorian standards, women were believed to be a notch higher than men in the moral sphere. It was argued, often by men, that if women could vote, crime and corruption in politics would disappear.

The quality of the debates was not high. There were no libraries for research, but that very fact stimulated logical and original thinking. I recall that I made my first public utterance at the Center Hill Literary Society at the age of ten when I upheld the affirmative of the question: Resolved that the Negro is the equal of the white man in intellect.

Except for topography, there was not much difference between Wirt County and the remainder of rural America in 1910. The whole country was agricultural rather than urban in outlook. It could have remained that way had it not been for the forces that were pushing the country toward industrialization. Among those forces the one that affected rural America the most was the invention and distribution of the Model T Ford Automobile.

I remember distinctly the very first automobile that made its appearance on the roads of Wirt County. In the summer of 1903 a man named John Russ drove an auto from Parkersburg to Spencer. My mother who is living in 1964 remembers the driver's name because she once attended school with him in Elizabeth. She does not, unfortunately, remember the manufacturer of the automobile. The dirt road he used is now State Route Number 14 over which hundreds and sometimes thousands of automobiles and trucks pass daily, but in 1903 neither the farmers nor their livestock had ever seen or heard an automobile. How long it took Russ to drive from Parkersburg to Spencer, a distance of about fifty miles, I never knew. All I recall is that I heard a great clatter down the highway, saw horses rearing and men running. The driver stopped near our house and showed a group of bystanders how the thing worked. He had blown a tire, and, after he passed on, I was the proud possessor of a piece of inner tube.

Thereafter, no other automobiles passed for three or four years. The horse and buggy era continued almost unmolested until the beginning of the second decade of the Twentieth Century, when, all of a sudden, Model T Fords began sprouting all over the countryside. Farmers who owned Fords became ardent supporters of road building programs. The car itself was an instrument of education. It broadened travel horizons and triggered a movement for rural high schools. It changed the outlook, the morals, and the economy of farm-oriented peoples everywhere. The hellfire preachers subsided and the literary societies withered and died. Victorian notions of feminine modesty and sexual conduct crumpled in the absence of prying eyes and informative lips. But the greatest impact of the coming of the automobile was on the economy of the nation, both urban and rural. The cities thrived and grew by leaps and bounds. Farm population dwindled. In the presence of better transportation and communication, labor-saving devices, refrigeration, and mass advertising, the little self-sufficient farms of Appalachia were doomed.

The change did not occur all at once and it is not thoroughly complete at this time. There were, of course, forces other than the automobile at work. World War I sent more than a million American soldiers to Europe, the first mass movement in that direction since America was first discovered. At the age of eighteen, I was one of them. Technology was on the move. The airplane was already a reality—radio, television, atomic energy, and space travel were around the corner. New knowledge from the microcosm of the atom to the macrocosm of space was being assembled. Chemists and medical men were discovering new compounds and remedies. Inventors were prolific with machines to replace hand labor, including farm labor, so that today a farm requires nearly as much machinery as a factory. The poor farmer, with only his hoe and his hands, cannot compete in such a market.

Ironically, the farmers of Wirt County, in drumming up support for good roads and modern high schools, did not suspect that they were legislating themselves out of business. The human animal is, undoubtedly, an optimist by nature. Prevailing opinion among Wirt County farmers was that good roads would open up the country to a great mass of people outside who were supposed to be falling over themselves to get in, though the truth was just the opposite. Roads carry traffic both ways and the roads of Wirt County, beginning with the decade 1900-1910, have carried out more people than they brought in.

One of the side effects of the coming of the automobile was the manufacture of automobile tires. For some reason the early tire manufacturers concentrated their efforts in the city of Akron, Ohio, and this fact must be noted in connection with the disappearance of small Wirt County farmers. I never knew how it happened, but before, during, and after World War I, the word was spread that the rubber factories in Akron would hire men from West Virginia in preference to all other labor. This was true. I worked in Akron twice myself, once at Firestone Rubber Company and once at Goodrich Rubber Company. As a result nearly all the young men and many of the young women of Wirt County trooped off to Akron, got jobs, and stayed there. These people, if alive, are now grandparents. In talking to some old acquaintances recently, I was told that Akron is almost wholly a city of transplanted West Virginians and their descendants. Of the 86 children with whom I attended the one-room Oak Hill School from 1909 to 1912, only three in addition to myself now live in Wirt County. Some are dead. Some are missing. The others almost without exception live in Akron or other Ohio cities.

What happened at Akron has happened at other places since, notably at Cleveland and Detroit, and more recently, as industry moved down the Ohio Valley, at places nearer home such as Parkersburg and Ravenswood. Some of our remaining farmers are only part-time farmers. They work a regular shift in Parkersburg or Ravenswood and raise cattle on the side. This is a far cry from the days when a farmer needed money only for taxes. Raising cattle, by the way, is a sure prescription for financial success to a factory worker. He benefits from the farm mess in Washington.

The population of Wirt County declined during the decade 1900 to 1910 and again during the decades 1910 to 1920 and 1920 to 1930. There was a gain during the decade 1930 to 1940, which is explainable on the same economic grounds as the decline. That decade was the time of the Great Depression, the period when industrial production dwindled and factory workers everywhere were unemployed. Rather than starve in the cities many of the workers returned to their old homes and became again self-sufficient farmers. In doing so, they were much better off economically than their friends in the cities for the reason that, when the chips are down for survival, the farms of Appalachia have been and will remain the very best places for survival. When the depression ended, through the intervention of war, when the factories started humming again, all the former factory workers and nearly all the young boys and girls graduating from high school, moved to the cities. Between 1940 and 1960 the population of Wirt County declined nearly one-third and the trend would have been even greater except for a slight trend in immigration in the opposite direction.

The people of Appalachia, and of Wirt County, like human beings everywhere, have an inborn nostalgia for the place in which they were born and reared. In my boyhood it was often said, *The man who drinks from the Little Kanawha River will return,* a proverb that probably goes back to the first settlements on the Euphrates and the Nile. Americans are a restless people, moving from place to place, and, oftener than is commonly suspected, their last move is back to the place where they were born. That very thing happened to me.

On my fiftieth birthday, with a law degree long behind me, I found myself in the City of Washington temporarily unemployed. I had just passed through one of those difficult periods that come to all men. My wife had died, my son was self-supporting. I had amassed, as the result of a lifetime of effort, some cash and some real estate. Both my father and my mother were still living in Wirt County, West Virginia. The thought came to me, why not get out of this Washington rat race? You don't have the money to buy a yacht and visit foreign countries, but you can live quite cheaply back home. Besides, you have always wanted to write a novel, and here is your chance.

So, I retired at fifty, went back home, and wrote a novel in three months time. In the book I drew heavily on my experiences in Washington, but I soon learned that it is one thing to write a book and quite another thing to get it published. The title of the novel was RENDEZVOUS AT FIFTY. No one liked it, and, after sitting around a few months waiting for rejection slips, I started looking for something else. Thirteen years later I had this novel published at my own expense, and to date have given away exactly thirty-eight copies.

It soon became apparent that the village of Elizabeth needed a lawyer. Rural county seats all over the country need lawyers, doctors, and accountants because young lawyers, doctors and accountants prefer the cities. Instead of remaining on the retired list, I started a new career at the age of fifty, and I am still embarked upon it in the very community in which I was born. An unforeseen side effect of this move was that I soon re-entered politics. In 1954, when I was fifty-five years old, I was elected Clerk of the Circuit Court, and in 1956 Prosecuting Attorney. In 1964, as this is written, I have just won the Republican nomination for Secretary of State of West Virginia. (This was written in May, 1964. I was defeated in November.)

Not many of my acquaintances retired, or attempted to

retire, at the age of fifty, but retirements are responsible, in one way or another, for much of the present day population of Wirt County. In nearly all corporations, retirement at 65 is mandatory. Now that self-employed persons, including farmers, business men, and professional men are entitled to Social Security benefits and the span of life is lengthening each decade, the county is saturated with people who draw government and other retirement checks. Those farm boys and girls who went to Akron fifty, forty, and even thirty years ago are now drawing Social Security, and, while most of them remain with their families in their adopted homes, a few are coming back. The young are still leaving, some of the old are coming back. The result is that Wirt County today is becoming a community of Senior Citizens. As such it furnishes a laboratory for a study of the effects of age on the social fabric.

2. Family Names

THE PEOPLE of Wirt County, as a whole, belong to the class that used to be called plain people, meaning the great faceless mass of citizens who never acquire wealth, panoply, or power. Plain does not necessarily mean poor, as I shall demonstrate later, but it does include people who are poor. After I established a law practice in Wirt County and became interested in politics, I got to know nearly every family in the county personally and was often made a confidant in their hopes and sorrows. Many of the family names intrigued me, particularly those that are French, and I made a point of inquiring of my clients what they knew of their own national origins.

Prior to this time I had never questioned the dictum of Fourth of July orators and some scholars that the people of Appalachia are of Scotch-Irish descent. To those interested in romance, it is fitting that the southern mountains should have been settled by Scottish Highlanders who brought along their tribal customs and family feuds. It is difficult, however, to fit names like Cheuvront, LaDeaux, Schreckengost and Kellar into the Scotch-Irish context. This is especially true when you find the names Cheuvront and Kellar mentioned in that famous book on Indian fighting called *Chronicles of Border Warfare* by Alexander Scott Withers.

Genealogy is not a strong point among plain people. In talking to my clients, I learned that they usually knew the names of their grandparents, seldom their great-grandparents, and that they preserved a family legend of their national origin. The legend is generally true with respect to origin, I believe, but it is overlaid with a myth concerning Three Brothers that cannot possibly be true in all cases and has been demonstrated untrue in some. Another legend common to many Wirt County families claims descent from an unknown Indian ancestor.

How widely dispersed the Myth of the Three Brothers is throughout America, I do not know, but I am beginning to believe it is widespread. The myth comes to light in a conversation such as the following:

Question: Your name is Fought. F-O-U-G-H-T. That is not a common name. Do you know where the Foughts came from originally?

Answer: I always heard it was from Germany.

Question: What part of Germany?

Answer: I don't know.

Question: Do you know when they came to this country?

Answer: No. All I know is that three brothers came to this country from Germany. One stayed in the East, one went South, and one went West.

Now this answer as to origin is probably correct. The name Fought (pronounced Fout) could well be a corruption of Vought. That part about the three brothers is pure myth. In the course of my investigation I heard of these three brothers from people who said their ancestors were German, English, Scotch-Irish, and French.

The legend of Indian ancestry probably has more substance, though I was able to pin down only a few names and dates. We are prone to forget that the frontier began at Jamestown and that for nearly two hundred years the Indian frontier remained in what is now the eastern part of the United States. Among descendants of frontiersmen, there is probably more Indian blood than is commonly suspected. There are two legends of Indian ancestors in my own family. As a boy, I was told that both my grandmothers were one-fourth Cherokee Indian, but no one told me how it happened. After they died no one knew. In recent years I have found a record wherein one of my great-great-grandfathers married a woman named Mary. The absence of a family name is circumstantial evidence that she was indeed a Cherokee.

The widespread legend of an Indian ancestor among Wirt County families is indicative of how long these families have lived in Appalachia. There have been few identifiable Indians, aside from travelling circuses, in what is now the State of West Virginia since 1795.

Though a list of the family names of the people living in Wirt County today is not an infallible guide to their national origins, such a list placed alongside the index to Withers' *Chronicles, Washington's Journals,* Caruso's *The Appalachian Frontier,* the tithables (tax lists) of Harrison County, Virginia, and other records, exhibits striking similarities. Of course, the common names such as Smith or Miller have little significance, but when you find a farm family named Cheuvront, with a legend of Indian ancestry, living in Wirt County today, and then learn from Withers' *Chronicles* that a man of that somewhat *unusual* name was living in present day West Virginia two hundred years ago, it may not be inappropriate to assume some sort of connection. Indeed, the present inhabitants of Wirt County are a reminder that as the frontiersman moved westward he always left some of his family behind.

According to my count there are exactly 545 family names among the 4,391 residents of Wirt County at the present time. The names and the count have been taken from the Voter's Registration Records in the Office of the Clerk of the County Court for 1962. There are, of course, some residents who are not registered and whose names therefore do not appear. Since the list is comparatively short, I am copying it in full, together with what is known or believed to be known of the national origin of the name. At the same time, I am indicating where the name appears in the source materials in the following manner:

Wi means Withers' *Chronicles*

Wa means *Washington's Journals*

C means Caruso's, *The Appalachian Frontier*

T means Tithables (tax lists) for Harrison County, Virginia, prior to 1810

Scotch-Irish means both Scotch and Irish

English means both English and Welsh

Name	References to Name	National Origin
Adams	T	English

Allen	Wi, Wa, T	Scotch-Irish
Allman		German
Alton	Wa	English
Amos	T	French
Anderson	Wi, T	English
Andrick		French
Archer	Wi	English
Arnold	T	English
Arthur	C	English
Ash	T	English
Ashby	T	English
Ashley	Wi (Ashly)	English
Ayres		Scotch-Irish
Bailey	T (Bayley)	
	Wi, T (different families—Balay)	French and English
Backhouse, (corruption Backus)	T (Backus)	English
Boone	Wi, C	Scotch-Irish
Baker	Wi, C	English
Baldwin	C	English
Ball	Wa	English
Ballengee		French
Barnes	T	English
Barr	T	Scotch-Irish
Batten		French
Bain	T (Bane)	English
Beck		German
Beckner		German
Bell	T, Wi, Wa	Scotch-Irish
Belt		German
Bennett	T	English
Bibbee	T (Bibby)	German
Bingman		German
Brannif		French
Black, (original name Schwartz)	T	German
Blair	T	English
Blankenship		German
Barton		English
Blosser		French
Bock		German
Beams		Scotch-Irish
Board	T	Scotch-Irish
Bonnell	T	French
Bonnett	Wi, T	French

Boston		Scotch-Irish
Boise		French
Boussman		German
Brannon		Scotch-Irish
Boggs		English
Brotton		French
Brown	Wi, C, T (different families)	English and German
Brookover	T	English
Bridges		English
Browning		English
Britton	Wi	English
Brohard		German
Bryan	Wi, C	Scotch-Irish
Bruce	Wa	Scotch-Irish
Buchanan	Wi, C	Scotch-Irish
Bumgarner	T	German
Bunner		French
Burr		English
Burrows	T	English
Bryant	Wi	Scotch-Irish
Burns	T, Wi	Scotch-Irish
Butcher	T	German
Buck		Scotch-Irish
Burch		English
Burdett		French
Busch	T	German
Cain	T	Scotch-Irish
Cale		Scotch-Irish
Calebaugh		German
Callison		Scotch-Irish
Caltrider		German
Campbell	Wi, C	Scotch-Irish
Caplinger	T	German
Carney		Scotch-Irish
Carpenter	T, Wi	English
Carter	C, T (Carder)	English
Chadock		French
Chambers		English
Channel		French
Cheatham		English
Chedester	T	English
Cheuvront	Wi	French
Clayton	T	English
Cline, (corruption of Klein)	T.	German

Clinton		English
Cochran	Wi	Scotch-Irish
Coe	T	Scotch-Irish
Collins	T, C	Scotch-Irish
Collums		English
Conger		Scotch-Irish
Conley		Scotch-Irish
Cooper	T, Wi, C	English
Copen		French
Coplin	T (Copeland) (Coplin)	English
Corbett and Corbitt	T	Scotch-Irish
Cottrill		French
Cottle		French
Courtney		Scotch-Irish
Cox	T, Wi	Scotch-Irish
Crew		English
Crislip	T	French
Criss		Scotch-Irish
Crothers		English
Curfman		German
Culver		Scotch-Irish
Cumbridge		Scotch-Irish
Cumberledge		Scotch-Irish
Cunningham	T, Wi	Scotch-Irish
Curry		Scotch-Irish
Daggett		French
Dailey	T (Delay)	French
Daniell		French
Daugherty	Wi (Dougherty)	Scotch-Irish
Davis	T, Wi	English (Welsh)
Davisson	T, Wi	Scotch-Irish
Dawson		Scotch-Irish
Deem	T	German
Delaney		French
Dennis	Wi	French
Dent		English
Depue		French
DeQuasie		French
Devaughan		French
Deviese		French
DeWeese	Wa	French
Dinnin		French
Dooley		Scotch-Irish
Dorsey		French
Dotson	T	English

Doty		Scotch-Irish
Douglas	T, Wi	Scotch-Irish
Dowler		Scotch-Irish
Drennen		French
Dulin		French
Dunbar		Scotch-Irish
Duncan	Wi (Dunkin)	Scotch-Irish
Duskey		French
Dye	T	English
Eagle		English
Earle	T (only Roman Catholic family in county)	Scotch-Irish
Eaton	T	English
Echols		English
Eckart		German
Eberhart		German
Eddy		English
Edwards	Wi, C	English
Elliott	T, Wi, C	Scotch-Irish
Ellison		Scotch-Irish
Emrick		English
Engelke		Dutch
Enoch	T, Wa	Dutch
Epler		German
Epling		German
Evans	C	English
Exline		French
Farley		Scotch-Irish
Ferguson	C	Scotch-Irish
Fields	C	English
Fierbaugh		German
Fint, (corruption of Findt)		German
Fisher		English and German
Flesher	T, Wi	English
Flinn	T (Flynn)	Scotch-Irish
Florence		French
Full		English
Floyd	Wi	English
Fluharty	T	Scotch-Irish
Foley	T	Scotch-Irish
Fought	T	German
Foutty	T	German
Frame		Scotch-Irish

Frazier	Wa, T (Frasure)	French
Frey	Wi	French
Frost		English
Fulmer		English
Furr		Scotch-Irish
Gabbert, (corruption of Gebhart)	T (Gabbard)	German
Gallagher		Scotch-Irish
Garretson		English
Gant		Scotch-Irish
Garrand		French
Gates	T	English
George	Wi	Scotch-Irish
Gibson	T, Wi, Wa, C	English
Giffin		French
Gilbert		English
Givens	T (Gibbens)	English
Glasscock		English
Goff, (corruption of Gough)	T, Wi	English
Goodwin	T	English
Graham	T, Wi, C	Scotch-Irish
Gray	T	Scotch-Irish
Griffin	T	Scotch-Irish
Grim	Wi	English
Gribble		English
Haines	T (Hain)	English
Hale		English
Hall	T, Wi, C (different families)	English, Scotch-Irish
Hamrick	T	German
Hancock	Wi	English
Hannah		French
Hardway	T	English
Harlow		English
Harrington		English
Harris	T, C	Scotch-Irish
Hays		English
Headley		English
Hefner		German
Heldreth		French
Hennen		French
Henthorn	T	French
Hersman		German
Hess	T	German

Hetzel		German
Hickman	T, Wi	German
Hicks		English
Higgins	T	English
Hill	T, Wi	Scotch-Irish
Hissam		French
Houchin		French
Hodgen	T	English
Hogue		English
Holbert		French
Hollingsworth		English
Honaker		German
Hoover		German
Hopkins	T	Scotch-Irish
Houck		German
Howard	T	English
Hudson	Wi, T (Hutson)	English
Huffman		German
Hughes	Wi	Scotch-Irish
Hulscher		German
Hunt	T	Scotch-Irish
Hupp		German
Hurd, (corruption of Heard)		Scotch-Irish
Husk		French
Hutchinson	T	English
Irons, (corruption of Iams)		French
Ingram		English
Jackson	T, Wi, C	Scotch-Irish
Jones	T, C (different families)	English, Scotch-Irish
James	T, Wi	Scotch-Irish
Javins		French
Jeffery		English
Jenkins	Wa	Scotch-Irish
Johnston	T	Scotch-Irish
Jordan	T	Scotch-Irish
Joy		French
Justice		French
Kastl (not native name)		Hungarian
Keeder		French
Keener		Scotch-Irish

Kellar	T, Wi	German
Kelly	T, Wi	Scotch-Irish
Kemp		Scotch-Irish
Kerns		Scotch-Irish
Kidder		French
Kidwell		Scotch-Irish
Kimble		English
King	T, C	Scotch-Irish
Kinney		Scotch-Irish
Kirby		Scotch-Irish
Kirchner		German
Kittle	T	Scotch-Irish
Knight	Wi	English
Knotts		German
Kohler		German
Koon, (corruption of Kuehn)	T	German
Koontz		German
Kreider		German
Kyer		French
LaDeaux		French
Lambert	T	French
Lambing		French
Lamp		French
Lasure	T	French
Law	T	Scotch-Irish
Lawson		English
Lee	T, Wa, C	English
Legg		French
Lehtomaki (not native name)		Finnish
Lemley		French
Lemon	T	French
Lett		French
Lewis	T, Wi, Wa, C	English
Licklider		German
Little		English
Littleton		English
Litton		French
Livingston	T	English
Lockhart	T	Scotch-Irish
Long	Wi, Wa	English
Longfellow		English
Lott		Dutch
Loudin	T	French
Lowe	T	Scotch-Irish

Lucky		French
Ledsome		Scotch-Irish
Ludwig		German
Mace	T	Scotch-Irish
Mackay	C	Scotch-Irish
Mahoney		Scotch-Irish
Malone		Scotch-Irish
Marcum, (corruption of Markham)		Scotch-Irish
Marks, (corruption of Marx)	T, Wi	German
Marshall	T, Wi, Wa, C	English
Martin	T, Wi, C	Scotch-Irish
Marlowe	T	English
Maser		French
Mason		English
Massey		Scotch-Irish
Matheney	T	Scotch-Irish
Mathess	T	Scotch-Irish
Maxson		Scotch-Irish
Maxwell	T, Wi, C	Scotch-Irish
Mayle (This name confined to a family part White, part Negro, and part Cherokee Indian.)		French
Maynard		French
Maze		German
McCarthy		Scotch-Irish
McCauley	T (McCulley)	Scotch-Irish
McClung		Scotch-Irish
McCoy	T	Scotch-Irish
McCray		Scotch-Irish
McCroskey		Scotch-Irish
McCue		Scotch-Irish
McCumbers		Scotch-Irish
McCutcheon		Scotch-Irish
McFee	T, C (McAfee)	Scotch-Irish
McGinnis		Scotch-Irish
McIntyre	T, Wi (McIntire)	Scotch-Irish
McKinney	T	Scotch-Irish
McVey		Scotch-Irish
McWilliams		Scotch-Irish
Meadows		English
Menefee		French
Merrill	Wi, C	English
Metz		German
Michael	Wi, Wa	Scotch-Irish

Milhoan		Scotch-Irish
Miller	T, Wi (different families)	English and German (Muller)
Mills	Wi	English
Minor		English
Mitchell	Wi	Scotch-Irish
Mitchem		Scotch-Irish
Moncrief		French
Monroe	Wa	English
Moore	T, Wi, C	Scotch-Irish
Morehead	T	Scotch-Irish
Morgan	Wi, Wa, C	English (Welsh)
Morris	T	English
Morrison	T	English
Mullen		German
Mullenax		French
Munday	Wi (Monday)	French
Murphy	T, Wi	Scotch-Irish
Murray	T	Scotch-Irish
Napier	Wa	French
Nay		French
Nelson	T, Wi	English
Neptune		French
Nestor		French
Newbrough		Scotch-Irish
Newell		English
Newhouse		German
Nichols		Scotch-Irish
Nicholson	T, Wi, Wa	English
Noble, (corruption of Nobel)		Swedish
Nottingham		English
Null		Scotch-Irish
Nutter	T	English
O'Dell		Scotch-Irish
Oldaker		German
Orr		Scotch-Irish
Osborne	T	English
Ott, (corruption of Odd)	T	Swedish
Owens	T, Wi	Scotch-Irish
Palmer		English
Parks		Scotch-Irish
Parsons	T, Wi	English

Patterson	T, Wi	English
Pavlick (not a native name. This man is an army officer married to a Smith.)		Polish
Pell		English
Perkins		English
Perrine		French
Pepper		English
Pickrell		French
Pettit		French
Petty	T	French
Pidcock		English
Phillips	T, Wi, Wa, C	English
Pomroy		French
Powell	Wi	English
Prather	T	Scotch-Irish
Pribble	T	English
Price	T, Wi	English
Prouse		German
Pyle		English
Quick, (corruption not easily identified. French legend.)		French
Rader	T	German
Randolph	T	English
Rathbone		English
Reed	Wi, Wa, T (different families)	English, Scotch-Irish
Reeves	T	English
Remmy	T	French
Reno		French
Rexroad	T	Scotch-Irish
Reynolds	Wi	Scotch-Irish
Richards	T, Wi	English
Rice	T, Wi	English
Riddle		English
Riggs	T	Scotch-Irish
Righter, (corruption of Richter)		German
Rinehart		German
Roberts	T (different families)	English, Scotch-Irish
Robinson	T, Wi, Wa	English
Rockhold	T	English
Rogers	T, Wi	English
Rollins	T (Roulings)	Scotch-Irish
Rowand		Scotch-Irish
Ruble	T	French

Runner	T	French
Russell	Wi	English
Salmons		English
Salyers		Scotch-Irish
Samples		English
Sams		Scotch-Irish
Sanson		French
Sarten		French
Schoolcraft	T, Wi	German
Schroeder		German
Scites		English
Scott	T, Wi, Wa	Scotch-Irish
Schreckengost		German
Seamon, (corruption of Simon)		French
Seibert		German
Settle		English
Shears	T (Shares)	German
Sheets		Scotch-Irish
Sheppard	Wi, Wa, T (sometimes Shepherd)	German
Shimer		German
Showalter		German
Shuck	T (Shook)	German
Sidwell		English
Siers		German
Simmons		Scotch-Irish
Simonton		English
Sims	T, Wi, C	English
Slack		German
Smith	Wi, Wa, C (different families)	English, Scotch-Irish, German
Snider	T	German
Snodgrass	Wi	Scotch-Irish
Snyder	T, Wi	German
Somerville		French
Spellman		German
Spencer	T	English
Springston	T	English
Staats	T	Dutch
Stalnaker	T, Wi	Dutch
Stallman		German
Staley	T (Staly)	Scotch-Irish
Stanley	T	Scotch-Irish
Starcher		Scotch-Irish
Stevens	T (Stephens)	Scotch-Irish

Stewart	T, Wi, Wa, C	Scotch-Irish
Stickley		English
Stout	T, Wi	German
Street		English
Strong		Scotch-Irish
Stuckey		French
Stull		Scotch-Irish
Sturm		German
Stutler	T	German
Sullivan	Wi	Scotch-Irish
Summers		English
Sutton	T	Scotch-Irish
Swisher	T	German
Taylor	T, Wi, C	English
Tanner	T, Wi	English
Thompson	Wi, C	English
Thorne (Thorn)		English
Tichnell		French
Tichener	T	English
Toncray		French
Toney		French
Tower		English
Townsend	C	Scotch-Irish
Trickett		English
Trippett	T, Wi	English
Tucker	T	English
Turner	T	Scotch-Irish
Twyman		German
Underwood		German
Veach	Wi (Veech)	French
Valentine		French
Vandale		Dutch
Van Horn	T	Dutch
Veon		French
Villers	Wa, C	French
Vincent		Scotch-Irish
Virtue		Scotch-Irish
Vlach (not native name)		Polish
Vogeding		German
Wade		English
Waggoner	T, Wi, Wa	German
Waldo	T	French

Ware		Scotch-Irish
Watkins		Scotch-Irish
Watson	T	English
Wease		German
Weaver		English
Weckesser		German
Weekley		English
Wells	T, Wi	Scotch-Irish
West	T, Wi, Wa (different families)	English, Scotch-Irish
Westbrook		English
Westfall	T, Wi	Dutch
Whipkey		French
White	T, Wi (different families)	English, Scotch-Irish, German
Whited, (corruption of Whitehead)		English
Whitecotton (Indian legend. This may be an Anglicized Indian name.)		English
Wigal		German
Williams	T, Wi, C	Scotch-Irish
Williamson	Wi, C	English
Wilson	T, Wi	Scotch-Irish
Wine		German
Winters		Scotch-Irish
Wise		English
Wiseman	T	German
Wix		French
Wolcott		English
Wolverton		German
Wood	T, Wi, C (different families)	English, Scotch-Irish, German
Woodring		German
Woodyard	T	English
Wright	T, Wi	English
Wyer	T (Wire)	French
Yeager		German
Yoho		French
Yonkins		French
Yost		German
Young	T	Scotch-Irish

There are doubtless errors in the foregoing list of national origins due to the manner in which it was made up. Family legends are sometimes unreliable because the person interviewed is not certain whether the legend applies to his father's or his mother's side of the house. In such cases I tried to learn something from the name itself. I have not had the leisure to trace all these family names back to the ship that brought them here, even if such a thing were possible, and in my opinion it would be impossible for the following reasons:

The frontier had few schools and even fewer records. In the early stages of each successive frontier, land was held by tomahawk rights. (On the Appalachian frontier, landowning was a complicated affair embracing land companies, veterans' tracts, settlement rights, pre-emption rights, and compensatory rights. Technically, a tomahawk right had no validity, but before settlement and pre-emption rights in Western Virginia were legalized by the statute of 1778 the tomahawk right was the outward symbol of ownership.) These tomahawk rights caused a great deal of trouble after the Revolution when the land was patented and surveyed. Spelling was atrocious, and spellings of proper names varied even for the same individual. A famous frontiersman, the progenitor of the far-flung Hite family, is known to have signed his name Justus Hite at one time and Yost Heid at another. Some names such as LaDeaux and McVey reveal their origin at a glance; others require study and research. How would you quickly classify such names as Fint and Sarten?

In some instances, I found that the person questioned knew of no family legend. This was unusual, but when it happened I had to study the name for other clues and make a guess. In one situation I learned of conflicting legends. The name was Marcum. One Marcum was certain that his ancestor came from England, and that the name was a corruption of Markham. Another, fortified by a family Bible, was equally certain that the first Marcum came from Ireland. This is probably a case of an English family emigrating to Ireland and later to America. For our purposes the Marcums are Scotch-Irish, but the incident suggests the pitfalls that open up in a study of this nature.

Though I freely admit that some of the national origins listed herein are guesses, I wish to make it clear that the guess in each instance is an educated one. I have not relied on myself alone. The list has gone to Judge Donald F. Black of Parkersburg, who is writing a History of Wood County, West Virginia, (Wood County adjoins Wirt), and to Dr. Hazel Roberts of New York City, Emeritus Professor at Hunter College, who has made a hobby of frontier genealogy for years and probably knows more about the beginnings of frontier families than any other person alive. Though some errors doubtless remain they have been minimized as much as possible.

Before leaving the subject of family names, it is appropriate to emphasize that this is not in any sense a genealogical chart. I have not proved, and cannot prove, that the Cheuvront family of Wirt County today is descended from the Cheuvront of Withers' *Chronicles*. The same statement is true of all other names on the list. All that can be said with certainty is that many of the present day inhabitants of Wirt County bear the same names, sometimes with variations in spelling as with the frontiersmen and their immediate successors.

3. Dark Ages of the Frontier

THAT THE INDIAN FRONTIER began at Jamestown is illustrated by the legend of Pocahontas. Unfortunately, there is more legend than fact in what is known of the relations between the white men and the red men in the early days of the Colony of Virginia. We learn of wars and massacres, but the issues are blurred. The Indians declined to be enslaved. Because Indian slavery was unworkable, the first Negro slaves were imported in 1619. Even before this time English wives were imported, like cattle at so much a head, to Jamestown.

These incidents have not received the attention they deserve in connection with the long and bloody history of the Indian frontier. The roving Indian tribes were proud, jealous, and warlike. They felt, not unreasonably, that the land belonged to them, but they seem to have been less concerned with land titles, in their early association with the white men, than they were with their own social status. When the white men first came, the Indians showed them, in their primitive way, how to make a living from the soil. They also provided the colonists with bedmates in accordance with their ancient, hospitable custom. The custom does not necessarily mean that the Indians held their women folk in low esteem. In return, the white men tried to enslave them, and, what may have been even more galling to Indian pride, showed their contempt for Indian women.

The true story of Pocahontas, as distinguished from the legend, sheds light on the racial prejudice of the English and on one of the recurring causes for conflict. To the rule that applied to Indian women, Pocahontas was the exception. Her husband made her his lawful wife and treated her with the respect due her station. We are told that the marriage of John Rolfe and Pocahontas preceded an extended period of peace and prosperity.

The great majority of the men of that place and time, however, subscribed to a different standard of conduct. To them, it was one thing to dally with an Indian girl and beget halfbreeds and quite a different thing to marry a white woman and raise a white family. Colonel William Byrd of Virginia believed that the colonists ought to marry Indian girls instead of importing wives from England. He based his argument on the ground that such a policy would amalgamate the races and insure peace. But his views did not prevail. Race prejudice seems to be inborn and ineradicable in private life. (At this moment the Negroes are protesting, with impeccable logic, against second class citizenship. Will it all end in amalgamation or in a race war?) Nearly all the families of Wirt County retain a legend of an Indian ancestor, but, aside from Pocahontas, few other names or dates have come down to us.

From the little that is known of the earliest frontier, we learn that Bacon's Rebellion in 1676 was a dispute over Indian policy. Bacon's Rebellion differed from the ordinary Indian affray in that white men, for at least once, started killing each other. Usually, it was white against red. Fighting was not continuous and wars, when they came, did not involve all Indians. The history of the frontier is a series of wars, conferences, and treaties, which were soon broken. Because the tribes were often at war with each other, some Indians were always on the white side and against their own people. The white men often sought and received the help of the Indians in their wars. Some historians have questioned whether the English could have won over the French in North America without the help of the Six Nations.

So long as the Colony of Virginia was weak, relations with the Indians remained relatively peaceful. It was only when the colonists began to spread out, to acquire larger and ever larger plantations, to seal off the Indians' traditional hunting paths, that disputes arose concerning the ownership of the land. If the Indians believed, with unerring logic, that the Creator had given them the land for a hunting ground, the white men, with equal logic, believed that the same Creator had given it to them for tobacco farms. In the final event history decreed in favor of agriculture, so that, within a hundred years of the founding of Jamestown, the tribes were forced out of present day Virginia. They migrated to Pennsylvania and across the great eastern mountain barrier to the waters of the Ohio and Mississippi Rivers.

This migration, this expelling of the tribes by war and diplomacy, from the eastern seaboard, contributed directly to the population of Appalachia and of Wirt County. Appalachia is perhaps the only remaining part of America that has not been inundated by successive waves of immigration. In withdrawing from the eastern seaboard, where the white man was now superior in numbers, to the north bank of the Ohio, the Indians left vacant a vast No-Man's Land comprising the mountainous region known today as Appalachia. There were a few exceptions. In the latter part of the Eighteenth Century there was still an Indian Village called Mingo Town in Randolph County, Virginia, and another called Bulltown in Braxton County. All this country was visited by Indian hunting parties and war parties, but for practical purposes the entire area, consisting of portions of nine states of the Union, was uninhabited. Into the void created by the Indian withdrawal filed the frontiersmen.

No customs officials guarded the Appalachian, or any other, frontier. For generations people were swallowed up there. Caruso in *The Appalachian Frontier* names Englishmen who visited the New River (Great Kanawha) Valley before LaSalle descended the Mississippi River. They wrote an account of their journey, and that account was used by the English to claim the Ohio Valley by right of discovery. The influx of settlers, as distinguished from explorers and traders, seems to have started late in the Seventeenth Century, and to have continued, in spite of the French and Indian War and the War of the Revolution, until 1794 when General Mad Anthony Wayne finally quelled the Ohio Indians at the Battle of Fallen Timbers.

Who were these frontiersmen, and what caused them to

choose a hard and dangerous life on the Indian frontier? The truth is that no one knows specifically, though generalizations are common. Caruso mentions certain ethnic groups such as the Scotch-Irish and the Germans that gravitated toward the frontier for economic reasons and because fighting was in their blood. Many Scotch-Irish and German names are preserved in Wirt County to this day. There were also the Englishmen, or rather the American born descendants of Englishmen, the Welsh, the French Huguenots, and a few descendants of the Dutch settlement at New Amsterdam and the Swedish settlement at New Sweden. Aside from sweeping generalizations, their motives are purely a matter of conjecture.

The frontiersmen may be thought of as people who were dissatisfied, for one reason or another, with their lot and with their opportunities on the eastern seaboard. We know that some of them were debtors and fugitives from justice. Others were mere adventurers. Still others, and this is a larger group than is commonly supposed, were younger sons and other relatives of the first families of the seaboard. In those days primogeniture, the law of the first born, was the law of the land. Younger sons were expected to shift for themselves. Although the exact connection is impossible to prove at this time, it is no mere coincidence that the following names are found in Wirt County today: Ashby, Buchanan, Burr, Bruce, Clinton, Culver, Douglas, Ferguson, Floyd, Hancock, Hutchinson, Jackson, Johnston, Lee, Lewis, Livingston, Longfellow, Marshall, Mason, Minor, Monroe, Morris, Nottingham, Phillips, Russell, Randolph, Rathbone, and Stewart. It is known that a man named Richard Lee, not the Richard Henry Lee of Revolutionary fame but a blood relative, according to legend, established a tomahawk claim at what is now Newark, Wirt County, West Virginia, in 1774, and later converted his tomahawk claim into a settlement warrant. He sold his land to Thomas Pribble in 1796. (This information comes from the Memoirs of Hiram Pribble, born 1793, died 1887.)

Wherever they came from and whatever their motives for coming, the frontiersmen were not weaklings. The criminal, unless he was also a desperado, had more to fear from the Indians than he had from the local authorities. Survival demanded quick thinking and a knowledge of Indian psychology. Daniel Boone, though captured more than once, was never tortured because his quick intelligence and brash actions appealed to the Indians' sense of humor and their honor. Lewis Wetzel, a far different and more dangerous type, inspired fear and won the ghostly appellation, The Wind of Death, because in woodsmanship and cunning he could beat the Indians at their own game.

The family names of Wirt County residents today serve the double purpose of identifying the inhabitants and of throwing a spotlight on the early history of the country. During most of the Eighteenth Century, the frontiersmen moved into the creeks and valleys of No-Man's Land and established their homes. How many did so and exactly who they were will never be known for their tomahawk claims are not recorded in any court house. The names listed in Withers' *Chronicles* represent only a fraction of the inhabitants of the frontier. He names those remembered in legend either as heroes, villains, or victims. There were unquestionably many more tomahawk claimants in present day West Virginia than is commonly believed. I have already mentioned Richard Lee at Newark. In 1770, a 20,000-acre Military Survey at the mouth of the Little Kanawha River was made for the benefit of veterans of the French and Indian War. With the fine disdain of legalists for frontiersmen, one of the surveyor's calls for this tract mentions "passing a cabin" without disclosing the cabin owner's name. I wish they had been more specific. There must be among the present day inhabitants of Wirt County a sizeable number of descendants of tomahawk landholders whose names do not appear in any of the source materials. I am led to this conclusion in part by what I have learned, or failed to learn, about the French families, soon to be related.

The process of filling up No-Man's Land between the Ohio Indians and the white settlements in the Valley of Virginia continued for nearly one hundred years. Think of it! Some people, if they were lucky, were born, married, became parents and grandparents, and died on the frontier, scores of miles in advance of the nearest outpost of civilization. They could do so because even Indians could not search every hill and valley of the vast mountain wilderness. From Parkersburg on the Ohio River to Winchester, Virginia, in the midst of the Blue Ridge Mountains today, on U. S. Route 50, is a distance of two hundred thirty-five miles. In between and up and down the spine of the Alleghenies are literally thousands of creeks, caves, and hideaways. Here, the frontiersman could stake his claim secure in his knowledge that his rights would be respected by other white men, if they were frontiersmen. Title troubles with lawyers and patent holders was a later development.

As more and more settlers poured into No-Man's Land at the close of the French and Indian War, blockhouse forts were erected in various places for mutual protection. Fort Neal at Parkersburg on the Ohio River was built in 1785, though there were tomahawk settlers nearby as early as 1770. This was eighteen years before the first settlement was made in the Northwest Territory at Marietta, twelve miles upriver from Parkersburg. The builders of Fort Neal bought the settlement rights of one Joel Reed, who may or may not have been my ancestor. Of this, more later.

It needs to be recalled that the Indian policy of the Crown of England was one of the contributing causes of the Revolutionary War. The frontiersmen wanted to acquire the land west of the mountains even if they had to exterminate either the Indians or themselves to get it; the Crown wanted to preserve the peace. Looking backward now, a great deal may be said for the English Government's position. The attempt of the Ohio Company to colonize the Upper Ohio Valley had touched off the French and the Indian War in 1754. To placate the Indians and detach them from the French, the English government had made solemn promises and entered into sacred treaties. At the same time the Colonial Government at Williamsburg, in order to spur recruiting, offered grants to volunteers to be effective when the war ended. The colony actually disposed of some land in this manner, though not enough to satisfy the frontiersman.

After the Declaration of Independence, the Commonwealth again used western lands as a means of financing the war. These war veterans, aside from tomahawk claimants who completed settlement rights, hold the first legal titles in Wirt County. Armed with their paper titles, the veterans, on taking possession, inevitably came face to face with the dispossessed tomahawk owners, with whom they customarily made a settlement. In those lawless days failure to make a satisfactory agreement with a tomahawk owner could lead to dire consequences. Some of the tomahawk owners then bought lands of their own, while others, being illiterate and bred to the ways of the wilderness, remained landless. The insuperable difficulty at this time is to determine who were and who were not tomahawk owners on the frontier.

Of the 545 family names now resident in Wirt County, 239 are found in the source materials. Of this number those mentioned in Withers' *Chronicles* may be thought of primarily as tomahawk people, and so may some mentioned in *Washington's Journals* and in Caruso's, *The Appalachian Frontier*. When we come down to the Tithables (Tax Lists) we are entering upon the final period of the eastern frontier. These people had recorded titles: Either a grant for services in the French and Indian War and the War of the Revolution, a completed settlement or pre-emption right, or a compensatory grant to those Virginians living in Western Pennsylvania whose titles were annulled when the boundary line between Virginia and Pennsylvania was finally established in 1779. This boundary dispute would fill a book by itself. Virginia originally claimed all the Monongahela Valley and the Ohio Valley. In the final settlement many native Virginians were dispossessed. Some of these received for a consideration compensatory grants farther down the Ohio River in newly-formed Virginia counties.

Though no settlements were completed on the west bank of the Ohio River until Marietta was founded in 1788, the mountainous region east of the Ohio was largely populated before that date: first, by the tomahawk people, who had been filtering in for a century, and later, by the grantees of patents issued by the Colony and the State of Virginia.

These later migrants often came down the Ohio River in flatboats and spread inland at the mouths of the creeks and rivers. Some of the dispossessed tomahawk people moved forward with the advancing frontier to Indiana and Illinois, but many stayed behind. They had already lived in the mountains for generations. The tomahawk people and their immediate successors are the direct ancestors of the inhabitants of present day Appalachia for an obvious historical reason.

When the Northwest Territory was opened to settlement after the Treaty of Greenville in 1795, the land-hungry immigrants of the following decades naturally preferred the plains to the mountains for agricultural purposes. The tide of immigration rolled westward leaving an enclave behind that was cut off by topography from the mainstream of American life. Appalachia was separated by hundreds of difficult miles from its own centers of government on the eastern seaboard. Kentucky and Tennessee soon set up governments of their own, but West Virginia remained a part of the Mother State until the Civil War. Isolated from the remainder of the country, cut off from intimate contact with their own government, the mountain people developed a culture of their own, a culture that combined the necessary hospitality of the frontier with the far-reaching principles of the Revolution, equality and freedom. In some of the more remote counties there was a reversion to primitive tribal customs based on ties of blood. This was true only in what is now southern West Virginia and eastern Kentucky, and was the result of remoteness from central authority. In the absence of strong law enforcement, families and communities naturally draw together for mutual protection. Wirt County never suffered from family feuds.

Because they were isolated, because they were imbued with the principles of the Revolution from earliest childhood, and because they had no overriding economic stake in slavery, the inhabitants of Appalachia were loyal to the Union, with notable exceptions, during the Civil War, even in the deep South. In Wirt County today, people are often Republicans and Democrats by inheritance. If I were asked to give a reason for being a lifelong Republican, though I have not always voted the Republican ticket, I would have to admit that it is largely because my Grandfather Reed was a Union soldier. Since the two-party system remains the best guarantee of our freedoms, I consider that as good a reason as any other.

For plain survival, Appalachia is superior to most of continental America. The climate is generally, not always, mild, the atmosphere healthy. Malaria, formerly the scourge of the lowlands south and west, is and always has been absent. Before the advent of coal mining and manufacturing, the streams were full of edible fish. There were wonderful virgin forests abounding in game. The soil, where it could be tilled, was highly productive in a plentiful rainfall. A man could make a living without too much effort and still have time for sports and such intellectual pursuits as the community afforded. These were not many, though illiteracy was not as widespread as is often thought. Even in the oldest land conveyances, only a few persons signed their names with a mark.

There was a long period from shortly after the Revolution to the close of the Civil War when immigration to the mountains fell far behind immigration to other parts of the country. At the same time many of the mountain people moved west. The people who remained in Appalachia married young and raised large families. In my boyhood I knew a family with twenty children, seventeen of whom reached maturity. The population increase during the first half of the Nineteenth Century was due in part to an unprecedented crop of babies. After the Civil War, when oil fields were discovered, and coal mining and timbering became profitable, there was a sudden and continuing influx of people from outside the mountains looking for economic and other opportunities. In West Virginia these persons are largely responsible for the growth of our cities and manufacturing centers. They are also responsible for the scars of coal mining, denuded forests, and stream pollution.

My mother's families, the Virtues and the Blacks, belonged to this latter group. My great-grandfather, Reverend Andrew Virtue, a Presbyterian minister, came to Wirt County from Emloenton, Pennsylvania in 1880. My grandfather, Amos Eckert Black, who had married Mary Virtue in Pennsylvania, followed two years later for a reason that sounds incredible today. My grandfather Black, who had never farmed in his life, contracted tuberculosis. His doctor advised him to give up his employment and move to a farm where he could get plenty of exercise. He bought a farm in Wirt County to be near his wife's parents. Strangely enough, he recovered, and became a useful citizen. In 1898 he became Overseer of the Poor in Wirt County and later President of the County Court. My mother, who was born in Pennsylvania in 1878, has an almost total memory of the early days of the family in Wirt County. The first crop was a failure, though later, the farm, a good one by Wirt County standards, became prosperous. She remembers that she was taunted at school with being a "foreigner," a term of opprobrium among her schoolmates.

There were five children in the Black family, excluding one who died young, and all five married locally. My grandfather Reed lived on a farm adjoining the Blacks. Since the Reeds are of frontier stock, I think it probable that I am related by blood to most of the inhabitants of Wirt County today, though it is, of course, impossible to prove anything of the kind.

The Appalachian frontier is a trial to genealogists. Both my cousin, Donald F. Black, and my son, William B. Reed, are genealogists by avocation, and have done useful work on the various family trees. Both have learned a great deal from records about my mother's ancestors, but the Reeds are a different story. To illustrate the genealogical problems of all frontier families, I am setting out here all that my son has learned of his and my own paternal ancestry, beginning in 1924.

(1) William Baldwin Reed, born in Norwich, New York, August 18, 1924. Married Mabel Gilbert, December 22, 1945. Now lives in Mesa, Arizona. He was the son of

(
(
(

(2) Louis Eckert Reed, born in Wirt County, West Virginia, October 1, 1899. Married Ruth Baldwin, July 5, 1923. Now lives in Wirt County, West Virginia. Married second wife, Mildred B. Johnston in 1961. He was the son of

(
(
(

(3) George William Reed, born in Ritchie County, West Virginia, May 10, 1871. Married Emma Belle Black, December 22, 1898. Died in Wirt County, West Virginia, October 1, 1957. He was the son of

(
(
(

(4) Amaziah Reed, born in Barbour County, Virginia (now West Virginia), 1843. Married Malinda Jane Keck in Ritchie County, West Virginia, 1869. Died in Hancock County, West Virginia, 1917. He was the son of

(
(
(

(5) John Reed, born in Harrison County, Virginia (now West Virginia), 1819. Married Martha Thompson, 1840. Died in Upshur County, West Virginia, 1892. He was the son of

(
(
(

(6) William Peter Reed, believed to have been born in Virginia in 1797. Married Mary ————. Died in Ritchie County, Virginia, (now West Virginia) in 1862.

Beyond William Peter Reed lies the frontier and nothingness. My father used to think that he was descended from the Reed who was Secretary to George Washington, but that is demonstrably wrong. Two Reeds on the frontier, against whom George Washington instituted land suits, are listed in *Washington's Journals,* and a John Reed is mentioned in Withers' *Chronicles.* There is also that Joel Reed, who owned the settlement right at Fort Neal, now comprising a sizeable part of the City of Parkersburg, West Virginia. It is possible, though by no means certain, that I am descended from one of these pioneers, but people in those days were too busy saving their own scalps to worry about blood lines. For genealogical purposes William Peter Reed had no father or mother, and that unwelcome truth applies to all the families that filled the void in No-Man's Land. We know some things about them in general but very little or nothing in particular. Only the family names and the family legends constitute a thread of continuity with the distant past. For that reason I have preserved the names and legends for this study.

The family names of Wirt County voters break down into the following national origins:

English	174
Scotch-Irish	163
French	101
German	93
Others	14
Total	545

This breakdown, allowing for errors and discrepancies unavoidable in a study of this nature, seems to dispose of the myth that the mountain people are of Scotch-Irish descent. Rather, they are a blend of English, Scotch-Irish, French and German nationalities, with a trace of other nationalities, and more than a trace of the American Indian. Not the Scotch-Irish but the English constitute the largest single group of family names, followed by the Scotch-Irish, the French, and the German in that order. We find reminders of New Amsterdam and New Sweden, and, in more recent times, reminders of the later immigration of the

Hungarians, the Poles, and the Finns. No Jews, Syrians, Greeks, Italians, Spaniards, or Spanish Americans live in Wirt County today, and it is believed that none have ever lived here. A farm family named Coen lives in adjoining Calhoun County. I have always suspected that this family descends from a Jewish trader on the frontier, but the Coens deny knowledge of a Jewish ancestor.

Of the family names that survive in Wirt County all are quickly accounted for in the historic context except the French. The English established the Colony of Virginia and were therefore the first frontiersmen in point of time. The Scotch-Irish and the Germans came later, and some of these gravitated to the frontier in search of opportunity. So did the French Huguenots. But there is a mystery all the same in that statistic showing that nearly one-fifth of all the families in Wirt County claim French descent. There simply were not that many Huguenots on the frontier, for the Huguenots, on the whole, were artisans and tradesmen rather than hunters and fighters. There is, of course, the historical fact of the Norman Conquest which established a number of French family names in England, Scotland, and Ireland. Such names, however, persist mostly among the aristocracy and are easily recognized. There was also a French settlement at Gallipolis, Ohio, in the 1790's, and at least one family, the LaDeaux, claims to have originated at Gallipolis. The Depues, the Cheuvronts, the Bonnetts and others are Huguenot in origin if we assume, what is impossible to prove at this time, that the present day bearers of those names are descended from known Huguenot families. That leaves a large number of French names unaccounted for.

The French families know no more of their ancestors than the other nationalities. They have now been so long intermarried with the other nationalities that the French language, customs, traditions, and religion have disappeared. Only the names remain, and the names constitute the mystery. So far as I know, no one has ever studied, or even commented on, the French contribution to the present day population of Appalachia. (I need to remind myself and the reader that this study is confined to a single West Virginia County near the Ohio River. Are the French family names concentrated in Wirt and nearby counties? Are they found in the same proportions in other parts of Appalachia? I simply do not know.) Because the names are so numerous and the people who bear them have obviously been here so long, I have searched in my reading for some explanation, and have come up with a theory of my own.

The French were the first white colonists in the Ohio Valley. How many there were and where they settled may not be ascertainable now, but we know from what has been written about the expeditions of General George Rogers Clark that there were still French towns in present day Indiana and Illinois as late as 1778. This was fifteen years after the Ohio country had been ceded to England. If the French had towns in Indiana and Illinois, what was there to prevent individual Frenchmen from becoming farmers and traders along the Ohio? We know about the traders of a later day, the famed French voyageurs of the Northwest, but nothing of the farmers. We know also that during the French and Indian War soldiers were dispatched all the way from New Orleans to Fort Duquesne. The French seem to have been the only white men in the Ohio Valley who had nothing to fear from the Indians after 1763. Without the backing of the Motherland, the French colonist in the Ohio Valley had to make his peace with the Indians, and he succeeded above other white men. In this context it is important to remember that the subject of this study, Wirt County, West Virginia, was a part of the Kingdom of France until 1763, a mere dozen years before the outbreak of the American Revolution.

What happened to the French in the Ohio Valley? In particular, what happened to those French soldiers and civilians at Fort Duquesne and other fortifications and establishments up and down the Ohio? No one really knows, but there are some interesting entries in *Washington's Journals* dealing with the French and Indian War. For instance, on the twelfth day of June, 1754, Washington wrote:

> I marched at the head of one hundred and thirty

men and about thirty Indians; but at the distance of half a mile I met the other Indians who told me there were only nine deserters, and I sent Mr. Montour with some Indians to bring them in safely. I had them clothed, and they gave us confirmation of what we had conjectured about the designs of M. deJumonvilles party, and that more than a hundred soldiers are waiting only for a favorable opportunity to come and join us. *(George Washington in the Ohio Valley* by Hugh Cleland, University of Pittsburgh Press, Page 85.)

There are other entries about deserters, and, while desertion is not an unusual occurrence in wartime, there is one peculiarity about these French deserters. Where desertion is ordinarily the act of an individual, or at most of two or three persons, these Frenchmen deserted in groups. I wish we knew their names. Obviously, there was a problem of morale among the French soldiers, but we can only guess at the cause. Were these soldiers residents of the Ohio Valley who had been impressed into service and had little stomach for helping Indians kill white men? More important, what happened to them after the War ended? Desertion in wartime was then, and still is, punishable with death. These French soldiers could not safely return to their regiments. What could be more natural for a deserter than to settle down after the war among his erstwhile enemies?

I do not mean to imply that the French families of Wirt County are descended from army deserters. Possibly, some of them are. What I am trying to say is that the French government exercised jurisdiction over the Ohio Valley until 1763, that the French established settlements there long before the English thought of doing so, and that these French frontiersmen continued to live there after the Ohio Country was formally ceded to the English.

A partial confirmation of this view comes from the *Memoirs of Hiram Pribble,* now in my possession. Pribble, whose father acquired the rights of Richard Lee at Newark in 1796, states that Lee had a hired farmhand named Joseph LaSure. The LaSure family is now widespread, and it has been established that the first LaSure (often corrupted to

Leasure or Lesher) did not acquire land in his own name until 1803. The native French could not obtain land titles in Appalachia for their services in the French and Indian War because they had fought on the wrong side. Like all frontiersmen their services in the War of the Revolution was a running battle with the Indians for survival. Of all the families on the frontier, the French alone appear to have been largely landless, a condition consistent with the theory that the French were a conquered people. If the theory is anywise correct, the French names of the present day inhabitants of Wirt County derive in part from the very first of the Trans-Allegheny pioneers, from the French who colonized the Ohio Valley before Daniel Boone was born.

It is instructive to note in this connection the difference between the French in the Ohio Valley and the French in Canada. The former have been so thoroughly amalgamated that only the French name or its corruption remains. There is not a single Roman Catholic among them. There were no Catholic priests on the English and American side of the frontier. Like the English, the Scotch-Irish, and the Germans, the French families were ultimately converted by the hell-fire preaching of the Methodist and Baptist Circuit riders. Like the other ethnic European stocks in America, they have forsaken their ancient customs and abandoned their racial and religious origins. By way of contrast the French Canadians have retained their language, their customs, and their religion, and there is a strong French Canadian party seeking independence of the British Crown at the present time.

4. Culture and Art

DUE TO ITS ISOLATION and its failure to attract new people and new ideas in the days when the West was being conquered for the white men, Appalachia is one of the few geographical divisions in America that developed a regional culture. It is apparent now that there were two main culture streams in American life. One was the culture of the North, often called New England culture, which had its roots in the concepts of free enterprise and mercantilism. The other was the culture of the South, based on the concept of human slavery, which proved to be profitable only in an agricultural economy. Though ideas are indeed more important than armies, as Victor Hugo noted, it is nevertheless true that the impact of reforming ideas is always directed outward and not inward. It is much easier to observe the mote in your neighbor's eye than it is to discover the beam in your own eye.

The conflict in ideas between the North and the South which culminated in the great Civil War of the 1860's needs detain us only briefly. Suffice it to note that at the time of the American Revolution the really important English colonies in America were the southern colonies. George Washington became Commander in Chief of the Continental Army not so much because of his military prowess as because he was a native of Virginia and Virginia was the largest and the most powerful English colony in America. After the Revolution, Virginia and the Southern States continued to dominate the political spectrum through many decades. Even such legendary liberal Presidents as Jefferson, Jackson, and Polk were Southerners and slaveholders. When the Civil War ended it was the agricultural economy of the South and not the alleged free mercantile economy of the North that was ruined.

Appalachia lay outside these two conflicting culture streams by reason of its topography. It is important now chiefly because of its contribution in the field of music. Though West Virginia was a part of Virginia until the advent of the Civil War and slavery was therefore legal within its present boundaries, there never were a large number of slaves in the mountains. There were not many places in the mountains where slavery was profitable, though Wirt County with its broad river bottoms in the Little Kanawha Valley, was an exception. The Steeds, the Enochs, the Blacks, the Foughts, the Beauchamps, the Creels, the Mayles, the Holberts, the Rathbones, the Pribbles, the Sims, the Roberts', the Mills, and the Bumgarners all owned slaves. Josephus Roberts is said to have been the first Wirt County planter to manumit his slaves in the 1840's. It is worthy of note that with the exception of the Roberts family, the Black family, the Rathbone family, and the Holbert family, all these families are Democrats today. The names Beauchamp, Creel, and Steed are no longer found in Wirt County. The Mayles who live here are all negroid. They, too, are Republicans.

There is no Negro problem in Wirt County such as afflicts the South and the Northern cities. As a matter of fact, only a few Negroes still live here. A generation ago there was a relatively large Negro farm community on Big Island Run in Clay District populated largely by the descendants of former slaves of the Mayle and Holbert families. There is a legend that the last white Mayle devised the Big Island Run lands to his manumitted slaves. If true, this happened before 1848 because I have not found such a will in the records of Wirt County. The colored Mayles and Holberts are a mixture of white, black, and Cherokee Indian. (I learned this fact from an anthropologist at the Library of Congress who has made a special study of the Mayle family. It seems that there is an older community of Mayles in Barbour County.) Most of the Wirt County Mayles and Holberts have joined the outward migration and have moved to Ohio where some of them have become economically prosperous. The Mayles and their connections own and control a number of business enterprises in Washington County, Ohio, where they customarily employ white workmen. I talked recently with an unskilled white laborer who had worked for a Mayle on a vegetable farm near Belpre, Ohio. He told me that the Mayles are good people to work for but that they "don't take any foolishness." Queried as to what he meant, he explained that, if a workman got drunk and failed to show up for work at the proper time, he was promptly fired.

There used to be a segregated one-room school on Big Island Run, but that school was discontinued long before the Supreme Court rendered its famed decision on segregated schools in 1954. Two years ago a young Negro named Ronald Costley, a Mayle on his mother's side, was captain of the football team and President of the Student Body at Wirt County High School. He died suddenly of a heart attack and more than a thousand white people attended his funeral. The Negroes have never constituted a criminal nor a welfare class in Wirt County. In sober truth they are among our most responsible citizens. Some cynics claim that they are not really Negroes and it is, in fact, difficult to distinguish some Mayles from white people, but the Mayles themselves are proud of their Negro blood. No Negro has been charged with a crime of any kind in Wirt County since 1915, though one Mayle was committed at the request of his family to Spencer State Hospital a few years ago for a mental aberration.

Nevertheless, and this seems significant, whites and Negroes, do not often marry in Wirt County. So far as I know, the old miscegenation statute, prohibiting marriages between whites and Negroes, has never been formally repealed, but most of the citizens of Wirt County seem unaware that such a statute ever existed. More than fifty years ago a Mayle married a white woman and lived with her openly near Elizabeth. The Clerk of the County Court tells me that in the past twenty years he has not had a single application for an interracial marriage license. The same situation prevails, I am told, in the City of Parkersburg where there is a considerable Negro community. There seems to be a reluctance on the part of both races to indulge in matrimony due no doubt to the circumstance that public opinion in both races frowns on such liasons. I recall an incident that occurred when I was in Washington. A young white college man and an almost white college girl sought my advice. I could not understand why until I learned that her mother was a Mayle. They wanted to marry and both their families objected. What did I think they ought to do?

Try that one yourself. He was a young Jew from New York and his father was a lawyer. Her father was no indigent sharecropper. He owned a prosperous trucking company in Ohio, and, though he could easily have passed for a white man, he chose to identify himself with the Negro community. There were no legal barriers to the marriage either in New York or in Ohio. I told them, "I think that everyone ought to have a free choice in marriage, but remember this. We all pay for everything we do in this world. What you are proposing exacts a specially heavy price because it means estrangement from both your families. It may also mean estrangement from your friends. Why don't you think about it for six months? If you find that you are willing to pay the price six months from now, go ahead and get married."

As it turned out these people did not marry. In marriage counseling, one can never be certain whether he gave the right advice, but I do know that her father came to me later and thanked me.

In West Virginia Negroes have all the legal rights that white people enjoy, but still there remains a definite barrier over which neither of the races cares to pass. The one truth we ought to have learned in our experience as a democracy is that no government can legislate love. Racial prejudice is not a one way street. The recent history of the Black Muslims, the racial riots in our northern cities, and our experiences in Africa should have taught us that the Negro is just as racially biased as the white man. There is a pecking order among hens and a caste system among dogs. One of the overriding problems of the white race is, "What race of men is going to be the superior race of men in the future?" From the noises that emanate from Red China, even against their Communist partners, the Russians, it is apparent that the concepts of brotherhood and the love of all mankind, irrespective of race, creed, or color, do not activate the policies of the Chinese government.

The culture of Appalachia predictably had its roots in the Middle Ages. The only musical instrument on the frontier that we hear about is the fiddle, possibly because the fiddle, though sturdy, has little weight or bulk and may be transported easily. The fiddle was and still is the accepted musical instrument in square dancing. Later came the banjo, the guitar, the harmonica, the organ, and by the time of my own boyhood a few pianos. Singing alone or in concert with others was a feature of everyday life. Group singing was largely confined to hymns, but old ballads were preserved in the privacy of the home where mothers rocked their children to sleep with lullabies and sometimes kept them awake with suspenseful theatricals. I recall three lullabies from my own childhood. The first was:

TWINKLE, TWINKLE LITTLE STAR

Twinkle, twinkle, little star,
How I wonder what you are,
Up above the world so high,
Like a diamond in the sky.

Another was:

ROCKABYE BABY

Rockabye, baby, in the tree top,
When the wind blows the cradle will rock,
When the bough breaks the cradle will fall,
Down comes baby, cradle, and all.

There was a bedtime prayer that the child memorized and repeated. It ran:

Now I lay me down to sleep,
I pray Thee, Lord, my soul to keep,
If I should die before I wake,
I pray Thee, Lord, my soul to take.

The song that impressed me most as a child and the one that I asked my mother to sing over and over again sounds as if it had originally been acted out on the stage, perhaps with dancing. My mother would sing all the parts with appropriate changes of voice and of gestures. I remember the words to this day, and for want of a better title shall call the song, HANGMAN, STAY THAT ROPE. There are five characters in the ballad: the condemned, his brother, his sister, his father, and his mother.

HANGMAN, STAY THAT ROPE

(Condemned agitatedly)
Hangman, hangman, stay that rope,
Stay it for a while,
I think I see my brother a-coming,
And he's come for many a mile.

(Condemned hopefully)
Oh, brother, brother, have you brought
the gold,
The gold to set me free,
Or have you come to see me hung,
Upon the gallows tree?

(Brother disdainfully)
No, my brother, I've not brought
the gold,
The gold to set you free,
For I have come to see you hung,
Upon the gallows tree.

(Condemned agitatedly)
Hangman, hangman, stay that rope,
Stay it for a while,
I think I see my sister a-coming,
And she's come for many a mile.

(Condemned hopefully)
Oh, sister, sister, have you brought
the gold,

The gold to set me free,
Or have you come to see me hung,
Upon the gallows tree?

(Sister flippantly)
No, my brother, I've not brought
the gold,
The gold to set you free,
For I have come to see you hung,
Upon the gallows tree.

(Condemned agitatedly)
Hangman, hangman, stay that rope,
Stay it for a while,
I think I see my father a-coming,
And he's come for many a mile.

(Condemned wearily)
Oh, father, father, have you brought
the gold,
The gold to set me free,
Or have you come to see me hung,
Upon the gallows tree?

(Father sorrowfully)
No, my son, I've not brought
the gold,
The gold to set you free,
For I have come to see you hung,
Upon the gallows tree.

(Condemned agitatedly)
Hangman, hangman, stay that rope,
Stay it for a while,
I think I see my mother a-coming,
And she's come for many a mile.

(Condemned almost hysterically)
Oh, mother, mother, have you brought
the gold,

The gold to set me free,
Or have you come to see me hung,
Upon the gallows tree?

(Mother joyfully)
Yes, my son, I've brought the gold,
The gold to set you free,
For I've not come to see you hung,
Upon the gallows tree.

Sometimes my mother would broaden the cast of characters to include aunts, uncles, and numerous cousins and I would sit entranced in a drama of near catastrophe, though I knew that ultimately there would be a happy ending. I never learned how or when this song originated, but it must spring from the very heart of Anglo-Saxon folklore. Other songs that my mother sang were not so obviously medieval ballads. One was:

THE LITTLE ROSEWOOD CASKET

In a little rosewood casket,
That is sitting on the stand,
Is a package of old letters,
Written by a cherished hand.

Go, and fetch them to me, sister,
Read them o'er and o'er to me,
For my eyes are growing weary,
And I cannot, cannot see.

Another was:

PUT MY LITTLE SHOES AWAY

I am going to leave you, mother,
So, remember what I say,
Do it, won't you, dearest mother,
Put my little shoes away.

Other songs that my mother sang were hymns such as "Rock of Ages," "Jesus, Lover of My Soul," and "Almost Persuaded." Still others were popular songs of the day. I remember a Negro song which ran:

Come along, get you ready,
Wear your brand, brand new gown,
For we're gonna have a wedding,
In this good, good old town,
Where you knows everybody,
And they all knows you,
And we'll take along a rabbit's foot,
To keep away the hoo-doo-doo.
Please, Oh please, Oh, do not let me fall,
I love you, I love you best of all,
If I don't get you I'll have no man at all,
There'll be a hot time in the old town tonight,
My baby.

There was also a cowboy song of which I remember only the chorus:

Oh, bury me not on the lone prairie,
Where the wild coyotes howl over me,
And the wildcat screams at the break of day,
Oh, bury me not on the lone prairie.

In suggesting that HANGMAN, STAY THAT ROPE may have originally been accompanied by dancing, I am thinking of the play parties that were still current in my boyhood. A play party was quite a different thing from a square dance. The square dance in my childhood and in the childhood of my mother was a public affair to which the dancers paid admission fees. Food and drink were served as a part of the entertainment. The play party, on the other hand, was strictly private, with a list of invited guests. Genteel and respectable, the play party perhaps has an even longer history than the square dance. There was no fiddle, which was considered an instrument of iniquity, nor any other musical instrument. The music was furnished by the dancers' voices and their clapping hands, and, young women who would never consider attending a square dance, would trip merrily to the beat of "Old Dan Tucker," "Skip to My Lou," "The Old Miller," "Chase the Buffalo," and many others.

The routine of "Old Dan Tucker" suggests the pattern of play parties. The routine made use of available dance partners plus an extra male. The dancers gathered in a circle, singing and clapping, while the male in the center executed a tap dance called the hoedown. The routine follows:

> (*The dancers sing and clap.*)
> Old Dan Tucker's in this town,
> Saluting the ladies all around,
> (*The male dancer in the center performs the hoedown and bows to the four corners of the room.*)
> First to the right,
> (*He dances to the right.*)
> Then to the left,
> (*He dances to the left.*)
> And then to the one he loves best.
> (*He advances to the girl of his choice and extends his arm. All the other males extend arms to their partners, and, arm in arm, they circle about the room chanting.*)
>
> Get out of the way for Old Dan Tucker,
> He's too late to get his supper,
> Supper, supper, supper a-frying,
> And Old Dan Tucker's left a-crying.

The routine leaves one of the males without a partner. He promptly steps to the middle of the ring. When the chant is over the circle is reformed with a new Dan Tucker.

It seems to me that I read something about the origin of

"Old Dan Tucker" somewhere, but I have forgotten what it was. If it is an English dance, as I strongly suspect, others are obviously American in origin. The routine of "Chase the Buffalo" was as follows:

(The circle forms. When the music starts the males all face in one direction, the females in the opposite direction. Again, there is a lone male dancer in the center of the ring.)

Oh, come my dearest dear,
And present to me your hand,
(The beat is slow. The male dancer in the center advances to one of the girls in the circle and extends his hand. He swings her completely around. Then they part, and moving in opposite directions, both the male and the female extend hands to the nearest dancers. The male without a partner retires to the center of the ring.)
And we'll all go together,
To a far and distant land,
Where the boys will reap and mow,
And the girls will spin and sew,
And we'll all go together,
For to chase the buffalo.
(The two original dancers move in opposite directions, extending hands, swinging, and performing the hoedown. The other dancers follow the same routine. At the word "buffalo" all the dancers face suddenly in the same direction. The men extend their arms to the girls with whom they are dancing at the moment. Everyone has a new partner. They circle the room chanting.)
For to chase the buffalo,
For to chase the buffalo,

And we'll all go together,
For to chase the buffalo.

There were a number of such songs with varying routines, but I find that I have forgotten most of them and no one else with whom I have talked remembers the routines. Play parties have been dead in Wirt County these fifty years. Curiously enough, the rowdy square dance has survived in the cities and in some places has even become fashionable while the genteel and respectable play party has completely disappeared.

I remember parts of some of the songs, such as:

THE OLD MILLER

There was an old miller,
And he milled all he could,
But he couldn't mill a bit,
For to do a bit of good.

With one hand in the hopper,
And the other in the sack,
The ladies step forward,
And the gents fall back.

SKIP TO MY LOU

Skip, skip, skip to my Lou,
Skip, skip, skip to my Lou,
Skip, skip, skip to my Lou,
Skip to my Lou, my darling.

(I have often wondered what these words really mean. All I know for sure is that they were part of a dance routine.)

THE DUKE OF YORK TOWN

He was the Duke of York Town,
He had a hundred men,

He marched them up a hillside,
And marched them down again.

Oh, when they're up they're up,
And when they're down they're down,
And when they're only half way up,
They're neither up nor down.

This particular song reminds one of the famous anonymous jingle about the King of France, which was first published in London in 1642. According to Bartlett's Familiar Quotations, the jingle reads:

The King of France went up the hill,
With twenty thousand men,
The King of France came down the hill,
And ne'er went up again.

Is the Duke of York Town a parody on the King of France or was the King of France itself a parody?

There was one dance song, now partially reconstructed with the help of my mother, which is indubitably American and which contains an unusual ceremony. It was confined in my boyhood to couples who were engaged to be married. I saw it performed but once. It ran:

We're marching down from Old Quebec,
The drums are loudly beating,
Americans have won the day,
The French are fast retreating.

The war's all o'er and we've turned back,
Never to be parted,
We open the ring,
And we all sing,
To cheer the broken hearted.

In this ceremony there was no hoedown. The dance partners constituted a line instead of a circle, and, with upraised hands, formed an arch. The engaged couple walked arm in arm under the arch until they reached the end of the line, where they turned to face the dancers. Then, a solemn voice intoned,

> I marry the Indian and the squaw,
> Under the old Virginia law,
> I pronounce thee man and wife.

There was a legend that this was originally a wedding ceremony, though the words of the song would not apply prior to 1763. Such a ceremony could have conceivably developed on the Indian frontier where there were no nearby licensing courts and very few preachers. The words and the tune remind us once again that Wirt County was once a part of the Kingdom of France.

The square dance is a subject of which I have little direct knowledge because my parents did not attend square dances. They were church people and church people did not even admit that play parties were dances. I recall attending only one square dance in the course of my life and that was after I left home at the age of fourteen. About thirty years ago, however, I had an interesting conversation with Dr. Cary Woofter, Professor of English at Glenville State College, who was gathering material for a book on Appalachian folklore. Dr. Woofter stated that the play party form of dance expression came first in point of time. The play party was a direct descendant of the morris dances of the Middle Ages, and the morris dances in turn probably go back to prehistoric times. When I talked to him, Professor Woofter was of the opinion that the square dance was a refinement of the morris dance and that it originated at the Court of the King of France. He based his judgment on the phrase do-si-do (pronounced dough-see-dough) which recurs in square dance patterns and which is a French phrase the exact meaning of which I have forgotten. My scant recollection of the phrase from the only square dance I ever attended is that in the dance itself it meant, circle with your partner.

The chief differences in the two art forms of the dance, as I recall them, were these: (1) There was no singing at square dances. While the fiddles screamed, the dance caller controlled the dance pattern with his voice. (2) The square dance was much more stylized and formal. There was a great deal of bowing and scraping. (3) Instead of a circle the dancers formed a square, which was better suited to the routines of a dance where individual partners advanced dancing to the middle of the square, and there bowed, swung, and retreated to their original positions. The square dance received its name, no doubt, because it discarded the traditional dance circle.

How and why the square dance lost its repute, though not necessarily its support, in Appalachia is properly a subject of religious history. At some point in the boisterous life of the frontier, square dances, card playing, and demon rum became symbols of sin. Sermons were preached denouncing one or the other and sometimes all three at once. My mother would not allow liquor in the house, if she knew of its presence, though my visiting Uncle Lon once showed me a bottle of whiskey that he kept locked in his valise. The common playing cards were also taboo, but we often played card games such as Authors, Flinch, and Old Maid.

It will be recalled that I grew up at a time when nationwide prohibition of alcoholic spirits and woman suffrage were crusading political issues. Crusades breed evasions and I am convinced now that the human mind is capable of infinite self deception. Not hypocrisy but self hypnosis, the will to believe what one wants to believe, the ability to make distinctions in words where no distinctions in fact exist, was responsible for the social distinctions between play parties and square dances and between a deck of Playing Cards and a deck of Flinch.

According to the tenets of a former generation, the vices ultimately triumphed. Prohibition was tried and failed, playing cards are now found everywhere, and square dancing is practiced at the colleges as an exercise in folklore and for the pure fun of dancing. These reflections make one wonder about the burning issues of the present time. Is disarmament the road to peace or to slavery? Is it possible to abolish racial prejudice by legislation? Is the abolition of poverty, owing to predictable defects in human nature, foredoomed to end in disaster? Only time will tell.

It is a curious circumstance that Wirt County, and, in fact, the whole of Appalachia, has never produced, to my knowledge, a single outstanding painter or sculptor. The mountain culture excluded these two disciplines for reasons that are today a matter of conjecture. Perhaps, the scriptural injunction against graven images was interpreted literally. Perhaps, and this is more likely, painting and sculpture flourish in an atmosphere of luxury and leisure. The visual arts are now taught in the elementary schools, but when I was a boy no one knew anything about them.

There were, however, some fine furniture makers, cabinetmakers, and woodcarvers, most of whose names have been forgotten. When I bought a house for my mother in Elizabeth, my wife discovered a beautiful, old, handcarved chair in the attic. The design of this chair does not appear in any of the anthologies on antique furniture. It is a genuine original, but no one, positively no one, knows where it came from or who made it. I did trace some other excellent handmade furniture to a cabinetmaker named Phil Meredith, who appears to have lived into the Twentieth Century. Phil Meredith operated a planing mill in Elizabeth. He built furniture as a hobby and the pieces that have been identified as his work were all gifts to his friends. I ought to mention in passing that one of my neighbors in the Beulah Hill Community is a famous gun maker. His name is Robert Milhoan. I had to go to Washington to discover that a Milhoan gun brings fantastic prices on the gun market.

Such sculpture as has been produced in Wirt County is all in the field of woodcarving. I own a handsome wooden pitcher that has, unfortunately, developed a crack. Household utensils on the frontier were often carved from wood, but wood is highly perishable and few such utensils remain. Decoration in carving was largely confined to wooden canes. There are still many examples of the woodcarver's art in canes in Wirt County. People have shown me polished canes decorated with carved serpents and other animals, and have told me proudly, "That was Grandpa's cane." They never know who made the cane.

While painting and sculpture are absent in the historic sense, Appalachia has produced exceptional business and professional men, military leaders, and authors. The business and professional men are listed later in a subsequent chapter. One of the recognized military leaders of all time was General T. J. (Stonewall) Jackson of Harrison County. Wirt County was once a part of Harrison County and the Jacksons who live in Wirt County today are related to the General's family. In fact, the Jacksons, like the Reeds, have been here so long that they are related to nearly everyone else.

Though there are no Pattons in Wirt County today, the Pattons used to live here. In 1861 a lawyer named George S. Patton organized a company of Confederate soldiers at Charleston. He rose to the rank of Colonel in the Confederate Army and was killed in the Valley of Virginia in 1864. He was the grandfather of the famous general of World War II, who bore the same name.

Appalachia and the South, to which the culture of Appalachia properly belongs, have produced a number of outstanding literary men and women. I recall in my own times such noted Southern writers as James Branch Cabell, Douglas Southall Freeman, Erskine Caldwell, Thomas Wolfe, and William Faulkner. Nearer home is Pearl S. Buck, a Nobel Prize Winner, who was born Pearl Sydenstricker at Hillsboro, in Pocahontas County, West Virginia. Sydenstricker was one of the German names on the Indian frontier. I am myself related to some Sydenstrickers, though not, so far as I know, to Mrs. Buck.

In addition to the famous writers there are all degrees of less famous writers. In my own family, my sister, Mary Jane Welch, is a published but not a famous poet. My mother has been a newspaper reporter and columnist for more than sixty years and still writes a weekly column for the Wirt County Journal in her eighty-seventh year. My cousin, Donald F. Black, has been working on a history of Wood

County for more than a decade. Not long ago he showed me his material and I calculated that, if he used it all, his history would run to at least ten volumes. Who, I wondered, would ever buy a ten volume history of Wood County. (This material has been placed at my disposal and I have drawn on it freely in this discussion.) It seems to me, when I talk to my friends, that nearly everyone I know is either writing a book, gathering material for a book, or thinking about gathering material for a book.

If it seems strange that Appalachia and the South should have developed a literary tradition and a host of hopeful literary workmen, the answer lies perhaps in the people who gravitated to the frontier. While it is just as hazardous to make generalizations here as it is in other fields of human endeavor, it seems plain that the frontiersmen were introspective by nature. They were certainly not disturbed at the prospect of loneliness and the demands of survival in a hostile environment where sudden death lurked always around the next corner predisposed them to violent action. Introspection and violence are attributes that often find expression in the pursuit of literature.

The culture of Appalachia was regional, and, except for music and literature, is rapidly being displaced in modern life. In recent decades there has been a growing interest in folklore music. Radio and television have spawned a new entertainment medium. Unfortunately, the demand for hillbilly songs exceeded the supply and most of the hillbilly songs I hear on television nowadays are new to me. They seem to be written by professional song writers for specific shows. *The Beverly Hillbillies* has been a top television show for the past two years, and, while it retains the traditional trappings of fiddle, guitar, and banjo, the songs are unrecognizable. Even the folksingers have taken liberties with their material. I once attended a folklore singing recital at Glenville State College. At the end I approached the performer, and said, "Miss ———, I recognized some of those songs, but the tunes were wrong."

Her reply disconcerted me. "I know, but what difference does it make? Many people who wrote down the words did not write down the music. Besides, when we find a tune we don't like, we improve it." Perhaps, I am old fashioned, but it seems to me that if "The Star Spangled Banner" were set to different music it would be an entirely different song.

Appalachia has always been comparatively poor in the economic sense, though much of the region is underlaid with coal, petroleum, and natural gas. Nevertheless, the longing for things of beauty is often illustrated in humble abodes by a profusion of wild and cultivated flowers. Once, when I was a small child, I was following my Grandmother Reed about the yard. In my innocence, I asked, "Grandma, where did the hollyhocks come from?"

My grandmother, you will recall, was one fourth Indian, which means that she was also three fourths white. She replied, "I will tell you the story just as it was told to me. Back in Indian times, one of my great-grandmothers came over the mountains from Virginia with her family. She was white, of course. The family had horses and cattle and all kinds of tools because this country was covered with woods. The men remembered to bring the tools—the axes, the mattocks, the shovels, and the hoes—but only my grandmother brought a package of hollyhock seeds. I have often thought that her remembering the hollyhocks illustrates better than anything else the role of women in the world. She was coming to a rough and forbidding land and she brought a reminder of beauty. Those hollyhocks are direct descendants of the seeds she carried over the mountains."

5. The Changing Age Pattern

THE APPALACHIAN FRONTIER was a melting pot of the nationalities, but it differs from other sections of the country in that most of the melting occurred nearly two hundred years ago. Since 1795 the outward migrations from rural Appalachia have exceeded the inward migrations. This is expecially true since the advent of the automobile. Most of the outgoing migrants and their descendants have remained plain people, but some have attained wealth, honors, and a measure of fame. Indeed, I shall not cease to wonder at the number of mountain farm boys and farm girls who have left their homes and carved a respectable niche for themselves elsewhere. In 1963 I was asked to speak at the French Creek Biennial Reunion in Upshur County, and there I was told that the French Creek Community, with less than a thousand inhabitants, has produced twenty-one native sons who are today serving professorships in American colleges and universities. Only one of them lives in West Virginia. French Creek, I believe, has an extraordinary record, but the information led me to make inquiry about migrants from Wirt County. This is what I have learned.

Wirt County, since its inception in 1848, has not produced a President of the United States, a Vice-President, a United States Senator, or a State Governor. The record in the realm of politics is quite modest. One native Congressman, Blackburn Dovener, moved to Wheeling after the Civil War, and represented the First Congressional District in Washington for many years. He was a Republican.

Howard B. Lee, a native of Wirt County and a Charleston lawyer at the time of his election, served as Attorney General of West Virginia from 1924 to 1932. He was a Republican.

Edgar B. Sims, a native of Wirt County and a resident of

Charleston at the time of his election, served as State Auditor from 1933 until his death in 1959, a total of twenty-six years. He was a Democrat.

Wirt County has produced a number of mayors, district attorneys, and lower court judges including Gordon Fought, former mayor of Wheeling; Duncan Daugherty, Federal District Attorney of Huntington; and Donald F. Black, of Parkersburg, incumbent Judge of the Circuit Court of Wood and Wirt counties.

The record in the realm of business is more impressive. Probably, the wealthiest of all former Wirt Countians is Ronald B. Woodyard, now in retirement at Fort Lauderdale, Florida, where he serves as angel to the Fort Lauderdale Symphony Orchestra. Woodyard, who used to own newspapers and radio stations, is reputed to be a large stockholder in three Dayton, Ohio, banks. I can remember when Ronald's father was a clerk in the Office of the County Assessor at Elizabeth. At that time Ronald worked for farmers, when he could, at fifty cents a day. He has recently given the Town of Elizabeth a library and a swimming pool.

Another native businessman who has made both reputation and money is French Robinson of Cleveland. Prior to his retirement, he was president of Consolidated Gas Company, one of the largest natural gas companies in the world.

Still another business executive is Howard West, president of Marathon Oil Company.

Another is William M. Batten, chairman of the board of J. C. Penney Company, one of the largest merchandisers in the world.

M. J. Rathbone, chairman of the board of Standard Oil Company of New Jersey in 1964, is not strictly a native of Wirt County, though his ancestors lived here and a number of less affluent Rathbones live here today.

Other prominent migrants are:

Dorothy Roberts, novelist and magazine writer, New York.

Mary Roberts Carter, novelist, Washington, D. C.

Dr. Amos H. Black, professor of mathematics, Southern Illinois University.

Dr. Lois Bing, nationally known optometrist, Cleveland, Ohio.

Dr. Hazel Roberts, emeritus professor of economics at Hunter College, New York.

Clay Williams. Even Wirt Countians know nothing of this man because his family never speaks of him. I know only because his brother married one of my cousins. Clay Williams became a henchman of the notorious Al Capone, but he never served a day in prison in his life. He was a police officer,—the Chief of Police at Las Vegas, Nevada, and later at Miami, Florida. He died in Miami, a very wealthy man.

At this point it is pertinent to add that not all the prominent businessmen of Wirt County are migrants. Roberts Brothers Hereford Farms of Elizabeth is one of the larger cattle raising operations in the East. Glen W. Roberts, who sends his sons to the University of Chicago and to Oxford, is an independent oil and gas producer.

In addition to the foregoing list of migrants, there are a large number of doctors, lawyers, and school teachers, especially school teachers. So many school teachers have left Wirt County for better paying jobs elsewhere that we have trouble staffing our own schools. As an example of what is happening to Wirt Countians who receive a college education I need only cite the example of my own relatives.

My Grandfather Black had thirteen grandsons, all of whom received at least one college or university degree. All are alive today. Of the thirteen, three are doctors of medicine practicing in the State of Ohio, three are lawyers, of whom one practices in Ohio and two, including myself and Judge Donald F. Black live in West Virginia, two own and operate retail businesses (one in West Virginia and one in Arizona), one is a university professor in Illinois, one a Presbyterian minister in Texas, one a high school principal in Cleveland, one a chemist for United Carbon Company in Ohio, and one a retired army officer in Florida. Of the thirteen only three live in West Virginia at this time. I, alone, claim Wirt County as my home, and I came back when I was fifty years old.

The story of the migrants is the saga of Twentieth Century America, with its headlong pace, instantaneous communication, and shifting values. The little self-sufficient farms are almost gone, perhaps forever. The urbanizing influence of the cities, with its broad horizons, penetrates the countryside just as far as, and no farther, than hard surface roads have been built. Where dirt roads remain the countryside is rapidly becoming a wilderness. I own two farms, on eight mile long Courtney Ridge near Elizabeth, that have been planted in pine trees. In 1910 more than five hundred people lived on this ridge, supporting a church and two schools. In 1964 not a single family remains. A few shells of decaying houses staving off the inexorable approach of the jungle are the only reminders that this was once a prosperous farm community. After all, the opportunities in Wirt County are limited. What has happened in my own family has happened in other families, and the sad truth is that the ones who have gone away and made the greatest successes in the material sense are the very ones who never return.

Practically all the present day population of Wirt County is concentrated in the Village of Elizabeth and along the all-weather roads. The State Road Commission classifies all-weather roads as Primary Roads and dirt roads as Secondary Roads. The Courtney Ridge Road is a Secondary Road. The rural community in which I now live, and in which I was born, is known as the Beulah Hill Community in honor of the nearby Beulah Presbyterian Church. The community is bisected by a Primary Road, State Route Number 14, and receives the following public services:

(1) Electricity is furnished by West Penn Power Company.

(2) Natural gas is furnished by Cabot Corporation.

(3) Dial telephone service is furnished by Chesapeake and Potomac Telephone Company, a subsidiary of American Telephone and Telegraph Company.

(4) A trash and garbage collection service operating out of Parkersburg is open to subscribers.

(5) There is no public water supply system, but plenti-

ful underground water is found in drilled wells. Using electric pumps, all modern houses in the neighborhood, and some older ones, have their own private water systems.

(6) Bus service, two trips daily between Parkersburg and Spencer on State Route No. 14, which passes through Elizabeth and also bisects the Beulah Hill precinct, is furnished by Reynolds Bus Company of Spencer.

(7) School bus service for all school children in the precinct is furnished by the County Board of Education. When I was a boy there were two one-room schools in the precinct. Now there are none. All school children attend the elementary and high schools in Elizabeth.

Electricity for light, running water, refrigeration, and television, natural gas for heating and cooking, and a dial telephone system for voice communication anywhere in the world place the Beulah Hill Community in the middle of the Twentieth Century. The visitor seeking evidence of the much advertised Appalachian poverty will have to go further afield. Yet, there is some poverty and what is even more discouraging a pervading apathy among a people that accepts declining population with stoic indifference and even public pride. The apathy, the inertia, the seeming progress that is not progress are all rooted in the social revolution, in the breaking up of the small farms and the acquisition of larger farms, in the declining birth rate, in the movement of young people to the cities, in the increasing span of life, in the paternalistic policies of the welfare state, and in the concentration of senior citizens.

How many senior citizens are there in the Beulah Hill Community? What are the ages of all the inhabitants? To find out I have canvassed each home in the Beulah Hill voting precinct for vital statistics. (On the election records the official name of the precinct is Center Hill, though no one ever speaks of the Center Hill Community.) My first conclusion is that the figures released by the Social Security Administration as to the number of persons above sixty-two years of age in Wirt County are misleading. According to the Social Security Administration only 14.9 per cent of the inhabitants of Wirt County are above sixty-two years old, but that does not include the old people who do not qualify for one reason or another for Social Security. Since I know practically everyone in the precinct personally, I am listing the households separately and am adding pertinent information as to size of households and employment.

HOUSEHOLDS	REMARKS
(1) E. W. Allman, age 75 Effie Allman, age 70	Prosperous farmers. He is president of County Court. No children at home.
(2) Theresa M. Anderson, age 85	Lives alone. No children at home.
(3) Larry D. Bailey, age 29 Dorothy Marie Bailey, age 27	He is a factory worker. She is housewife. Three small children.
(4) Forrest F. Bailey, age 54 Inez M. Bailey, age 53	Farmer and factory worker. Parents of Larry D. Bailey. One child at home.
(5) Olin L. Bell, age 43 Mary E. Bell, age 33	Factory worker. Housewife. Three children at home.
(6) Harry L. Bibbee, age 64 Icie Bibbee, age 62	Farmer and factory worker. No children at home.
(7) Lyle R. Bibbee, age 34 Thelma M. Bibbee, age 35	Factory worker. Son of Harry L. Bibbee. No children at home.
(8) William T. Boise, age 60 Ellen O. Boise, age 53	Factory worker. No children at home.
(9) Annie E. Buchanan, age 81	Lives alone. No children at home.
(10) Lawrence Buchanan, age 40 Bonnie Buchanan, age 40	Chemist at Viscose Company, Parkersburg. Two children at home.
(11) Everett R. Buchanan, age 54 Alma G. Buchanan, age 50	Farmer and factory worker. No children at home.
(12) Wayne C. Buchanan, age 53 Opal B. Buchanan, age 53	Farmer and factory worker. No children at home.
(13) Wilmer W. Burns, age 47 Mary E. Burns, age 47	Farmer and factory worker. Five children at home.

(14)	Estella Butcher, age 74	Widow, lives alone. No children at home.
(15)	Henry C. Caltrider, age 66 Audrey Caltrider, age 52	Retired farmer and factory worker. No children at home.
(16)	John Alva Collins, age 75 Wife, age 72, and daughter, age 52, not registered to vote	Retired farmer. Part-time Methodist minister. No children at home.
(17)	Ritchie E. Cooper, age 42 Beulah K. Cooper, age 38	Farmer and factory worker. Three children at home.
(18)	Ernie F. Cumbridge, age 30 Lorene B. Cumbridge, age 24	Farmer and school bus driver. One child at home.
(19)	Donaldson R. Earle, Sr., age 74, Donaldson R. Earle, Jr., age 27	Father and son. Son employed as factory worker. No children at home.
(20)	Harrison C. Edwards, age 23 Father and mother, with whom he lives not registered to vote. Both in late forties	Factory worker. Unmarried.
(21)	Wallice J. Ellison, age 44 Marvella J. Ellison, age 42	School bus driver. Retired master sergeant, U. S. Army. No children at home.
(22)	Solomon B. Exline, age 66 Bonna M. Exline, age 53	Retired factory worker. One child at home.
(23)	Howard Fought, age 50 Anna M. Fought, age 38	Factory worker. Five children at home.
(24)	Edward Fought, age 78 Cora Belle Fought, age 80	This couple lives alone. Parents of Howard Fought.
(25)	Jessie L. Fought, age 78	Widow. Lives alone.
(26)	Morton Frey, Jr., age 47 Ruth Frey, age 40	Farmer and factory worker. Three children at home.
(27)	Ellsworth L. Gabbert, age 62 Kathryn R. Gabbert, age 43	Retired factory worker. One child at home.
(28)	Elizabeth S. Gibson, age 83	Widow. Lives alone.
(29)	Verna H. Hague, age 82	Widow. Lives alone.

(30) Clayburn J. Hanna, age 49 Garnet R. Hanna, age 48	Farmer and factory worker. Wife also employed in Parkersburg. One child at home.
(31) Ralph E. Hupp, age 56 Martha A. Hupp, age 51	Factory worker. No children at home.
(32) H. C. Jones, age 49 Eva Jones, age 40	Farmer and factory worker. Two children at home.
(33) Johanna S. Keener, age 47 Husband not registered to vote	Husband is career soldier serving overseas. Three children at home.
(34) Otha King, age 51 Amy King, age 42	Farmer and factory worker. Five children at home, three of whom are adults and two minors. Adult children in 21 to 30 age group.
(35) Ruby Pearl Lee, age 60	Widow. Lives alone.
(36) Robert C. Lee, age 34 Norma M. Lee, age 29	He is steel construction worker. She is employed at glass factory. He is son of Ruby Pearl Lee. One child at home.
(37) McKinley Ludwig, age 66 Genevieve Ludwig, age 60	Retired farmer. No children at home.
(38) Gail P. McCroskey, age 35 Geraldine McCroskey, age 33	Factory worker. One child at home.
(39) Nellie B. Mace, age 76	Widow. Lives alone.
(40) Corba J. Mace, age 72	Widow. Lives alone.
(41) Harry D. Matheney, age 47 Janice J. Matheney, age 46	Farmer and factory worker. One child at home.
(42) Robert U. Milhoan, age 78 Georgia A. Milhoan, age 63	Farmer. Former clerk of the Circuit Court. No children at home.
(43) Victor V. Morgan, age 51 Marie Morgan, age 51	Farmer and factory worker. No children at home.
(44) Raymond F. Morgan, age 57 Ruth Morgan, age 55	He is dairy farmer and former member of State Legislature. She works for Parkersburg newspaper. No children at home.
(45) Harley Morgan, Sr., age 61 Vinnie Morgan, age 61	Factory worker. No children at home.

(46) Harley Morgan, Jr., age 41 Eileen Morgan, age 40	Factory worker. Son of Harley Morgan, Sr. Two children at home.
(47) Paul V. Morgan, age 26 Anna Morgan, age 22	Farmer and factory worker. Son of Victor V. Morgan. Three children at home.
(48) Charley Morgan, age 54	Bachelor. Lives alone. Cattle farmer.
(49) Harvey H. Nicholson, Sr., age 65 Wife not registered to vote	Retired. No children at home.
(50) Harvey H. Nicholson, Jr., age 41 Freda Nicholson, age 41	Employed in Parkersburg. Three children at home.
(51) Arthur Nutter, age 78 Mary Nutter, age 74	Retired oil field worker. One adult child, above 40, and three grandchildren at home.
(52) George H. Nutter, age 54 Gertie Nutter, age 48	Chief maintenance employee of County Board of Education. No children at home.
(53) William E. Nutter, age 31 Patty Lou Nutter, age 26	Factory worker. Son of George H. Nutter. Three children at home.
(54) John W. Pidcock, age 74 Alma Pidcock, age 56	He is retired lumber worker. She works for Viscose Company at Parkersburg. No children at home.
(55) Walter Powell, age 45 Bonnie Powell, age 41	Farmer and factory worker. One child at home.
(56) Louis Reed, age 65 Mildred J. Reed, age 65	He is retired lawyer. She is retired civil servant. No children at home.
(57) Emma Belle Reed, age 86	Widow. Lives with housekeeper. Mother of Louis Reed. No children at home.
(58) Myrtle Reed, age 83	Widow. No children at home.
(59) Philip Shears, age 23 Janet Shears, age 22	Factory worker. One child at home.
(60) Sarah E. Sims, age 70	Widow. Lives alone.
(61) Johnny Smith, age 73 Laura Smith, age 63	Retired farmer. One adult child in 30 to 40 age group at home.
(62) Lowell D. Somerville, age 39 Marian Somerville, age 37	Factory worker. Three children at home.

(63)	Harvey Staley, age 74 Effie Staley, age 64	Retired factory worker. No children at home.
(64)	Roxiana Strong, age 83	Widow. No children at home.
(65)	Okey Strong, age 54 Merle M. Strong, age 45	Farmer. One adult child in 21 to 30 age group and three minor children at home. He is son of Roxiana Strong.
(66)	Cecil J. Taylor, age 35 Charlotte Taylor, age 32	He is manager of a pesticide company. Four children at home.
(67)	Okey L. Turner, age 78 Anna B. Turner, age 55	Retired factory worker. No children at home.
(68)	Harry A. Virtue, age 66	Bachelor. Retired Farmer.
(69)	Dennis J. Wease, age 65 Lyda J. Wease, age 68	Retired merchant and landlord. No children at home.
(70)	George R. West, age 75 Mabel West, age 65	Retired farmer. Former member of State Legislature. No children at home.

The canvass shows that there are 70 households in the Beulah Hill voting precinct. The precinct is irregularly shaped, but it contains, according to my estimate, an area of approximately nine square miles. The population is rural in character, though many of the wage earners are employed in Parkersburg. There is not a single village nor a commercial establishment of any kind in the precinct. Farming is largely confined to raising cattle and hay, though nearly every household has its vegetable garden and a few raise hogs and chickens. All the residents of Beulah Hill Community live on State Route No. 14 or on all-weather branches of the same. Nearly all use electric power. A majority of the houses are equipped with natural gas, running water, and dial telephones. At least one house owned by an eccentric bachelor has no modern conveniences whatever.

Except for the people themselves and their historical and genealogical background, the Beulah Hill Community is not strictly typical of Appalachia. There are no coal mines. We are so close to Parkersburg, fifteen miles from my home, that we are almost a distant suburb. That circumstance alone accounts for our living conveniences. While electric power lines span most of rural America in 1964, natural gas and dial telephones are still the prerogatives of suburbia. Actually, dial telephones came to Wirt County as late as

1956 and much of the county still does not have natural gas distribution lines. There are 140 registered voters in the Beulah Hill precinct, divided almost equally between Democrats and Republicans. Of this number 15 are absentee voters. Absentees represent persons serving in the armed forces, residents of the District of Columbia who formerly lived in the precinct, and voters who have moved away and have failed, for one reason or another, to change their registration. That leaves 125 adult registrants, 7 unregistered adults, and 65 persons under 21 years of age, a total of 197 scattered among 70 different households.

These 70 households are occupied by persons in the following age groups:

Above 60	50
50 to 60	23
40 to 50	30
30 to 40	14
21 to 30	15
Under 21	65
	197

Percentages of population for the same age groups are:

Above 60	25.4%
50 to 60	11.7%
40 to 50	15.3%
30 to 40	7.2%
21 to 30	7.6%
Under 21	32.8%

Unfortunately, I cannot list similar statistics for the precinct in 1900 or 1910. The United States census figures for those years do not list voting precincts, and I find that my memory is unreliable with respect to numbers and ages of persons living in the various households in 1910. It did not occur to me as a boy that I would ever be writing a discourse of this nature, and no one has preserved a written list. On one point, however, my memory is sharp and clear.

In 1910 there were two one-room schools in the precinct, the Oak Hill School and the Center Hill School. I attended both schools at different periods, and I recall the seating arrangements. Attendance varied with changes in the weather. It was an unwritten law that when a school gained more than fifty pupils, the school authorities built a new school. The majority of the pupils were between eight and fifteen years of age, though six-year olds were admitted and it was not uncommon for older boys and girls to attend. I am convinced that the two schools in 1910 had an average enrollment of forty-five each, making a total of ninety. Remembering that children under six and often under eight years of age did not attend school (my sister Mary, who was frail in childhood, did not attend school until she was almost nine years old), that boys of fifteen or younger frequently left school and went to work, and that girls usually married in their teens, I think it safe to state that approximately 240 persons under 21 years of age lived in the precinct in 1910.

For some reason, I remember the houses better than I remember the people. Since 1910 many new houses have been built and many old ones torn down. Counting the old house sites and comparing them with the new house sites reveals that there are actually eight more households in the precinct now than there were in 1910. While I am unable to cite specific figures for age groups in those former years, it is apparent from estimated school enrollments and house sites that the population percentages were quite different then and now. I cannot recall old people living by themselves fifty-five years ago. To do so was difficult because wood for heating and cooking had to be cut daily. Every household had children and many had grandfathers or grandmothers who helped with the chores. People died earlier—a person over eighty was a rarity. My four grandparents died at ages 55, 59, 74, and 75 respectively. There was more youth and vigor in the community, and, while living conditions were harsher, there was less apathy and more hope.

The conclusions drawn from the foregoing discussion in which some of the figures are admittedly deficient are as follows:

(1) Wirt County now has a population less than half of what it was in 1910.

(2) The percentage of the population under 21 years of age has decreased to about one third of what it was in 1910.

(3) The percentage of the population above 60 years of age has increased from a negligible fraction to more than one-fourth of the total.

(4) More households than not in Wirt County now have no children under 21 years of age. I have spot checked the municipality of Elizabeth and have learned that there are more old people and fewer children there than there are in the Beulah Hill precinct. The difference arises because retiring farmers often move to the village.

(5) Families with children generally live in less affluent circumstances than those without children. The more spacious and expensive homes in Wirt County are almost all owned by older couples with no children at home. The old twenty-two room house in Elizabeth is still standing, occupied by one unmarried school teacher.

(6) The automobile, motion pictures, radio and television, together with widely disseminated birth control methods, an increasing life span, and government welfare have transformed not only the way of life in Wirt County but also the thoughts and the motivations of its people. The old virtues are declining. I am thinking particularly of hard work, scrupulous honesty, responsibility, self reliance, and thrift. In place of the themes of liberty, fraternity, and equality that stirred men's souls less than two hundred years ago, our people are straining toward a great regimented society with unmistakable aspects of dictatorship and tyranny. The human spirit soars in cycles. We have cringed in fear before the threat of the nuclear bomb, but our scientists and philosophers have failed to note that the real strength of a nation lies in the self reliance, some call it the morale, of its people.

6. Economics

SINCE WORLD WAR II the State of West Virginia has suffered a painful economic decline and mounting unemployment, due in a large measure to automation of the coal mines. In an era of prosperity West Virginia, and indeed all of Appalachia, has become known as a pocket of poverty. The displacement of workers by machines is one of the potent factors in the developing American welfare state.

Prior to World War II much bituminous coal mining was performed by hand labor. Minable coal seams rest on beds of slate. Coal miners dug out the slate with pick and shovel, shot the coal down with a charge of explosive, and then loaded the coal with shovels on hand carts. The famous miner's song, SIXTEEN TONS AND WHAT HAVE YOU GOT?, describes the back breaking effort required to load sixteen tons of coal on a hand cart in a single day.

Nowadays, the mines have cutting machines to cut out the slate and loading machines to fill the carts. The coal miner is no longer a laborer—he is an operator of expensive machinery. As such, he requires education and training. With the installation of automatic machinery, the minimal qualifications of coal miners drastically changed. The man with the strong back who could load sixteen tons was displaced by the high school graduate who could read and understand instructions.

Throughout the preceding century, coal mining had become a way of life. Coal towns were invariably drab, dreary, and soot blackened. Accidents and sudden death were common. Coal miners were barely literate and the nature of their work encouraged a fatalistic attitude toward life. They expected little and often received less. It was these men and their families who were spewed forth by the great upheaval in mining methods when the mines were automated.

The automation of the mines gave West Virginia the highest unemployment rate in the nation for many years and contributed greatly to the State's loss of population. I remember reading, perhaps twenty-five years ago, a newspaper story to the effect that one person in three in West Virginia was directly or indirectly dependent on coal mining for a living. Where there were once two hundred thousand coal miners in the State there are now forty thousand, and the forty thousand produce more coal than was formerly mined by two hundred thousand.

The short term effect of automation was an enormous increase in the number of welfare recipients and the long term effect to this date shows a disproportionate percentage of the population receiving welfare payments. The more aggressive displaced miners emigrated to other states. Only recently I talked to a motel manager in Bonham, Texas, who had been a West Virginia coal miner for twenty-seven years. Those who remained behind often became permanent relief clients. One of the continuing problems of the day is the family without pride or ambition, content to live in idleness on the government dole.

Though Wirt County has no coal mines of its own, it must be remembered that economics are subject to the law of proximity. There are coal mines in nearby counties. Besides, West Virginia coal miners are often descended from those pioneers who infiltrated NO MAN'S LAND two hundred years ago. The family names of Wirt County citizens can frequently be matched in the coal towns. The motel manager in Texas, previously mentioned, bore the name Rader and there are many Raders in Wirt County. In short, the Appalachian people are usually related by blood one way or another, and, over the years, some strains have degenerated. This condition is by no means confined to Appalachia. The same thing has happened in the royal and noble families of Europe.

Relief and welfare are administered in West Virginia by the Department of Public Assistance, commonly called the

DPA. The DPA in turn is a creature of the United States Department of Health, Education, and Welfare. Operating under Federal and State Law the DPA is a semi-secret agency, and it is difficult to obtain specific information about its activities. When I was Prosecuting Attorney of Wirt County I asked for the names and addresses of unwed mothers who were receiving public assistance, but I was told that such information is classified. Nevertheless, the local supervisor of DPA has favored me with a revealing mass of general information. I have learned, for instance, that welfare in Wirt County is categorized as follows:

(1) Persons who receive Old Age Assistance. These are men and women above sixty-five years of age who are needy and who do not receive Social Security pensions or other regular income.

(2) Persons who receive aid to the blind. This includes both the blind person and his or her wife or husband and their dependents.

(3) Persons who receive aid to Families with Dependent Children. This category is divided into two sub-categories.

- (a) Those families in which the wage earner is either deceased or temporarily disabled.
- (b) Those families in which the wage earner is furnished work, usually on the roads or other public property.

(4) Persons receiving aid because of Permanent and Total Disability. This category includes the disabled and his or her dependents.

(5) Persons receiving General Relief for the Unemployed. This category covers unemployed persons and their dependents who are not covered by some other relief program such as unemployment compensation.

(6) Persons receiving Aid to Crippled Children. This category is designed to furnish aid, usually of a medical or surgical nature, to parents of crippled children who may, or may not, be otherwise eligible for welfare payments.

(7) Persons receiving the services of the Child Welfare Program. This category is designed for neglected and delinquent children, including the children of unwed mothers.

Its specific activities are classified, but I know from my tenure as prosecuting attorney that the DPA frequently goes into court to obtain custody of children who have no legal fathers and also of children who are neglected or delinquent. The agency makes an investigation and recommendation to the court in all cases of juvenile delinquency irrespective of whether the parents are welfare recipients. Juvenile court judges customarily follow such recommendations with respect to probation, commitment, award of custody, and adoption.

(8) Persons entitled to surplus foods and commodities. This category covers all welfare recipients and also all other families in the county with a total income of less than ninety-five dollars a month. I know of some families who, from a sense of pride, decline this proffered help even though they are eligible.

(9) Persons entitled to other services. In practice, this category is confined to the children of welfare recipients, above eighteen years of age, who are still in high school. It is an exception to the general rule that welfare aid stops when a person reaches the age of eighteen.

(10) Persons entitled to medical aid for the aged. This category, under the Kerr-Mills Act, covers old people who have a sufficient income under ordinary circumstances but who are confronted with illnesses requiring expensive medical care and hospitalization.

General information for these categories as of December 31, 1964, follows:

Category	Total Cases	Total Recipients
Old Age Assistance	62	69
Aid to Blind	2	2
Aid to Families with Dependent Children	43	180
Aid to Permanent and Totally Disabled	21	23
Aid to Unemployed	2	2
Aid to Crippled Children	2	2
Aid to Child Welfare	Classified	Classified

Medical Aid for Aged	44	44
Aid for Other Services	1	2
Aid in Form of Food and Commodities	109	313
TOTAL	286	637

Total cost of the above described programs for 1964 is not available at the time this is written because the final figures for that year have not yet been audited. I have, however, been provided with such cost figures for 1963 as are kept at the local DPA Office. It appears that the bookkeeping for the categories Aid to Crippled Children, Aid to Child Welfare, Medical Aid for the Aged, Aid for Other Services, and Aid in Form of Food and Commodities is kept either at the State or the National levels. The local office of the DPA is concerned only with taking applications, making investigations, and forwarding recommendations in these programs. Furthermore, the following figures do not reflect costs of administration.

The figures furnished me for 1963 follow:

Category	Total Expenditures
Old Age Assistance	$ 29,688.00
Aid to the Blind	2,012.00
Aid to Permanent and Totally Disabled	12,994.00
Aid to families with Dependent Children	
Sub-Category (a)	33,389.00
Sub-Category (b)	40,715.00
Aid to Unemployed	855.00
TOTAL	$119,633.00

It is obvious that the figure of $119,633.00 is far wide of the mark with respect to the total cost of welfare in Wirt County. Administration costs, Medical Aid to the Aged, and Aid in the Form of Food and Commodities are bound to be expensive. Aid in the Form of Food and Commodities is particularly expensive because the government first pays the farmer for his surplus product, then pays the processor to process it and then pays an additional sum to transport and distribute the processed product to the consumer. In this connection I am reminded that nearly all the taxpayers I know serve oleomargarine on their tables which costs about thirty cents a pound, while those who receive commodities are issued butter which costs about one dollar a pound at the stores.

Nevertheless, the figures are revealing not so much for what they conceal as for what they tell about welfare payments. Persons who receive old age assistance are ineligible if they have more than one hundred dollars in the bank or if they receive Social Security or pension payments. The local supervisor tells me these qualifications are being liberalized, but they were not liberalized in 1963. Old age recipients in 1963 received about $35.00 a month out of which they were expected to pay rent, if they were renters, and taxes and utilities if they owned their own property. They were also expected to buy all their own clothes and such food items as are not furnished under the heading of commodities. The blind were somewhat better treated, receiving approximately $84.00 a month. The permanent and totally disabled received $47.00 a month, while families with dependent children received about $30.00 a month for each dependent in the family.

It should be noted here, though I expect to go into the matter in more detail later, that the County's share of the welfare costs for Wirt County for 1963 was $2,100.00.

It is noted that DPA categories do not include cases of mental illness and mental retardation. Such of these cases as become public charges are still committed to a State or a Federal institution by the County Mental Hygiene Commission consisting of the county clerk, the prosecuting attorney, and the president of the county court. I was a member of this commission when I was prosecuting attorney. Commitments to an institution, either State or Federal, were made after an open hearing in the presence of and upon the recommendation of two physicians. Only war veterans were committed to Federal institutions.

One of the concerns of modern living is that persons committed to an institution are often forgotten. They may spend their entire lives in an institution, though in many instances they could return home if relatives wanted them. The condition however is not as heartless on the part of the relatives as may be assumed. Mental illness is a recurring malady, and relatives who try to be helpful often assume an intolerable burden. Family life is difficult at best—it can be thoroughly disrupted by an individual not amenable to necessary household discipline and routine.

As an example of how these people are really forgotten, I find, to my chagrin, that no one knows exactly how many men and women of Wirt County are confined in State or Federal mental hospitals at the present time. The total, however, is not large, possibly because mental patients often die soon after commitment. I do know of one male patient at Spencer State Hospital who has been there for fifteen years, and who, to all outward appearances is perfectly sane. Nevertheless, this man has a history of recurring attacks. His father brought him back four or five times. After his father died, his brothers and sisters committed him permanently.

The population of Wirt County in 1960 was 4,391. It is probably no less today and possibly a little more, as I shall point out presently. Of this total six hundred thirty seven persons are known to be receiving welfare services of one kind or another, which works out to about one person in seven. Though this figure seems high, the picture is not as bleak as it looks. Persons who receive old age assistance, for instance, often own their own homes and so do those who receive food and commodities. Nearly all the families in all categories own an automobile.

Nevertheless, a large number of Wirt County citizens are definitely poor. Without public assistance it is difficult to see how they could survive in today's economy. Their ancestors, of course, dug a living from the hillside farms, but no one digs a living from anything nowadays. The welfare law discourages individual effort. A disabled man receiving aid to dependent children receives less if he raises a garden. Some families increase income by raising babies instead of vegetables. There is a special section of the law relating to unwed mothers. When I was prosecuting attorney, a middle-aged woman, the mother of three illegitimate children, consulted me. Her fifteen-year-old daughter was pregnant. When I suggested that she swear out a warrant for statutory rape, the woman was horrified. All she wanted, she assured me, was to make certain that her daughter received welfare payments.

In addition to those receiving aid from the Department of Public Assistance a substantial number of workers receive aid each year from the Department of Unemployment Compensation. These are employed persons who, for one reason or another, became unemployed temporarily. This program is likewise administered by the Federal Government, and I know from personal observation that the number of recipients increases during the winter months. Unemployment compensation is payable only for a period of twenty-six weeks. The worker must then become re-employed for a specified time to attain re-eligibility. The chief beneficiaries are workers in the construction trades and other types of seasonal employment.

In analyzing the welfare statistics with special reference to the Beulah Hill precinct, I am conscious that my home community is more prosperous than some other sections of Wirt County. Only one person, to my knowledge, receives welfare payments. Ten others are eligible for old age assistance, medical help for the aged, and food and commodities. Of the seventy houses in the precinct, sixty-seven are owned by the occupants. At least eleven are encumbered with mortgages. Only three householders in the precinct are renters. Nearly all the houses have natural gas, running water, and dial telephones, in addition to electricity, and that is not uniformly true throughout the county.

It is uniformly true that the great majority of Wirt County families own their own homes. Rental properties are few and far between. Four years ago I wanted to rent a house for my mother in Elizabeth so that she could be near a physician. None were available. I finally bought a house in self defense. The absence of rental properties follows the tradition established in the days of small hillside farms.

A different face of the Wirt County economy than that

shown by the welfare rolls is reflected in the condition of the Wirt County Bank, of which I was until recently an officer and director. The Wirt County Bank, the only bank in the county, was founded in the 1890's following the closing of a former bank in the Panic of 1893. For many years in the early part of the present century the dominating figures at the bank were Mr. George W. Roberts and Mr. Herbert Roberts. George W. Roberts died about 1929. After the stock market crash of that year, banks in West Virginia failed right and left, but the Wirt County Bank survived. Mr. Herbert Roberts, now deceased, told me that at one point in the depression the total deposits of the bank declined to a mere $116,000.00.

For purposes of comparison, I am copying here the latest published statement of the bank as follows:

REPORT OF CONDITION OF WIRT COUNTY BANK OF ELIZABETH IN THE STATE OF WEST VIRGINIA AT THE CLOSE OF BUSINESS ON OCT. 1, 1964

ASSETS

Cash, balances with other banks, and cash items in process of collection	$ 435,273.06
United States Government obligations direct and guaranteed	884,699.65
Obligations of States and political subdivisions	194,362.50
Other bonds, notes and debentures	None
Bank premises	3,000.00
Furniture and fixtures	2,526.67
Other Assets	13,044.53
Loans and Discounts	1,488,323.96
Total Assets	$3,021,230.37

LIABILITIES

Demand deposits of individuals, partnerships, and corporations	$ 981,168.68
Time and Savings Deposits of individuals, partnerships, and corporations	1,522,775.06
Deposits of United States Government, including postal savings	421.83

Deposits of States and political subdivisions..	239,635.83
Certified and officer's checks, etc...........	5,812.11
Rediscounts and other liabilities for borrowed money........................	70,000.00
Other liabilities...........................	17,578.77
Total liabilities...........................	$2,837,392.28

CAPITAL ACCOUNTS

Common stock, par value $50..............	$ 50,000.00
Surplus....................................	100,000.00
Undivided profits..........................	33,838.09
Total Capital Accounts...................	$ 183,838.09
Total Liabilities and Capital Accounts.....	$3,021,230.37

It will be apparent to any banker that the above statement of condition falls short of the ideal for bank profits. There is too much money in savings accounts on which the bank pays interest and too little money in checking accounts for which the bank pays nothing other than its services in keeping money in circulation. Mr. Herbert Roberts and I often discussed this problem, but we were unable to devise a more profitable formula. The bank was and is a community institution. As such it was and is the very heart beat of the community's economy. If a community wants to save its money instead of spending it, the astute banker understands that savings accounts are a cushion against possible "hard times" in the future. Despite the discrepancy, the bank has paid its stockholders an annual dividend of eight per cent for many years and on two occasions has declared an extra dividend of two per cent. The bank's common stock, with a par value of fifty dollars a share, now sells at one hundred twenty-five dollars a share on the rare occasions when any of the stock is available for purchase.

That item of $1,522,775.06 in savings accounts tells more about the economy of Wirt County than the welfare rolls. It means that in 1964, in the very year when President Johnson designated Wirt County as a poverty stricken area, there was actually in savings alone, in the County's only bank, an amount equal approximately to three hundred fifty dollars for every man, woman, and child in the county. Three hundred fifty dollars is higher, I am told, than the yearly earnings of many workers in other parts of the world.

Savings accounts, of course, are not evenly distributed among the population. It may be assumed that persons drawing welfare payments, except unemployment compensation, do not own savings accounts. At least, they are not supposed to own them under the law. Young married couples with families are concerned more often with meeting installment payments than with building up a nest egg. There are people in Wirt County as elsewhere who spend all they earn as soon as they earn it, and sometimes more. Still, it is illuminating to learn that the sum of $1,522,775.06 in savings accounts in the Wirt County Bank belongs to one thousand nineteen different depositors. No one depositor has more than ten thousand dollars, and the average for all depositors is around One thousand four hundred dollars. About two-thirds of all the accounts are under one thousand dollars.

Comparing the number of savings account depositors with the number of persons receiving public assistance underscores the hazards of generalizing in economics about nations, states, and even small communities. To the intellectual steeped in altruism and to the politician seeking votes the people of Wirt County appear to be depressed, underprivileged, and unhappy. To a distant banker these same people may well appear to be exceptionally energetic, thrifty, and prosperous.

Neither view is entirely correct. If the comparative ages of all the residents of Wirt County is reflected in the percentages shown for the Beulah Hill Community, and I believe that the comparison is conservative, then 52.4 per cent of the population of Wirt County is above forty years of age. That circumstance more than any other, in my opinion, is responsible for the large number of savings accounts. Persons above forty tend toward conservatism in all things. They remember the Great Depression of the 1930's and they are not convinced that hard times will not recur. They put their surplus money in savings accounts for various reasons. Among older people the reason is often the very human desire for a proper funeral. Another inducement is the law whereby the Federal Deposit Insurance Corporation guarantees bank deposits up to and including ten thousand dollars. The conservative citizen reasons that a savings account, guaranteed by the government, is a better investment than common stocks or even government bonds because he always knows exactly what his investment is worth and he can withdraw his account at any time simply by writing a check.

In my experience as a lawyer, a banker, and a public official I have found that the ordinary citizen of Appalachia is a conservative at heart no matter how he votes on election day. In the voting booth the voter is given a choice between the men and the issues, and he narrows that choice, perhaps subconsciously, to the men and the issues that come closest to his own personal interest and political thinking. In this limited context, we are all bought one way or another. The Democrats have understood and exploited this political maxim since 1932.

A curious corollary to the principle of self-interest in voting is that the very individual who is thoroughly committed to spending other people's money is often the most careful in protecting his own. I recently read an article in the Saturday Evening Post about silver coinage. It appears from the article that coin collectors and vending machines are tying up so many silver, nickel, and copper coins that banks and business places everywhere are finding it difficult to make change. The government is considering the issuance of aluminum coins to foil the speculators. I have a message for the government.

About four years ago I was in the bank one day when a man I have known all my life appeared at the teller's window with a sizable check and asked to be paid in half dollars, quarters, dimes, nickels, and pennies. After he received the money, I called him into a side office, and said, "Harry (his name was not Harry), what in the world are you going to do with two thousand dollars in small coins?"

He replied, "Reed, this is really none of your business, but I'll tell you. I'm scared. The way I see it, a country is just like a business firm or an individual. If a country keeps spending more than it takes in, that country will eventually go broke. If the United States goes broke, bonds, stocks, savings accounts, and paper money won't be worth a dime. Neither will pensions, insurance, or Social Security. You ask about this Two Thousand Dollars. I'm going to bury it."

Now, the astonishing thing about this disclosure to me was that the man who made it is a petty politician of the Far Left persuasion. He is not a Communist, though he believes in much Communist ideology. He is a dedicated proponent of the Great Society envisioned by President Johnson. I believe that he is sincere and that he looks forward hopefully to a better world in the future. His political beliefs, however, do not blind him to the possibility that the future may be less a Garden of Eden than a maelstrom of chaos. He is hedging his bets by burying some of his money. Our society, in the final analysis, still bears the forbidding aspect of the jungle and a man of prudence understands that he must look out for himself and his family.

We have no large coin collectors in Wirt County, but I noted over the years many other withdrawals of large numbers of small coins that failed somehow to return to the bank. People who bury money do not talk about it for obvious reasons. While I have no proof that large amounts of small coins are buried in Wirt County, I suspect strongly that such is the case. The plight of the government makes one wonder if hundreds of thousands of other people all over the nation are not doing the same thing. If they are, propaganda and lectures will prove futile because one law of human nature that no man can change is the law of self preservation.

While the tradition of owning one's home has largely persisted in Wirt County, other facets of the economy have changed beyond recognition. Nowadays everyone needs money not just periodically but constantly, day by day and hour by hour. Consequently, there is a great deal more money in circulation than there was half a century ago and everyone has more to spend. Installment buying, particularly of automobiles, houses, and furniture, accounts for a large proportion of credit transactions. Consumer buying habits have altered to the point where many housewives, even farm housewives, shop at the supermarkets in Parkersburg and the semi-supermarkets in Elizabeth for the next day's provisions. Fewer people are engaged in the retail trade. There were four country stores and two post offices in the Beulah Hill precinct in 1910. Now there are no stores and mail is delivered by a rural mail carrier from Elizabeth.

Though the country store has practically disappeared merchandising still flourishes in the Village of Elizabeth. In fact, it is surprising, when one considers how close we are to Parkersburg, that Elizabeth retains the number and variety of business places that it does. Remembering my own disappointment because George Washington failed to list the names of the French deserters, I am setting down here what I hope is a complete list of business institutions and retail outlets in Elizabeth together with pertinent personnel data.

(1) The Wirt County Bank. Statement of condition already noted. Officers of the bank are Harry L. Righter, President; Denver R. Roberts, Executive Vice President and Cashier; Robert B. Black, Secretary. Directors are Harry L. Righter, Denver R. Roberts, Robert B. Black, E. C. Andrick, and William Gene Davisson. I was myself an officer and director of this bank until I retired in 1964. Bank has eleven employees.

(2) Wirt County Industries, Incorporated. This is a local development corporation designed to bring industry to Wirt County. It owns the land and the buildings occupied by the aluminum fabricating company hereinafter described. Assets are approximately $125,000. Organized in 1956, I was the first president of the company. Present officers and directors are Roger E. Roberts, President; Louis Reed, Vice President; Eloise Sturm, Secretary and Treasurer; R. W. Coplin, E. C. Chambers, B. B. Sims, and Faustine Huffman. For the past two years this corporation has paid a six-

percent dividend to its stockholders. Company has but one paid employee, a bookkeeper.

(3) Glen W. Roberts, independent oil and gas promoter and developer. He owns two drilling outfits. In recent years he has been active in acquiring leases for western oil and gas companies. Oil and gas men are notoriously secretive, but if there is a millionaire in Wirt County I think he is the likely prospect. Seven regular employees, but has employed fifty.

(4) Altech Division of Financial Development and Research Corporation. This is the aluminum fabricating plant which now employs eighteen men and two women. Plans are afoot to increase the working force to fifty men during 1965. FDR Corporation is a subsidiary of Ravensmetal, Inc., of Parkersburg of which Lloyd C. Cook is President, Lowell Morgan is Vice President, and Howard Smith is the local superintendent. The plant is now engaged in subcontracting for the United States Department of Defense.

(5) Curry Lumber Company. This company operates a sawmill on Standing Stone Creek. The owner is C. D. Curry of Uniontown, Pa. Company employs about fifteen men.

(6) Roberts Hereford Farms. This is a partnership owned by two brothers, Roger E. Roberts and Walter M. Roberts. They raise registered Hereford cattle, and keep the winter herd down to about seven to nine hundred head. The farms employ from twelve to twenty-two men, depending on the season.

(7) Sturm Insurance Agency. This company deals in insurance of all kinds and is owned by Fred Sturm and Eloise Sturm, husband and wife. In addition to the owners, the company has one regular employee.

(8) Roberts Store. This is a partnership owned by Leslie V. Roberts and his son, James H. Roberts. Grocery department is operated like a supermarket. Estimated investment, $200,000.00. Store has five employees in addition to owners.

(9) Sims and George Store. This is a general store comparable to Roberts Store. Owned by B. B. Sims, Jr. and Carl

George, brothers-in-law. Store has five employees in addition to owners.

(10) Dick's Market. This is a semi-supermarket owned by Richard Thorn. Two employees in addition to owner.

(11) General Store owned by Dale and Maggie Goodwin, husband and wife. Also deals in lumber and cement. No employees.

(12) A. W. Thorne and Company Store. Owned by J. Cecil Thorne. Two employees.

(13) Chambers Furniture Store. Owned by E. C. Chambers. One employee.

(14) The China Store. Owned by Paul E. Black and Mary Black, husband and wife. Deals in chinaware, second-hand furniture and appliances. No employees.

(15) The Elizabeth Pharmacy. Owned by Faustine Huffman. One employee.

(16) The Wirt County Journal. A weekly newspaper owned by Woodrow Wilson. No employees.

(17) The Casual Post. A woman's dress shop owned by Ethel Eberhart. No employees.

(18) Litton Electronics Company. A radio and television sales and repair shop owned by R. M. Scott. No employees.

(19) Western Auto Sales. An automobile and appliance store owned by Charles Flesher. Two employees.

(20) Robinson's Trucking Company. A general hauling business owned by Elvin Robinson. Two employees.

(21) The Dairy Queen. A dairy outlet owned by E. C. Chambers and Carl George. Two employees.

(22) One laundryette. Owned by E. C. Chambers and Carl George. One employee.

(23) State Liquor Store. Owned by State of West Virginia. Two employees.

(24) Three one-man barber shops owned by Beverly Morgan, W. A. Stanley, and Larry Shears respectively.

(25) Four one-woman beauty shops owned by Sue Davisson, Zelma Simonton, Belva Morgan, and June Sheppard respectively.

(26) A. A. Rice Repair Shop. Repairs clocks and watches. Owned by A. A. Rice. No employees.

(27) Seven gasoline filling stations owned by Edna Smith, Joe Cheuvront, Rex Watson, Charles Cline, Jr., Elvin Robinson, Chester Boggs, and Denzil Blair. All these filling stations sell tobacco, soft drinks, automobile tires, lubricating oil, and automobile accessories. Joe Cheuvront and Chester Boggs also carry a line of groceries. They have a total of fourteen employees in addition to the proprietors.

(28) Lowe's Shoe Repair Shop. Owned by Bernard Lowe. One employee.

(29) J. Frank Lee Ford Agency. Lee has recently sold this business to a man named Dowler. Deals in new and used automobiles, and conducts automobile repair business. Four employees.

(30) Marcum Motors. Owned by Glen Marcum. This man is expert automobile mechanic and used car dealer. One employee.

(31) Hancock Motors, which used to be a Chevrolet automobile agency, closed its doors in 1964. It appears that automobile agencies require a larger market than Wirt County affords in order to survive. Small town agencies throughout the State are moving to the cities or discontinuing business.

(32) Elizabeth has two funeral homes. One is Pomeroy Funeral Home owned by Don Pomroy. The other is McCray Funeral Home owned by Harry McCray. Both furnish ambulance service and each home has three employees.

(33) There are three cafes or lunch counters owned by Maggie Goodwin, Earl Henthorn, and June Hudson respectively. They have a total of nine or ten employees among them.

(34) Villers Nursing Home. A home for aged men and women who do not require hospital care. Four women employees.

(35) There are no plumbing or electrical shops in Elizabeth, though plumbing and electrical supplies are sold at Roberts Store and at Sims and George Store. Plumbers and electricians subject to call include William McFee, Carl Clinton, and Ralph Caltrider. These men also serve as carpenters and painters. Elmer McFee is an expert at install-

ing water pumps. Many farmers install their own plumbing. The best carpenters, who are also cabinetmakers, are Doral Lockhart, Harry Lockhart, Charley Kidwell, and Heraldy Cline.

(36) R. W. Coplin, M. D., is the county's only physician and surgeon. He operates a small clinic with four nurses and aides. He performs surgical operations at the Camden-Clark Hospital and the Saint Joseph's Hospital in Parkersburg.

(37) Stark M. Snyder is the county's only dentist. He has one regular employee.

(38) Two lawyers are active at Elizabeth at the present time. One is Lewis D. Archer, aged 84; the other is Robert B. Black, aged 27. I was active in the practice of law myself until 1964 when I retired and sold my practice to Robert B. Black. Black has two stenographers and Archer, one.

(39) Elizabeth has five churches, but only four ministers. The resident ministers are the Reverend Harry Foley, Methodist; the Reverend K. D. Finch, Baptist; the Reverend Maynard Kreider, Presbyterian; and the Reverend Gaylord Van Horn, Church of the Nazarene. All these ministers, except the Methodist, have rural charges. The Church of Christ has had no minister for the past two years.

(40) There are two taverns, or beer joints, in the County. One is Bill's Tavern in Elizabeth, operated by William Reed; the other is The Bend, on State Route 14, operated by John Hamrick. Under State law, taverns may sell beer but not liquor by the drink. Intoxicating liquors, other than beer, must be bought in packages at the State Liquor Store.

(41) Conner and Amos Tree Nursery. Owns tree and shrub farms. Employs four to fifteen employees, depending on season.

(42) Elizabeth has one transport company operating a fleet of tank trucks in the gasoline business. It is owned by Jake and Faustine Huffman, husband and wife. They have, I believe, four trucks, and employ four truck drivers. The Huffmans also own and operate a tugboat on the Ohio River and a six-hundred-acre cattle farm. Their exact number of employees is not known.

(43) In addition to the retail outlets listed above, Wirt County still has three country stores: Scite's Store at Burning Springs, owned and operated by Mr. and Mrs. O. F. Scites; LaDeaux's Store at Palestine, operated by Mae LaDeaux; and A. F. Fought's Store at Newark operated by a daughter of A. F. Fought. Both the LaDeaux Store and the Fought Store were once flourishing businesses. All are now outmoded. There are also two country stores near the boundary line between Wirt and Calhoun counties. One is owned by Noble Busch, the other by Harley Shimer.

(44) Both Harley Shimer and Noble Busch are also independent oil and gas operators. Busch, in particular, has been highly successful. To my personal knowledge Busch recently was offered $35,000.00 for one of his gas leases.

(45) The biggest businesses in Wirt County are the utility companies with headquarters elsewhere. The Monongahela West Penn Power Company is a subsidiary of some company operating out of New York City. This electric company keeps two employees in Elizabeth but its maintenance crew comes from Parkersburg. The Chesapeake and Potomac Telephone Company is a subsidiary of American Telephone and Telegraph Company, possibly the world's largest utility. It has no employees in Wirt County. Cabot Corporation, which supplies natural gas, has its base in Boston, Massachusetts. It retains two regular employees in Wirt County. Reynolds Bus Company of Spencer has no employees in Wirt County. The County Board of Education employs fifteen bus drivers.

There is no railroad in the County at the present time. Wirt County used to be served by the Little Kanawha Railroad which discontinued service about 1932. In 1938 the Federal Government abandoned its locks and dams in the Little Kanawha River. One of my instructions from the County Republican Executive Committee, when I delegated my duties as Prosecuting Attorney of Wirt County in 1956 to become again Administrative Assistant to Senator Chapman Revercomb in Washington, was to make certain that the Federal Government rebuilt Dam No. 3 below Elizabeth. This washed-out dam had lowered the municipality's water tables. With the help of my employer and friend, Senator Revercomb, a construction bill was passed in Congress in 1958 and the dam was re-built in 1959 and 1960.

Since government has become the biggest and the costliest business in the country, no discussion of the economy of Wirt County would be complete if it failed to include the budgets of the County Court, the County Board of Education, and the Town Council of the Municipality of Elizabeth. These three government agencies are the only tax-levying bodies in the county. To understand how these local agencies function, two circumstances must be borne in mind; (1) All are corporations, with limited powers, descended directly from similar corporations established in England during the Middle Ages, and (2) the spending power of all tax-levying agencies in West Virginia is sharply curtailed by the Tax Limitation Amendment to the State Constitution.

Because counties were formed originally on the horse and buggy concept, there is no provision in the State Constitution whereby a county may be discontinued or abolished just as there is no provision in the Federal Constitution whereby a State may be discontinued or abolished. That is why many counties both in West Virginia and elsewhere in the nation must look to the Federal or the State governments for aid in carrying out their assigned duties. The legalities are otherwise with respect to Town Councils. Municipal corporations are chartered by the Legislature of the State and the charter may be suspended, annulled, or revoked by the Legislature.

7. County Budgets and State Aid

THE COUNTY as a unit of government in Virginia, and indeed in America, is a bequest of our English ancestors. First, there were colonies. As the colonies grew in population and expanded geographically, divisions and subdivisions of the central authority became necessary. These divisions and subdivisions acquired the names of counties, towns, townships, and magisterial districts because those terms were familiar political units in England. In Virginia there never were towns or townships in the New England pattern. Such subdivisions were and still are called magisterial districts.

New counties appear to have been formed at the central authority of the colony and later at the central authority of the state upon considerations of a growing population and the maintenance of law and order. In Virginia from early colonial times, the procedure for forming a new county was inaugurated by a petition on the part of the inhabitants to the colonial governor and the legislature. The creation of magisterial districts within the counties seems to have been left largely to the counties themselves. At least, this was true in the later stages of county making.

The formation of new counties in Virginia was a matter of concern to the colony and later to the Commonwealth because of the conflict of interest between the rapidly growing West and the entrenched East. New counties inevitably diminished the geographic limits of the older counties from which the new counties were formed. Nevertheless, the colonial governments and later the state governments exhibited remarkable foresight in planting County court houses within a reasonable distance of every English speaking citizen. Wherever the white man went, English law, English speech, and English customs followed. This policy of Anglicizing everything in its path (which accounts today for one language and one general concept of law from coast to coast) was initiated not by the Founding Fathers but by various and sundry anonymous gentlemen in the colonial capitals.

Most of West Virginia in the colonial period was a part of the District of West Augusta, but we have enough counties formed before the Revolutionary War to discern the pattern of colonial county building. Hampshire County, West Virginia, (originally Virginia) was formed in 1753 from parts of Frederick and Augusta Counties. This was prior to the French and Indian War. Berkeley County, the second oldest in the State, was formed in 1772 from the northern third of Frederick County. Monongalia and Ohio Counties were formed in 1776, the year of the Declaration of Independence, from the District of West Augusta. After the Revolution and up to the outbreak of the Civil War, forty-seven new Virginia counties were created in what is now West Virginia. In this list Wirt County is thirty-seventh in point of time; its boundaries having been carved from adjoining Wood and Jackson Counties. Only five of the fifty-five counties were formed after West Virginia became a separate state in 1863: Grant County in 1866, Mineral County in 1866, Lincoln County in 1867, Summers County in 1871, and Mingo County in 1895. Of all the counties, Summers County alone is named in honor of a white Virginian who was born and reared west of the Allegheny Mountains. George W. Summers, a man who is otherwise unknown, led the anti-Secession forces in the fateful Virginia Assembly Session of 1861.

There is a mine of untapped history in America in the spread of county government. While I have not explored the subject in depth, I strongly suspect that the formula for admitting new states to the Union under the Federal Constitution was based on colonial experience in county making. Certainly, in the eastern part of the United States, the pattern for ultimate statehood was to create a county and magisterial districts or townships which county and magisterial districts or townships were soon divided and subdivided into additional counties and magisterial districts or townships to become a half state known as a Territory. The process of county making continued under the Territorial government and later under the State government when the Territory was admitted to the Union. County making in West Virginia lasted from the formation of Hampshire County in 1753 to the formation of Mingo County in 1895, a total of one hundred forty-two years.

The list of county names in West Virginia, which appears in the index, reflects the political changes that occurred during that one hundred forty-two years.

County names were voted on by the Legislature, often from a list placed in nomination. Hampshire County was obviously named for the shire of that name in England. Berkeley County was named for Norborne Berkeley, the Baron de Botetourt, Colonial Governor of Virginia from 1768 to 1770. Indian names began with the formation of Monongalia and Ohio Counties in 1776. Other counties bearing Indian names are Kanawha, Mingo and Wyoming. Logan County was named for the famous Mingo Chief, Logan, and Pocahontas County was named for the wife of John Rolfe. Boone and Wetzel Counties were named for famous frontiersmen and Indian fighters. Revolutionary War figures were commemorated in the county names of Braxton, Fayette (for LaFayette), Hancock, Harrison, Jefferson, Lewis, Marion, Mason, Mercer, Morgan, Preston, Putnam, Randolph, Wayne, and Wood. Many later counties were named either for national personalities such as Monroe, Jackson, Wirt, Clay, Calhoun, and Webster or for governors, jurists, and other politicians of Virginia whose names are otherwise mostly forgotten. In 1850 the Legislature departed from its current custom of naming new counties in honor of contemporaries and created Raleigh County in honor of Sir Walter Raleigh. The stability of county names, once the name is affixed, is worthy of note. The county names of West Virginia have withstood two civil wars. No county has ever changed its name.

These county names preserve at least one curious historical paradox. West Virginia has four contiguous counties named Jackson, Wirt, Calhoun, and Clay, all of which were formed in the thirty years preceding the Civil War. Jackson

County, named in honor of Andrew Jackson, was formed in 1831. Thereafter, the Legislature, whether intentionally or not, surrounded Jackson County with memorials to his bitterest political enemies, Wirt, Calhoun, and Clay. Today, Jackson County is a staunch Republican County while the others, especially Calhoun, exhibit registered Democrat majorities.

An important thing to remember about county government is that it is uniform throughout the State. Wirt County officials, whose duties are prescribed by law, are duplicated in every other county of the State. The county officials elected by the citizenry consist of:

(1) The Sheriff. The sheriff is the chief county law enforcement officer and also the collector of taxes. Under the State Constitution, the sheriff is the only county official who cannot succeed himself in office. The present Sheriff of Wirt County is C. D. Powell. His term is four years.

(2) The Clerk of the County Court. The clerk keeps the records of the County Court including deed books, administration of estates, probate of wills, births, marriages, and deaths. The clerk also grants a variety of licenses such as junk dealing, hunting and fishing, and marriage licenses. The Wirt County Court now has its first woman clerk, Miss Lella Ingram, elected in 1962. The term is six years.

(3) The Clerk of the Circuit Court. The clerk is the recorder of the actions of the Circuit Court, the only trial court of record in Wirt County. The Court is presided over by Judge Donald F. Black of Parkersburg. The clerk is also the chief election officer of the County and has other duties prescribed by law. The present clerk is also a woman, Mrs. June Hudson. The term is six years.

(4) The County Assessor. The assessor appraises real and personal property and assesses such property for tax purposes. He is therefore an official who exercises considerable discretionary power. The assessor at the present time is Kendall Amos. The term is four years.

(5) The Prosecuting Attorney. The prosecutor represents the State and its subdivisions in all public litigation including criminal prosecutions. Robert B. Black is now the prosecuting attorney. His term is four years.

(6) The County Court. This corporate body is comprised of three members whose terms are staggered so that one comes up for election each two years. The Court is a fiscal and not a judicial body. Under the law only one commissioner at a time may be a resident of a given magisterial district. The present members of the Court are E. W. Allman, Hubert Full, and Donald F. Lockhart. The term of office is six years.

(7) The Board of Education. This corporate body is comprised of five members whose terms of office are likewise staggered. Unlike the County Court, members of the Board are chosen at the primary election on a non-partisan ticket. The members of the Board in the month of March, 1964, were George Robinson, president; John Hale, Clyde Cale, Donald Hickman, and Preston Andrick. The term is six years.

(8) The Town Council of Elizabeth. This corporate body is comprised of a mayor and six councilmen which acts as the fiscal and the governing body of the municipality. The members of the Council in the month of March, 1964, were Charles A. Cline, mayor; Harley Lee, Albert Cain, Foster McClung, Walter Dailey, Earl Villers, and Frank Munday. The term of office is four years.

(9) Justices of the Peace and Constables. These are the only remaining officials of the magisterial districts. Under the law each magisterial district is entitled to the services of two justices and two constables. Since justices and constables have no salaries but depend on fees, candidates seldom offer themselves for election in rural areas nowadays. Wirt County has seven magisterial districts: Burning Springs, Clay, Elizabeth, Newark, Reedy, Spring Creek, and Tucker. Of these, six have no justices or constables. Only Elizabeth District has two justices, Virgil Snider and Olive Hays Smith, and one constable, John Hutchinson. Justices of the peace have limited county-wide civil and criminal jurisdiction. They hear civil suits if the amount in dispute is three hundred dollars or less. They try and render judgment in specified misdemeanors and are authorized to conduct preliminary hearings in felony cases. Constables serve

legal papers and also execute arrest warrants. There is a growing sentiment among lawyers, educators, social workers and others that justices of the peace, once the very backbone of our legal system, are now outmoded and ought to be abolished. The term of office is four years.

While the names and duties of county officials are uniform throughout the State, except that some counties have intermediate courts, the salaries for the same officials vary widely from county to county. The Sheriff of Wood County, for instance, receives a salary of twelve thousand dollars a year and is provided with a dozen deputies while the Sheriff of Wirt County receives three thousand fifty dollars a year and is limited to one deputy. Salaries for other county officials vary in like degree. Attention is called to the Wirt County Court estimate, for 1964-1965, which appears in the Appendix.

The County Court is self sustaining, partly through earnings and partly through taxation, but counties are prohibited from plunging unwisely in debt by the Tax Limitation Amendment to the State Constitution. Sparsely populated counties such as Wirt have a difficult time making financial ends meet. A glance at the County Court Levy Estimate in the Appendix for the fiscal year 1964-65 reveals that the estimate for that year was $42,075.00. The Estimate having been approved by the State Tax Commissioner is now the Budget. Out of the budgeted sum of $42,075.00, the Court must pay the salaries of the county officials and their deputies or assistants, expenses of the Circuit Court which includes per diem and mileage allowances for jurors and the mileage and fees of State witnesses, the cost of maintaining a court house and jail, the transportation and support of inmates in State institutions, the expenses of primary and general elections, the cost of insurance and official bonds, and the county's contribution to the Fire Department, the Welfare or Relief Fund, and the Social Security Fund. This Estimate and Budget was prepared, to my certain knowledge, by the Clerk of the County Court and her deputy, who receive between them a total salary of four thousand three hundred dollars.

Particular attention is directed to the following items of the budget:

Salaries of the Clerk of the County Court, and one deputy	$ 4,300.00
Salary of the Clerk of the Circuit Court, no deputy	1,800.00
Salaries of the Sheriff and one deputy and traveling expenses	5,375.00
Salary of the Prosecuting Attorney, no assistant or stenographer	1,500.00
Salaries of the Assessor, two deputies, and traveling expenses	4,990.00
Contribution to salary of Clerk of County Agricultural Agent. The Agent is a Federal employee	1,200.00
Salary of Janitor for Court House and Jail	1,200.00
Salaries of members of the County Court, $640.00 each	1,920.00
Total	$22,185.00

The first time I saw the County Budget I had just served a term as administrative assistant to a United States senator in Washington and I wondered how Wirt County could induce competent people to work in important elective positions at such ridiculously low salaries. In sober truth that is a perennial problem. Yet, the work gets done somehow, and, on the whole, it is competently done. Not only are the salaries low but other expenses are cut to the bone. Note the following items:

Jail expense	$ 100.00
Feeding prisoners	475.00
Court House expense	200.00
Furniture and fixtures	100.00
Repairs	500.00
Water, light, fuel, and ice. These are furnished by utilities and cannot be cut lower	1,200.00
Record books	700.00

Stationery and office supplies for all county offices	500.00
Postage for all county offices	200.00
Advertising. The Court is required by law to advertise the Levy Estimate at the beginning and the Financial Statement at the end of the fiscal year	500.00
Telephone and telegraph service for all county offices. This includes the monthly rental on four telephones as well as tolls for long distance calls and telegrams	750.00
Total	$ 5,225.00

People certainly do not run for elective office in Wirt County for the sake of the salary and other emoluments. Their motives are likely to be less self-interest than personal and public spirited. Take the office of Sheriff. The newly elected Sheriff, C. D. Powell (This portion of the report is being written in the month of February, 1965) is a retired farmer over seventy years of age. His office deputy is a widow, Florence Morehead, the wife of a former Sheriff who was familiar with the office and who probably was tired of sitting at home with folded hands. Both are Democrats.

The Clerk of the County Court, Lella Ingram, has been employed in the same office for more than twenty years. She was formerly a legal stenographer in Parkersburg but returned to Elizabeth to care for her aged, invalid mother. She was deputy clerk to Emory N. Davis for eighteen years. He stepped down. She ran for the office, was elected, and promptly made him her deputy. Emory N. Davis is about eighty-five years old. He was a retired Civil Service employee when he first ran for the office in 1944. Both are Republicans.

The Assessor, Kendall Amos, has likewise served in that office either as assessor or deputy assessor for about twenty years. Apart from his official duties, he is a prosperous cattle farmer. One of his deputies, W. H. Callison, known as the outside man, is also a prosperous farmer and works only three months a year. The other deputy, Ruth Stanley, is the wife of a local barber. All are Republicans.

The Prosecuting Attorney, Robert B. Black, is a young lawyer who relies on his law practice for a livelihood. He is a Republican. The Clerk of the Circuit Court, June Hudson, serves in the double capacity of clerk and private secretary to the prosecuting attorney. She is a Republican. The members of the County Court are all prosperous farmers. Two are Democrats and one is a Republican. Even the Court House janitor is retired and is glad to work for $100.00 a month because he can earn $1,200.00 a year and still draw Social Security payments. His name is Russell Wiseman and he is a Democrat.

The question of money for operating purposes is a continuing problem for Wirt County officials. The clerks of the County Court have served traditionally as guardians of the public purse. When I first became clerk of the Circuit Court, I found that the office had no private telephone. For that matter, it has none to this day. I recall that the clerk of the County Court at that time, Mr. E. N. Davis, showed me the budget, and said, "Reed, if you can figure a telephone from that budget, go to it." In the event I installed my own telephone and even paid for official calls.

An important point to remember about the County Court is that the Court is no longer responsible for the care of the indigent. In the old days, before the advent of the New Deal, the County Court operated a poor farm and appointed one of its members to the post of Overseer of the Poor. Nowadays, the care of the indigent has been assumed by the Federal Government, though the County is still required to contribute a token amount to the welfare fund. In 1964-65 the County contributed $2,100.00 to the fund, an insignificant sum when compared to the grossly deflated $119,633.00 listed heretofore as welfare expenditures in the County. In addition, the County provides the Department of Public Assistance with office space in the Court House, plus utilities. The contribution of $2,100.00 will pay less than one-half the salary of one welfare investigator and there are two in the County. While the Court receives no direct aid from either the Federal or the State government, the poor farm is no longer in use and part of it has been sold to Wirt County Industries for industrial development.

Budgetwise, the Board of Education differs from the County Court in two important particulars: (1) The Board receives direct payments, known as State Aid, from the State of West Virginia in the operation of the county school system, and (2) the Board has more money to spend, but is subject to stricter supervision and control. Not the Board, but the county superintendent of schools, an appointive official, is the key administrator of the school system. Minimum salaries of administrators and teachers are set by State Law. The Levy Estimate of the Board of Education for the fiscal year 1964-65 appears in the appendix.

The Levy Estimate of the Board of Education for the year 1964-65 shows that the proposed expenditures for education in Wirt County for the fiscal year amount to $339,694.00. Of this amount the sum of $108,702.00 is proposed to be raised from local taxes and the balance of $230,992 is to be furnished by the State of West Virginia. The Levy Estimate was approved by the State Tax Commissioner and is now the Budget. The people of Wirt County, therefore, are now paying slightly less than one third of the total cost of their school system, though this fraction does not include the cost of the bond issue for buildings and the cost of the excess levy for teachers. Obviously, without State Aid, Wirt County could not afford even the minimal school system that it now has.

While the Board of Education is subject to many restrictions in the matter of salaries, qualification of teachers, and minimum standards of transportation and equipment, it exercises, nevertheless, considerable discretion and power. It employs administrators, teachers, bus drivers, maintenance men, and custodial employees throughout the school system. It owns all the school property in the county and is the sole judge of whether or not particular schools are to be abandoned and others built. It is authorized to enter into contracts with employees, suppliers, construction companies, and other persons, firms, and corporations with which it does business. It has the right under the law to name the poll clerks and commissioners in school bond and school levy referendums.

The five members of the Board of Education in the month of March, 1964, when the Levy Estimate was made, were all parents of children enrolled in the school system. All were high school graduates and four were graduates of Wirt County High School. None were college graduates, though I believe that one attended Glenville State College. Board members were younger than other County officials and their official duties are less demanding. Ordinarily, they meet with the county superintendent a couple of hours each month at which time they approve all that the county superintendent has done in the meantime. Only the president's signature is required on official documents. The salary is twenty dollars a month.

Attention is directed to the following items of the budget:

Administration............................$ 17,870.00

This item covers the salary of the County Superintendent, $6,360.00; the salaries of the members of the Board of Education totaling $1,200.00; the salaries of the secretaries to the County Superintendent; and certain contracted services and miscellaneous expenses.

Instruction...............................$206,925.00

This item covers the salaries of one high school and seven elementary school principals, teachers, other instructional staff, secretarial and clerical assistants and teachers' sick leave. It also covers textbooks, school libraries and audio visual materials, teaching supplies, and related expenses.

Pupil Transportation Services..............$ 56,548.00

This item covers salaries of bus drivers, maintenance men, and custodial employees, replacement of vehicles, pupil transportation insurance, expenditures in lieu of transportation, and a fund for contingencies.

Operation of Plant........................$ 19,100.00

This item covers janitor service, heat, water, electricity and supplies.

Maintenance of Plant......................$ 6,775.00

This item covers maintenance workers and supplies.

Fixed Charges.............................$ 15,703.00

This item covers the Board's contribution to the teachers' and employees' pension funds and fire and other hazard insurance on school buildings.

Community Services........................$ 1,263.00

This item covers contributions to the Four-H Club, a nation-wide association of rural pupils, and the amount proposed to be spent for adult education. (Frankly, I was not aware that Wirt County offers a course in adult education and I have not yet found anyone who takes it.)

Capital Outlay............................$ 12,500.00

This item covers proposed acquisition of new school sites and buildings. Except for completion work on the new elementary school at Elizabeth, no school acquisition or building is in progress at this time.

In the year 1961, the voters of Wirt County at a special election approved a bond issue in the amount of $320,000.00 for the construction of a new elementary school at Elizabeth and other schools throughout the county and in the same election approved an excess levy designed to add about $40,000.00 a year to teachers' salaries. Neither the County Court nor the Board of Education had any outstanding bonded indebtedness in 1961 and the bond issue and the excess levy raised county taxes to the limits permitted under the Tax Limitation Amendment. The bond issue is now being retired on the following schedule:

1963	$27,000.00
1964	28,000.00
1965	29,000.00
1966	30,000.00

1967	31,000.00
1968	32,000.00
1969	34,000.00
1970	35,000.00
1971	36,000.00
1972	38,000.00

Unlike the bond issue, the excess levy was imposed on the total valuation of land and personal property at specified levy rates. Since 1961 a re-evaluation of land for tax purposes has increased total assessed valuations in the county from $7,180,750.00 to $9,269,165.00, so that the rates of levy for school bond purposes have decreased while the rates of levy for the excess levy have remained the same. Both the bond issue and the excess levy are temporary in nature, but they must be considered a part of the county's tax contribution to the school system.

The Budget of the Board of Education is much larger and more complicated than the Budget of the County Court. Having once walked two miles each way to school in all kinds of weather, I find it interesting to note that transportation of pupils in Wirt County costs more than the entire operation of the county government apart from the school system. The Budget of the County Court for 1964-65 amounts to $42,075.00 while the Budget of the Board of Education for pupil transportation services amounts to $56,548.00. Since there are but 989 pupils in the school system, I am beginning to have some doubts about our standardized school procedures. Do we have here a case of trying to fit square pegs in round holes?

The educational system, above all else, is directed from Washington and guided by bureaucrats. It may well be that each separate county ought not to have a separate educational system, that education should be directed from one central authority on a regulated basis; but to do that would require an overhaul of our State and County system of government that is not authorized by the Federal Constitution or by the Constitution of the State of West Virginia. Though much has been written and said, since the inception of our Republic, about States' Rights under the Constitution, the problem of States' Rights is inextricably bound up with the problem of county rights and county prerogatives. The kernel of the controversy is the freedom of local communities to govern themselves, a concept of freedom that is losing validity in a push-button world. The current regimentation of public schools on a county basis, irrespective of size and population, is highly inefficient and wasteful, but a change either for better or for worse could be imposed only by a complete change in our governmental structure and in the ideology upon which our nation was founded. The county is one of the oldest concepts in the English tradition. To attempt to abolish a county and its prerogatives would in itself be a revolutionary action.

The Levy Estimate of the Municipality of Elizabeth exemplifies the problems of municipalities everywhere in a miniscule form. Municipal corporations traditionally provide public services to their citizens. They deal with streets, alleys, water supply, sewer lines, zoning restrictions, building permits, fire protection, traffic control, and general law enforcement. Elizabeth is provided with electricity and natural gas by private utilities under long-term monopolistic contracts. The utilities are regulated and taxed by the State Public Service Commission. The Municipality owns and operates its own water and sewer systems and charges its customers monthly fees. Sewer fees are fixed at one dollar a month per household but water fees are based on the amount of water consumed. Parking meters have been installed by a Pittsburgh company under an exclusive agreement whereby the Municipality collects the coins from the meters and pays the company fifty percent of the proceeds. The other fifty per cent goes into the general fund of the Municipality. The Municipality also receives income from various licenses, fines, and a consumers sales tax on whisky, wine, and other intoxicating liquors. The Municipal sales tax is in addition to the State Consumers Sales Tax.

To provide the required services the Municipality, acting through the Town Council, has one full-time employee who serves as policeman, superintendent of the water plant, and supervisor of streets. For many years past, this manyhatted position has been filled by Virgil Snider, who receives compensation of $3,180.00 a year. Part of his salary is paid him as chief of police and the remainder as superintendent of the water department. In addition to his seven days a week duties with the Municipality, Snider is also a justice of the peace and a prosperous cattle farmer. Whenever a water line breaks or a street needs repair, Snider recruits a crew of laborers who are paid by the Municipality on an hourly basis. The Levy Estimate of the Municipality of Elizabeth for the fiscal year 1964-65 appears in the appendix.

It will be observed that the Municipality earns much of its operating expenses from its services. This is a matter of necessity for the Tax Limitation Amendment to the State Constitution is particularly harsh on small municipalities. Reference to the Levy Estimate shows that taxable property, both real and personal in Elizabeth, is valued for tax purposes at $1,779,340.00. Due to complications in assessment, this figure is about half the market value. On this valuation the proposed rates are the highest permitted a municipality, and the tax itself amounts only to $5,623.00. Hence the Budget of the Municipality of Elizabeth amounts to estimated receipts from earnings of $16,740.00 plus the tax levy of $5,623.00, a total of $22,363.00. It should be noted that if for any reason, earnings or taxes fall below the estimates, the Municipality cannot spend more than it takes in. A few years ago the Mayor and the Town Council of Parkersburg were removed from office because they bought official automobiles on the installment plan.

The population of Elizabeth in 1960 was 767 and it is believed that no sizeable changes have taken place since that time. Possibly the population has increased a little, say to 800. To maintain a municipal government and to provide municipal services including police and fire protection, water and sewer service, heating, street lighting, traffic control, and street construction and maintenance is a complicated problem at its best. The problem is magnified by (1) the policies of the Federal Government which extracts an income tax from each wage earner and an excise tax on many items of commerce such as liquor, long distance telephone calls, gasoline, jewelry, and furs, and (2) the policies of the State Government which likewise extracts an income tax from each wage earner, an excise tax on liquor, gasoline, soft drinks, and other items, and a consumers sales tax of three per cent on each commercial sale and many services within the municipality. The Budget of $22,363.00 is insignificant compared with what the citizens of Elizabeth pay into the Federal and State treasuries in income, excise, and sales taxes. Federal and State taxes on gasoline alone amount to eleven cents a gallon. During the year 1964 I paid in gasoline taxes on one Ford automobile the sum of $283.26. The Assessor advises me that there are approximately two thousand licensed motor vehicles in Wirt County. If they all paid as much as I did, and of this I have no proof, then the gasoline taxes taken from Wirt County by the Federal and State Governments almost equal the combined budgets of the County Court and the Town Council. If gasoline taxes are high, what can be said of the consumers sales tax? How about the income tax and the tax on alcoholic beverages?

What the Federal Government and the State receive from the income tax is not available on a county basis; nor is the amount of taxes received from the sale of alcoholic beverages. At least, I have been unable to obtain reliable figures. I do know that some years ago in Washington I was approached with a proposition to buy bonded warehouse liquor for shipment to and sale in South America, thereby eliminating the Federal Tax. I declined because I believed that the deal involved something akin to smuggling into a foreign country. The thing that arrested my attention, however, was the price of the liquor. The brand in question could be bought without tax at four dollars a case and the same brand was selling at retail in Washington at forty eight dollars a case. Obviously, someone somewhere is making a lot of money from the whisky business.

I once read an article on Communism which explained how the Soviets have been successful in Russia in spite of the gross inefficiency of their bureaucratic form of government. The answer, according to the author, lay with the people in the lower echelons of the hierarchy, with the farm managers, the doctors, the lawyers, and the lower orders of party workers. These people are less interested in ideology than in performing assigned tasks in a workmanlike manner. They persist in getting the job done in spite of the obstacles.

The analogy applies to Wirt County and to the Municipality of Elizabeth. The human race seems to be blessed with a minority of competent people who will persevere and finally overcome under the most adverse conditions. I have seen the members of the Town Council of Elizabeth working as laborers on the streets, though their salaries as councilmen amount only to $16.00 a year. Sixteen dollars is less than the average daily wage of a factory worker in Parkersburg.

Though I have already named the members of the Town Council, I am constrained to add some personal data for the sake of a better record. The members are:

(1) Charles A. Cline, Mayor. Age 51. Cline is also the county superintendent of schools. Married. Family. Graduate of West Virginia University. As mayor, he is ex-officio justice of the peace and judge of the Municipal Court. His salary is $50.00 a year.

(2) Foster McClung. Age 47. He is a cattle farmer and is also employed as salesman at Sims and George Store. Volunteer fireman. Adjutant, local Post of the American Legion. Married. Family. Graduate of Wirt County High School. Salary is $16.00 a year.

(3) Harley Lee. Age 68. Retired farmer. Married. Family. Graduate of old fashioned one-room school. Salary is $16.00 a year.

(4) Walter Dailey. Age 44. Employed by Kaiser Aluminum Corporation at Ravenswood. Part time refrigerator salesman and repairman. Volunteer fireman. Married. Family. Graduate of Wirt County High School. Salary is $16.00 per year.

(5) Earl Villers. Age 50. Employed by State Construc-

tion Company of Parkersburg. Married. Family. Graduate of elementary school. Salary is $16.00 per year.

(6) Albert Cain. Age 45. Chicken farmer and land owner. Married. Family. Graduate of Wirt County High School. Salary $16.00 per year.

(7) Frank Munday. Age 43. Employed by duPont Company at Parkersburg. Married. No children. Volunteer fireman. Graduate of Wirt County High School. Salary is $16.-00 a year.

Employees of the Municipality as of March 1, 1964, were:

(1) Virgil Snider. Age 56.

(2) Eloise Cline, Clerk. Age 48. She is the wife of the mayor. Her salary is $50.00 a year.

(3) Robert B. Black, Attorney. Age 27. He is also prosecuting attorney and an officer and director of Wirt County Bank. Graduate of Marietta College and West Virginia University Law School. Salary is $100.00 a year.

It should be noted for the record that the Municipality of Elizabeth owns one fire truck and the Wirt County Volunteer Fire Department owns another fire truck. Both are manned by a volunteer fire company from Elizabeth of which Edward Ott is the fire chief. Ott earns his livelihood as a clerk in the Elizabeth Post Office.

The Levy Estimate of the Municipal Council of Elizabeth by one omission illuminates the whole field of growing bureaucracy in the United States. I have stated heretofore that the Municipality owns its own water and sewer system. That is true, but you would never guess it from the Levy Estimate. You will learn from the Estimate that the chief of police receives a salary of $1,200.00 per year, but nothing whatever is said about his receiving an additional salary of $1,980.00 a year for his services as superintendent of the water department. Nor is anything said about the revenue bonds, which are still unpaid and by which the water department was originally financed.

These discrepancies are not attributable to local officials. They result from an Act of the Legislature whereby municipally owned utilities are required to form a separate corporation even though the new corporation is comprised of exactly the same people as the old corporation. This country suffers from a plethora of new legislation. When the Town Council of Elizabeth deals with matters affecting the water supply, it acts in its capacity as directors of the water department and not in its traditional capacity as Town Council. The division of executive powers at the municipal level proliferates the extension of bureaucracy at higher levels of government. Not finding the water department in the municipal budget reminds me that we have erected a monstrous bureaucracy in this country, a bureaucracy so complicated, in fact, that there may be little to choose between the notorious inefficiency of the bureaucrats of Russia and the inefficiency of the equally numerous bureaucrats of America.

8. Education

THE NATIONAL EDUCATION ASSOCIATION has devised a formula, based in large measure on teachers salaries, whereby it rates the educational facilities of the various States. According to the Association, West Virginia ranked 48th among the fifty states of the Union in 1963. Twenty years ago, before the mines were automated and the State began losing population heavily, West Virginia was ranked 38th by the same Association.

While I am not always an admirer of the National Education Association, for reasons that are separate from this study, I concur in the conclusion that the West Virginia educational system leaves much to be desired. For the past ten years two thousand trained teachers have left the State annually for employment elsewhere.

An incident that occurred during World War II first opened my eyes to the inadequacies of West Virginia High Schools. At that time I was Administrative Assistant to Senator Chapman Revercomb in Washington. The Senator had the privilege of nominating two cadets to the Military Academy and two midshipmen to the Naval Academy. In such cases it was and is traditional to nominate a principal and three alternates to each position, a total in this instance of sixteen nominations. Because it was war time, the Senator decided against the usual political appointments and made all the nominations, without reference to party affiliation, from a list of West Virginia boys in the proper age group who were high school graduates and were already in the Army or the Navy. The appointees, no matter where they were at the time, were promptly flown to service preparatory schools in the continental United States. In fairness to the preparatory schools it should be added that they had only two or three weeks time to prepare the appointees for the examinations.

The result shocked us all. Sixteen West Virginia boys passed the physical examination, but not a single one passed the mental examination. While we knew that entrance examinations to West Point and Annapolis are difficult and that many fail, we were certainly not prepared for sixteen successive failures on the same day. I talked to some of the boys at the time and all told the same story. They had taken examinations in subjects that are not even taught in West Virginia High Schools.

What is wrong with the educational system in West Virginia and why is the State ranked forty-eighth among the fifty States of the Union? The answer seems to lie in the field of regional history and geography. The Southern States, on the whole, are less progressive in education than the remainder of the country, and West Virginia, despite its stand with the North in the Civil War, is a product of southern society.

The best study of education in West Virginia was made some years ago by Dr. Charles H. Ambler of West Virginia University in a book called THE HISTORY OF EDUCATION IN WEST VIRGINIA, published in 1951. In this book Dr. Ambler comments on the varying attitudes toward education in the English colonies. For all their narrow thinking in religious matters the Puritans of New England encouraged general education. In Virginia and throughout the South the slave economy operated in the opposite direction. Some of the best educated men in America in colonial times were Virginians, but all of them belonged to the planter aristocracy. Education was the privilege of the few and the earliest schools in Virginia were plantation schools.

Dr. Ambler describes plantation schools in more detail than is required for this discussion. Suffice it to say that plantation owners operated their own schools, often by importing tutors from Europe, that the schools were attended by the planter's children, by the children of his relatives and sometimes by the children of his neighbors, and that in all such schools the poor whites and the negroes were rigidly excluded. Such schools were thoroughly incidental to private enterprise.

Public schools in the colony of Virginia developed from the Poor Law patterned on the current Poor Law in England. Though we tend to forget it, there seems always to have been a Poor Law of some kind in countries with a recorded history. Concern for the plight of indigent white families who could not afford the plantation schools was finally expressed in the enactment of laws providing for public instruction to indigent children. These Poor Schools never approached the plantation schools in prestige or in breadth of instruction, but they did serve the useful purpose of diminishing illiteracy. The Poor Schools were the first public schools in Virginia.

Neither the Plantation Schools nor the Poor Schools extended to the No-Man's Land of the Indian frontier. Frontier people were generally ill-educated, though many learned to read and write somehow. After the Indian wars some Plantation Schools appeared in West Virginia. Hiram Pribble states that his father owned many slaves at Newark in what is now Wirt County, West Virginia, and there is a legend of a Plantation School at the Steed plantation nearby. The Pribbles, the Foughts, and the Steeds were neighbors and they intermarried. Robert B. Black, who was elected Prosecuting Attorney of Wirt County in 1964, is the great-great-great-grandson of Henry Steed, who was the first Sheriff of Wirt County in 1848. My mother, who grew up with some of the grandchildren of Henry Steed in the 1880's, recalls that the Steeds, even at that late date, were opposed to public schools.

There is no legend of a Poor School in Wirt County and no record of one has come to my attention. School records in Virginia and in West Virginia are woefully deficient. The whole subject of education is complicated by the process of county making and the two civil wars. Wirt County, in the English and not in the French phase, was originally a part of Augusta County, Virginia. Later, it was a part of Monongalia County, then of Harrison County, then of Wood County, then of Jackson County, until finally, in 1848, the subdividing terminated with the formation of Wirt County. All the former counties are still functioning and the records pertaining to Wirt County for the periods of time when Wirt County was a part of another county are found at the parent court house. Land and estate records in these older counties, where the records have not been destroyed by war or fire, are often informative, but school records generally are confined to real estate transfers. Even today the County Board of Education does not record its proceedings at the Court House in sharp contrast to the County Court and the Circuit Court, both of which act officially on the record. What is known of schools in former times is, therefore, largely a matter of legend in the local sense, though much has been written about frontier and rural schools in general.

The chief educational institution on the frontier and in West Virginia down to the end of the Civil War in 1865 was the Subscription School. Both my Grandfather, Amaziah Reed, born in 1843, and his wife, Malinda Jane Keck, born in 1844, attended subscription schools, and I recall that both of them spoke to me of these schools when I was a boy. Subscription schools lasted anywhere from a month to six months, depending on the financial resources of the community.

Subscription schools were conducted by journeymen schoolmasters. In the early and middle 19th Century, western Virginia, except for small river towns such as Wheeling, Parkersburg, and Charleston, was a patchwork of rural communities conveniently divided by geography into creeks. People usually built their homes along the river and creek banks, where there was level bottom land, even though they obtained a living from the surrounding mountains and forests. These creek communities persist in rural areas. If a Wirt County resident today is asked where he lives, he may reply, "On Tucker Creek", or "On Reedy Creek", or on some other creek. When I was a boy, residence identification for country people was always by creeks, but nowadays it is often by State Highways. A study of creek communities with special reference to loyalties in the Civil War dispels the romantic notion that residents of the border States invariably went North or South after individual soul searching. They did exactly what one would expect them to do under the principle of leadership in human affairs: that is, they went North or South as communities rather than as individuals. Reedy Creek was generally Confederate, Tucker Creek leaned toward the Union, Reedy Creek votes Democratic and Tucker Creek votes Republican to this day.

The journeymen schoolmasters were products of the frontier and later of the harsh conditions inherent in the task of conquering a wilderness. In a sense they were adventurers just as the people with whom they lived were adventurers. Some were men of considerable learning while others were frauds only slightly more literate than the people they attempted to teach. Some married, settled down, and became prosperous citizens, others continued to wander.

A school master would appear at the home of a leading citizen of a creek community and announce his intention of conducting a school. Sometimes, he was known already because he had taught schools in nearby communities, sometimes he was a total stranger. In either event he had no credentials other than his word and possibly a framed diploma. There would be a public meeting at the community school, if the community had a school, or at a church, or at a private home, at which the parents of potential "scholars" subscribed what they thought they could afford toward the proposed school. There was always some money, but many patrons subscribed commodities such as homespun clothes and furs. Some furnished the schoolmaster with room and board. The amount of the subscription determined the length of the school term.

Many communities built log school houses in anticipation of the arrival of a teacher, so that the building was available from time to time. Such schools have often been described in literature and I shall not take the space to describe them again other than to remark that a subscription school is still standing on Hughes River near Smithville in Ritchie County. The building is constructed of logs shaped by an adze and daubed with clay. Its dimensions are twenty-four feet by eighteen feet, and it has no windows. When I first saw it more than forty years ago an old man living nearby told me that his mother had attended school there and that the teacher was known as Professor Snodgrass. The building is now used as a cow stable and the present owner was surprised when I told him its original purpose.

My Grandfather Reed attended two subscription schools for a total period of twelve weeks. I wish now that I had written down the names of his teachers. He was clearly not an educated man, yet he must have gained something more than a superficial knowledge of the three R's from his schooldays. Among his books, when he died, was a set of Scott's Waverly Novels and a two-volume translation of the works of Josephus. My Grandmother Reed likewise attended a subscription school, though I recall from her conversation only one circumstance about it. In her school the pupils were taught Singing Geography. The knowledge contained in the geography book was set to a tune. One side of the room would sing:

Name and declaim
The Capital of New York.

The other side of the room would reply:

The Capital of New York is
Albany on the Hudson.

The song covered the capitals of all the States of the Union and all the countries of the world, together with the rivers upon which they were located. I remember particularly my Grandmother singing:

Name and declaim
The Capital of Kentucky.
The Capital of Kentucky is
Frankfort on the Main!!!

Subscription schools, of course, were not the only institutions of learning in western Virginia in the early 19th Century. There were Academies, somewhat resembling modern Preparatory Schools at Morgantown and Huntington, which later became West Virginia University and Marshall University respectively. Alexander Campbell was organizing the religious sect known as The Disciples of Christ and also laying the foundations for Bethany College. There was a fashionable seminary for young ladies at West Liberty, to which my other grandmother, Mary Virtue, was dispatched from Pennsylvania. Other academies, seminaries, and boarding schools in western Virginia have been largely forgotten, notably the Academy at Saint Albans where the abandoned buildings were still standing thirty years ago. Nearly all towns had a school of some kind, but the mass of the population lived in the creeks and hollows and the creeks and hollows knew only the journeyman schoolmaster.

The long-standing quarrel between Tidewater Virginia and the western counties is too complicated to be detailed here. Yet, no rational assessment of the history, economics, religion, politics, law, education, social structure, legend, and tradition of West Virginia can be made without postulating (1) that there was a fundamental cleavage which began in colonial times, and (2) that the quarrel finally terminated in bloody civil war.

The quarrel had its beginnings in geography. Eastern Virginia was the oldest English colony in America. As the settlements spread out from Jamestown and Williamsburg, the nature of the land and of the times favored the development of huge plantations and slave labor. The government of the colony and later of the State gravitated toward a few favored families who owned the land and who exemplified the aristocratic, paternalistic tradition. There came a time when the topography changed, when, instead of the wide level plains, there was nothing left for cultivation but the valleys between the mountains. These valleys, however, were fertile enough. They had a bounteous rainfall and the mountains swarmed with wildlife. While the terrain was unfavorable for cultivation with slave labor, it was ideal, except for the Indians, for the landless farmer who was not too proud to work with his own hands. Restless people, people who left nothing behind but who hoped to gain lands of their own in the mountains ahead, swarmed into No-Man's Land. They were by nature aggressive, turbulent, and violent, and as soon as they settled with the Indians, often by extermination, they began to quarrel with their supposedly more effete brethren on the eastern seaboard. As early as 1776 the Trans-Allegheny pioneers were clamoring for a State of their own.

The grievances of the people of the western counties were grounded in the circumstances of their life and times. Appalachia was better suited to industrial than to agricultural development. Salt wells were drilled near Charleston before 1800. The mountains were covered with virgin forest and nearly every county had rich, visible seams of bituminous coal. The West was filling up. Steamboats plied the Ohio, the Mississippi, and the Missouri Rivers, and there was a constant demand for salt, coal, and lumber on the treeless plains. The population of the western counties increased by leaps and bounds, but their influence in the State Legislature was restricted by the law permitting a planter to count his slaves for voting purposes. As the preponderance of political power remained in the East, the East received a disproportionate share of the roads, the state institutions, and the schools on a statewide basis. Hence, the educational standards in western Virginia were low even by the standards of the aristocratic South.

When war came, when western Virginia turned against the Mother State and became a State by itself, one of the first Acts of the new State was to provide for a public school system. The Constitution of 1863 contained a provision for public schools in all counties, with a designated school term of six months. But here, as elsewhere, in the complexity of counties and magisterial districts, the problem was money. Some counties and some magisterial districts had more tax money than other counties and other magisterial districts. Some counties and districts were able to establish the six months school system with little delay, others suffered serious delays and some had to cut the school term from six months to three or four months.

In rural areas, during the forty to fifty year period following the Civil War, the one-room schools were known as common schools. This was true not only in West Virginia but also in many other parts of the nation. Much of the older generation in America today attended common schools. All had certain common characteristics. A one room school had one teacher who was certified upon written examination, called the Uniform Examination, by the State and the County Superintendents of Schools. The whole country was divided into geographical school districts, and a pupil attended the school in the district in which his parents lived. The school district was a subdivision of the magisterial district. There were two school districts in the Beulah Hill voting precinct which was itself a subdivision of Newark Magisterial District.

Each school district elected three unpaid School Trustees, who served as the District Board of Education. The duties of the Trustees were (1) to employ the teacher, and (2) to enforce discipline. If the teacher found that he had an incorrigible pupil, the Trustees were authorized to take such action, within limits, as was deemed necessary. At its broadest authority the Trustees could expel a pupil from the school system.

The one-room country school in West Virginia, under the public school system, was a vast improvement over the unlighted log schools with dirt floors and puncheon seats of an earlier generation. The type became standardized. The white painted frame building was rectangular in shape, about forty feet long and thirty feet wide, with three windows on each side and no windows at all at the ends of the building. One end housed the entrance, the other was covered with blackboard and supplied with chalk and erasers. The teacher sat at a desk in front of the blackboard facing the entrance and the pupils at their three-seat benches and desks.

Those old fashioned benches and desks seem to have disappeared. They were really quite ingenious in that they served the double purpose, when placed in rows, of providing a seat for three pupils in front and a desk with a book shelf, for three pupils behind. Usually, the younger pupils sat up front while the older pupils occupied the rear. In these combination desk-seats there was, unfortunately, at the seat level an aperture about an inch wide through which the behinders could insert frogs, snakes, pins, and other instruments of torture, often to the detriment of discipline and good order.

The schools were modeled on the English Form System, except that the forms were known as Readers. Each Reader provided auxiliary instruction in other subjects such as penmanship, spelling, and arithmetic in the lower Readers and geography, history, civil government, and bookkeeping in the Advanced Readers. Throughout my life I have kept a ledger based on the double entry bookkeeping that I learned in the common school. McGuffey's Five Readers were standard when my mother attended school in the 1880's and the 1890's, and they continued to be standard until about 1907 when Elson's Readers were substituted. I started in the First Reader with McGuffey and ended in the Fifth Reader with Elson.

My mother tells me that in the 1880's Wirt County had only four months of school each year. This had changed before 1905 when I lived with my Grandfather Black and first entered the Center Hill School for a six months school term. The six months school term persisted until after I left the common school system, in fact, until after World War I.

I cannot leave the subject of one-room schools without making a few observations gleaned from experience both as a pupil and as a teacher. The one-room schools had serious limitations, but they also had advantages in the area of imparting knowledge on a group basis that we have since lost. One teacher taught the whole common school curriculum. Classes were seated on the recitation benches at the front of the room and were conducted within sight and hearing of pupils of all ages. In the course of a single day the whole school watched six year olds struggling with their ABC's and Fifth Formers learning square root, cube root, and algebra. The bright pupil learned from the classes ahead of him, the dull pupil benefited from repetition.

In the grade school, by way of contrast, there is much rigidity of form. The pace is often geared to the abilities of the stupid. While I am aware that this problem is approached in progressive school systems by having special classes for the gifted and other classes for the retarded, I am also aware that such refinements cost money. In Wirt County there are so few people that, without State Aid, we could not support even a minimal school system.

The trouble with the common school system in rural America was that it was the be-all and end-all of education for the great mass of its pupils. Wirt County had no high school, and, unless relatives had money for boarding schools, there was no place else to go. I passed all the required examinations of the common school when I was ten years old and then loafed for five years until my relatives entered me as a boarding student at Davis and Elkins Academy at Elkins, West Virginia. Later, with time out for war service, I received the Bachelor of Arts degree from Cornell University and the Bachelor of Laws degree from West Virginia University. I did not distinguish myself in scholarship at either university, and I make no claim to being an expert in education. In the role of victim rather than expert, I submit that present day educators would do well in some instances to adopt the methods of instruction used in the one room schools, while dispensing with their obvious limitations.

Today, Wirt County has a modern high school with a library, a gymnasium, and a football field, a comfortable new elementary school in Elizabeth, and seven two-room elementary schools throughout the county. An elementary school in Wirt County is defined as a school in which instruction is given in Grades 1 to 6. Grades 7 and 8 comprise the Junior High School. Grades 9, 10, 11, and 12 comprise the Senior High School. All Junior High School and Senior High School students attend classes in Elizabeth and are transported from and to their homes by bus. The seven elementary schools outside Elizabeth provide instruction only in Grades 1 to 6. Each has two teachers. One teacher teaches Grades 1 to 3, the other Grades 4 to 6. In a limited sense these auxiliary schools resemble the one-room schools of a former generation.

In obtaining detailed information about the Wirt County School system today, I am indebted to Miss Louise Roberts, the Librarian of the Dora Bee Woodyard Library at the

Wirt County High School. This library was made possible through a gift of Ronald B. Woodyard, heretofore mentioned. Since the information was supplied in response to written questions, I am setting forth here the questions propounded by me and the answers supplied by Miss Roberts. The information pertains to the school year, 1963-64.

Question: How many pupils are there in the Wirt County High Schools and how are they divided by classes?

Answer: There are two High Schools, Junior and Senior.

The number of pupils in Junior High School are:

Grade 7	68
Grade 8	67
Total	135

The number of pupils in Senior High School are:

Grade 9	69
Grade 10	76
Grade 11	63
Grade 12	69
Total	277

Total number of pupils in Junior High School and Senior High School....................................412

Question: How many pupils are there in Elizabeth Elementary School and how many pupils are there in other elementary schools in the county?

Answer: Number of pupils in Elizabeth Elementary School....................................288

Number of pupils in other elementary schools....289

Total....................................577

Total number of pupils in Elementary Schools, Junior High School, and Senior High School............989

Question: How many elementary schools outside Elizabeth are now operating in the county?

Answer: Number of elementary schools outside Elizabeth.................................... 7

Question: How many teachers are employed in the High Schools?

Answer: 20

Question: How many teachers are employed in the elementary schools?

Answer: Number of teachers at Elizabeth Elementary School 12

Number of teachers at other elementary schools .. 14

Total 26

Total number of teachers employed in county school system 46

Question: How many high school teachers have college degrees?

Answer: .... All

Question: How many high school teachers have advanced degrees?

Answer: .... One

Question: What courses are taught in Senior High School?

Answer: Categories are: English, Foreign Language, Social Studies, Mathematics, Sciences, Commercial Studies, Vocational Studies, and Miscellaneous Studies.

Courses offered in English are:

English (four years)
Journalism
The Bible as Literature
and History

Courses offered in Foreign Language are:

French (two years)

Courses offered in mathematics are:

Algebra I
Plane Geometry
Algebra II
Business mathematics
General mathematics

Courses offered in sciences are:

General Science (9th Grade)
Biology (10th Grade)
Chemistry (11th and 12th Grades)
Physiology

Courses offered in commercial studies are:

- Typing (11th and 12th Grades)
- Shorthand
- Bookkeeping

Courses offered in social studies are:

- Civics (9th Grade)
- American History (11th Grade)
- Problems of American Democracy (12th Grade)
- American Government
- World History
- Geography

Courses offered in vocational studies are:

- Home economics (three years)
- Vocational agriculture (three years)
- Farm Mechanics (one year)
- Shop (two years)

Miscellaneous courses are:

- Art
- Physical Education
- Band music

Question: What courses are taught in elementary schools?

Answer: Reading, writing, spelling, English, American history, World history, West Virginia history, arithmetic, geography, music, art, and physical education.

Question: How much mathematics is required for a high school diploma?

Answer: Five courses are offered and two are required. Students who do not intend to go to college may choose their own. College entrance requires that the student pass algebra and plane geometry.

Question: How much science is required for a high school diploma?

Answer: General Science and biology.

Question: How many courses must a student pass in order to obtain a high school diploma and what courses are required?

Answer: To obtain a high school diploma a student must have a minimum of seventeen credits. The required credits are:

Subject	Units
English	4
American History	1
Problems of Democracy	1
Civics	1
Biology	1
General Science	1
Mathematics	2
Physical Education	2
Elective	4
Total	17

Question: Over the past ten years what percentage of high school graduates have gone on to college?

Answer: Approximately fifteen per cent.

Question: What is the average annual salary of a high school teacher? What is the salary of the high school principal? What is the salary of the County Superintendent of Schools?

Answer: All salaries are based on degree and type of certificate. The average annual salary of high school teachers $3,889.47. The salary of the high school principal is $5,253.50. He serves as principal of both the Junior and Senior High Schools. The salary of the County Superintendent is $6,360.00.

Question: What are the average salaries of elementary school teachers and principals?

Answer: Elementary school teachers average $3,591.00 annually. Elementary principals average $4,119.83.

Question: What inducements are made to teachers with respect to social security, and fringe benefits?

Answer: All teachers are covered by social security and there is also a Teachers Pension Fund over and above Social Security. The only fringe benefit is a Sick Leave Fund required by law.

Question: How many school buses are owned by the Wirt County Board of Education and how many bus drivers are employed?

Answer: Fifteen buses and fifteen drivers.

Question: Are bus drivers full time employees? How much are they paid?

Answer: Bus drivers are all part time employees. Nearly all have some other regular employment. They are paid on the average $2,156.38 per year.

Question: Apart from administrators, teachers and bus drivers, how many persons are employed by the Board of Education and what do these persons do?

Answer: The Board of Education employs four clerks in administrative offices. The Board also employs four full time janitors, one part time janitor, and one full time maintenance man. Under the hot lunch program thirteen cooks are employed at an average wage of $5.00 per day.

Question: When was the Wirt County High School established?

Answer: 1918-19.

Question: Can you furnish me a list of the high school principals and county superintendents since the high school was established and the dates of their terms of office?

Answer: High School Principals and their terms of office are:

1919-1922........................C. H. Snodgrass
1922-1923........................Marvin Cooper
1923-1931........................Camden Sims
1931-1932........................R. A. Lee
1932-1933........................E. H. Knabenshue
1933-1936........................Austin Dearman
1936-1943........................Truslow Waldo
1943-1945........................Gordon Eismon
1945-1948........................James E. Brown
1948-1951........................Ray Walter
1951-1961........................Sam Williams
1961-1963........................Roy Jarvis

County Superintendents and their terms of office are:

1863-1865........................Jesse Little
1865-1869........................L. C. Rogers
1869-1871........................M. B. Edmondson

1871-1875 .... Zaccheus Hickman
1875-1879 .... D. C. Casto
1879-1885 .... M. B. Edmondson
1885-1887 .... David Martin
1887-1889 .... M. B. Edmondson
1889-1891 .... Wellington Lister
1891-1893 .... George Harris
1893-1895 .... Willie Fought
1895-1899 .... John A. Davis
1899-1903 .... Ralph E. Davis
1903-1911 .... J. F. Haverty
1911-1919 .... Ross Wilson
1919-1923 .... Leonard Dailey
1923-1931 .... C. H. Snodgrass
1931-1935 .... Ross Wilson
1935-1941 .... Clarence Ray
1941-1945 .... Robert Hickman
1945-1948 .... Gordon Eismon
1948-1951 .... Glendon Yoak
1951-1961 .... Charles A. Cline
1961-1963 .... Waymond Riley

It is noteworthy that school enrollment in Wirt County in 1963-64 was the highest in a decade. Based on that circumstance the State Board of Education estimated the population of Wirt County for 1963 at eighty persons above the 1960 Census, and that estimate, if correct, would establish the present population at 4471. Using the Beulah Hill percentage base on a county wide basis, there ought to be 1464 persons in the county under twenty-one years of age, and of this number 989 were in school in 1963. The comparative figures for Junior and Senior High School Grades indicates that there are not many dropouts in the school system. A factor against dropouts is that Parkersburg and Ohio factories often require a high school diploma for prospective employees. Dropouts are frequently girls who marry someone employed elsewhere. Nearly all high school graduates leave the county immediately upon graduation, either to take employment or to continue their studies. The difference between 1464 minors and 989 in school represents roughly the number of children in the county who are not yet old enough to attend school. If the present trend continues approximately eighty-five percent of today's elementary school pupils will eventually finish high school.

On the quantitative scale the Wirt County High School is highly successful. It prepares more than eight out of ten of its pupils in the minimal qualifications for employment in an industrial society. Actually, the new generation is better educated, on the whole, and far more sophisticated than earlier generations. With the advent of the Machine Age, with the widespread use of the automobile, the airplane, radio, and television, education has shifted from the classroom to the mainstream of American Life. Machines and compulsory military service, which together carry young men and young women to the far corners of the earth, make the new generation less provincial and more cosmopolitan in character than the old. The distant frontiers are shrinking. Soldiers serving overseas bring home new ideas and often new brides. On quantity alone the Wirt County school system performs a highly useful service in preparing its pupils for the nonspecialized work of the problematical world of tomorrow.

Qualitatively, the rigid grade system and the standardized curriculum are definitely faulty. Wirt County High School has no physics course in 1964! There is no solid geometry. I was introduced to algebra, plane geometry, solid geometry, and trigonometry at Davis and Elkins Academy nearly fifty years ago. The only foreign language is French. Why French? Why not Russian, Spanish, or German? (A telephone call reveals that French is a product of our lack of finances. The foreign language teacher is qualified in no other foreign language.) I am intrigued by the abundance of studies in the social sciences. History and geography are excellent, but why so much emphasis, in a limited curriculum, on Civics, American Government, and Problems of Democracy. The school system is trying, no doubt, to prepare its pupils for responsible citizenship, but none of the studies cover the most urgent problems of all, namely (1) the exercise of raw power through patronage, the welfare rolls, control of communications media, vote buying, vote stealing, corruption, cynicism, and fraud, and (2) the apathy and sometimes the active connivance of an unaroused public that no longer expects plain honesty in its officials and has deluded itself into thinking that Santa Claus will never die.

The thought intrudes here that what I am saying does not apply to the school authorities of Wirt County. They have no more control over what is taught in the schools than I have. Wirt County High School is an accredited high school. Accreditation, by devious channels, goes back to the National Education Association and the Department of Health, Education, and Welfare in Washington. The courses taught in Wirt County High School are probably duplicated in thousands of other little high schools all over the nation, and, under the circumstances, the duplications will doubtless continue.

There is too much emphasis on athletics, band marching, public images, and showmanship, though the public obviously thinks otherwise. Football is all the rage. In 1964 a candidate for Governor drew only three hundred people to an open court house rally in Elizabeth, but the annual football game between Wirt and Calhoun County High Schools attracted approximately four thousand paying spectators. Football is replacing baseball as the national sport. The ruggedness of the game, the marching bands, the flashing colors, and the ever increasing feats of showmanship make one wonder if America is following the footsteps of the populace of ancient Rome in its craving for bread and circuses.

While the Wirt County school system seems to be turning out students who are, in general, well adjusted to their surroundings, there is no place in it for the gifted student. The pace is too sluggish. If it surprises anyone to learn that there are gifted students in Wirt County, let it be noted that within the past ten years two fifteen-year old boys have passed the entrance examinations and have been admitted as undergraduates at the University of Chicago. Gifted children are rare in any environment. Our universities are starting to search for them. Talent scouts from Yale University have been in Wirt County, and I understand that other universities have similar programs. The few students who win scholastic excellence in Wirt County do so in spite of their public school training and not because of it.

Having said so much in criticism, I think it is only fair to add a few words of commendation as follows:

(1) Considering what they are paid, it is a wonder that Wirt County can keep a teaching staff at all. The teachers are all college trained, yet they earn on the average about one half the annual wages of a steelworker. Obviously, there is an economic factor in West Virginia's losing two thousand trained teachers a year.

(2) Generally, the teachers are young though a few, such as Louise Roberts, have taught for many years. There is a heavy turnover, and it is whispered that some teachers are merely seeking experience before moving on. They are, nevertheless, sober and industrious as a rule, and they seem to be conscientious in their work.

(3) The commercial courses, manual training shop, vocational agriculture courses, and home economics courses are each of inestimable value. I employed a girl in my law office who had received training in typing and shorthand at the high school. Her name was Ruth Ellison, and she turned out to be the best secretary I ever had. She was so good in shorthand that she was often used as a substitute court reporter. The shop is an excellent training place for factory employees. Vocational agriculture is invaluable to potential farmers, and home economics is undoubtedly a factor in successful marriages.

(4) For all the relaxation of discipline under modern teaching techniques, I am convinced that high school students are better mannered and less inclined to troublesome mischief than they were when I was a boy. This development, no doubt, is a result of adjustment programs.

(5) While the students seem to spend an inordinate amount of time on athletics, intricate band marching, social committees, and other extracurricular activities, it is undeniable that such activities consume much of the leisure time of modern society.

(6) No educational system will ever be perfect. Education in the final analysis depends on individual effort.

(7) On the whole, considering teachers salaries, changing values, the uncertainties of the times, and the problems of enforced leisure, the Wirt County school system is about as good as could reasonably be expected.

9. Politics

POLITICS HAS so many aspects and definitions that a mere catalogue would exceed the limits of this discussion. The human animal has undoubtedly reached its present predominance in the animal kingdom through a genius for organization. Organization is the key to all human political systems.

Life Magazine recently carried an article about colonies of baboons. It appears that baboons have a political hierarchy, somewhat resembling certain human institutions, in which one of the males is recognized as the unquestioned leader of the colony. The leader, however, is not necessarily the best fighter of the group. The leader is rather the statesman and the diplomat among baboons, the baboon who is able, through the force of his personality, to attach other baboons to his party. He retains his chieftainship only so long as he retains the loyalty of his followers. While the language of baboons has not been thoroughly interpreted, their system of government bears a strong resemblance to unadulterated but primitive democracy.

Here is an illustration of the leadership principle. In human society this principle, the desire of the mass of followers for a protective leader who in return demands obedience, extends from the heads of great nations to any group containing more than two individuals. Even small boys and girls instinctively choose a leader. A citizen of Wirt County cannot be elected constable, now the lowest office in the political spectrum, unless he is able to persuade a requisite number of his fellow citizens to vote for him.

Everyone knows how these matters are handled in America. Leadership is required and taken for granted. In some countries defeated candidates resort to revolution and bloodshed, but in America, at least since the Civil War of the

1860's, being a good loser is considered mannerly and good form. Manners and good form, in this instance, are fortified by the plausible hope that there will be another election and a different result.

In looking back over the course of my life, I find that I have always been mixed up in politics somehow, though I could not possibly tell why. It must be some kind of compulsion. I have been a candidate for public office at the lower levels of government on eleven different occasions, and, in spite of having belonged to the minority party during most of my adult life, I have been elected to the office for which I was a candidate seven times and defeated four times. Two of my defeats were at the state-wide level when the entire Republican ticket went down the drain. The Offices I have held have all been minor. I have been a member of the Board of Education, a Town Councilman, a Clerk of the Circuit Court, and a Prosecuting Attorney. Between times I served as Chief Investigator for the Office of Price Administration in Charleston and Administrative Assistant to a United States Senator in Washington.

Politics in Wirt County has a relatively simple meaning. It represents the party, the machine, and the choice offered between the candidates and the issues. Voters may register in three categories, Democrat, Republican, and Independent. Registration figures in Wirt County for the General Election of 1964 were: Democrats 1435, Republicans 1271, Independents 8. Since there is no organized Independent Party in West Virginia, the voter who registers Independent is not entitled to vote in a Primary Election but he can vote for whomever he pleases in the General Election.

The choice of the voter under our election laws is frustrating, particularly in Presidential primaries. The ballots are long and may be complicated by constitutional amendments, bond issues, and levy increases, so vaguely worded that even lawyers are not sure what they mean. Machine organization and the voters preference for one of the Presidential candidates often result in straight ticket voting in General Elections. Both parties have machines, or party organizations, but Republicans in West Virginia at the statewide level must depend on voluntary contributions to their campaign fund while Democrats have a ready-made machine in the State employees. Politics in Wirt County is inextricably bound up with politics at the State and the National levels because of our traditional two-party system.

At this point I wish to interpolate a comment with reference to human nature. Philosophers from earliest times have recognized the forces of good and evil in human relationships. Human beings seem to have a built-in moral sense that tells them what is good and what is bad. While nearly everyone wants to be good, the mechanics of living offer many temptations to be bad. The bad side of human nature, the forces of evil decried by theologians and moralists, comes to the surface most frequently, in my experience, in four different situations: crime, divorce, distribution of estates, and partisan politics.

Crime will not detain us here because Wirt County has one of the lowest crime ratios in the world, and, besides, crime is probably a pathological and/or a psychological manifestation. Divorce is less common in Wirt County than in other parts of the country, but it is present, and here, as elsewhere, some divorces are arranged ahead of time while others are fought out in court. There is no more dirty, bitter, underhanded exhibition of jungle warfare in the world than a contested divorce case. As counsel for one side or the other, I have often marvelled that two persons, who have enjoyed the familiarity of marital embraces, could learn to hate each other so intensely that they take leave of the refinements of civilization and even of common sense. Yet, these same people are often good people, once they extricate themselves from their miseries. Another throwback to prehistoric times occurs in the distribution of estates. Estates more often than not are settled amicably, but, if brothers and sisters once start quarreling over heirship property, they will stop at nothing to gain their ends. Enemies are unreasonable wherever they come from but an enemy who is also related by blood is the most vindictive and dangerous of all. Finally, an area of conduct that encourages the worst in human nature lies in the field of partisan politics.

Some people, usually those who know the least about them, believe that all political machines are immoral and ought to be abolished. Nothing could be further from the truth. A political machine is as essential to government as breath is to life. In America, there are always at least two political machines opposed to each other. One is the machine in office and the other is the machine trying to attain office. The machine out of office is always honest and idealistic, except in the places where it retains power, because it has nothing but hope to offer its adherents. The machine in office, no matter how it got there, soon becomes corrupt simply because power corrupts. If our electorate is intelligent it will not keep either party or any candidate in office for a period of more than eight successive years. Under the table of probabilities it takes a machine in power a maximum of four years to learn the ropes. During the next four years the machine will find ways to reward its stalwarts at the public expense and to protect its party prerogatives.

The story of the two dominant political parties in West Virginia contains some curious paradoxes. Before the Civil War of 1861, West Virginia was a part of Virginia. While I have not found reliable election returns for the western counties in the early days of the Republic, other sources such as biographies of Gideon Draper Camden and George W. Summers indicate that the mountain region was predominantly Jeffersonian Republican and Jacksonian Democrat in the period 1800 to 1860. Nevertheless, there was always a lively opposition from the Federalists and the Whigs. The Federalists vanished in the face of Jeffersonian Republicanism and the Whigs dissolved on the issue of secession.

When Virginia seceded from the Union, the western counties set up a government of their own, not for western Virginia alone but for the whole Commonwealth of Virginia, called the Restored Government of Virginia. Throughout the War, Virginia had two separate governments and two separate Governors, one at Richmond and one at Wheeling. The Richmond Governor was a Democrat, the Wheeling Governor a Republican. This situation persisted after West Virginia was admitted to the Union on June 20, 1863. After the surrender at Appomattox the Wheeling Governor, Francis H. Pierpont, moved to Richmond where he served as Governor of Virginia until 1868. During the same period Arthur I. Boreman was Governor of West Virginia. One of the first acts of the new Republican Administration in West Virginia in 1863 was to abolish slavery.

In Appalachia and in the Deep South the Civil War fostered hatreds, enmities, and family feuds that sometimes survive to the present time. In the Deep South the defeat of the Confederacy and the Federal Government's reconstruction policies converted nearly all Southerners, including Whigs, into Democrats solely because the Democrats were in opposition to the Republicans. The issues were regional rather than ideological. In Appalachia, and particularly in West Virginia, the victors and the vanquished were forced to live side by side, and each side retained memories of the anarchy that had prevailed during the war years. In many counties there had been no law enforcement officers and no law. Partisans had robbed, pillaged, and killed with impunity. Such incidents are not soon forgotten among people who cling to the same land for generations. One result of the War was that the younger generation was brought up to be Republicans or Democrats by inheritance. Politics in Appalachia was a continuation of the War in times of peace with all the oppression, chicanery, and fraud that war exploits.

From 1863 to 1932 West Virginia was generally a Republican State, but the Democrats always mustered enough strength to insure an active opposition. They consistently retained control in a number of counties, especially those bordering on the Mother State of Virginia. Between 1863 and 1932, the Democrats elected some Governors, but the Republicans usually managed to control the Legislature and the Board of Public Works. The latter is important because West Virginia is one of the few States of the union in which the executive power is shared by seven different officials. The Board of Public Works consists of the Governor, the Secretary of State, the Auditor, the Treasurer, the Attorney General, the Commissioner of Agriculture, and the Superintendent of Schools. The Governor has no authority over the Board except such as he can maintain by persuasion. While the Governor cannot succeed himself under the Constitution, members of the Board may be re-elected indefinitely. In a very real sense the Governorship is ceremonial in nature because the Board of Public Works exercises the real executive power of the state. When the Governor belongs to one party and the Board of Public Works to the opposition party, as has happened at least twice in our political history, you have a situation in which the Governor is practically helpless. It is as if the President of the United States had been saddled with a Cabinet holding a veto power over his programs.

The Republican Party, which began humbly as a weak protest against slavery, became identified, after a few years in office, as the party of big business and special privilege, illustrating once again what I have already said about parties and their swift corruption. Our history is studded with such paradoxes. The Democrat Party, which now claims to be the accepted vehicle for liberalism, survived partly because the defeated Southern leaders continued to believe in slavery and the racial supremacy of white men. In West Virginia the big business influence reached its apogee in the coal and lumber industries.

After the Civil War most coal miners and lumber workers, both white and Negro, were Republicans by inheritance. It was relatively easy in those early days for a coal mine operator or a mill owner, to transport his entire working force to the polls on election day and deliver a one hundred percent Republican vote. Later, as labor disputes arose between the owners and the employees, the coal operators and the mill owners, at first triumphant, made voting compliance a prerequisite for employment, and such compliance extended even to primaries. As late as 1930 I saw 135 coal miners from Raymond City in Putnam County brought to the polls in a primary election. They were in the charge of the mine foreman and each miner voted the company's choice on an open table. Besides, West Virginia, in common with other portions of this planet, has produced a minority of voters and office holders who can be had for a price. It is always disillusioning to a young politician when he learns exactly who can and must be had for a price.

Politics is another field in which it is dangerous to state generalizations. Corruption or lack of corruption in elections and in local government depends in large measure on an active opposition and on the political traditions of each community. In Raleigh County, West Virginia, many precincts have no secret voting booths, though such booths are required by law. Everyone votes openly on a table and no one objects because elections have always been conducted in that manner. Logan County, which merited an article in Life Magazine because of its election frauds, has voting machines, but the voter may not approach the machine. The voting machine is operated by a pair of election clerks, nicknamed the Lever Brothers, who manipulate the machine's levers without the slightest regard for the voter's preference. Such practices are not statewide, and it is instructive to observe that flagrant election violations and general corruption recur in the very counties in which the mine owners and the lumbermen used to deliver lopsided majorities to the Republicans. It is, perhaps, only poetic justice, though it certainly bodes ill for the future of republican institutions, that the labor union leaders in the same counties now deliver the same lopsided majorities to the Democrats. These counties are conditioned to fraud because they have never known honest opposition or honest elections and government.

In some counties in West Virginia elections always have been and still are relatively clean, but the clean counties have had an active opposition. Wirt County is a clean county with respect to the casting and counting of ballots. But even where elections are clean the traditions of the past in which no quarter is asked or given, where some people still vote Democrat or Republican by inheritance—even in such clean elections tradition favors mass appeal and machine politics. Mass appeal will be the ruination of this country yet. One of the most effective campaign gimmicks for Lyndon B. Johnson in 1964 was a television picture of a pair of hands, obviously Goldwater's hands, tearing up Social Security cards. Actually, Goldwater's record on Social Security was as good as Johnson's record. The picture however convinced many oldsters and younger people that their security was threatened. The campaign of 1964 was a mishmash of many issues, notably the class struggle of the Negroes, but the outcome demonstrated once again that the citizens of a democracy are less interested in corruption in high places and in low places than they are in their own personal welfare.

Republican domination of the executive branch of the government, the Legislature, and the Judiciary in West Virginia ended abruptly with Franklin D. Roosevelt's elevation to the Presidency in 1932. That occurred in the third year of the Great Depression when banks had failed or were failing everywhere, when the crash of the stock market had wiped out a large portion of the country's savings, when unemployment had reached staggering proportions, when debtors by the hundreds of thousands had lost their real and personal property, and when values of all kinds had plummeted to an unprecedented low. Now, the mines and the mills were mostly shut down. The mine and mill employees, cast adrift, lived as best they could by their own efforts and in dependence on public and private charity.

Though much was said in the course of the campaign of 1932 about starving miners, and rations were indeed skimpy, I never heard of a single American anywhere who actually died of starvation. At its worst, more people were employed during the Depression than were not employed. There was always money in circulation. Adjustments were made in accordance with the age-old capacity for survival. The people who had money, and a minority as usual made money out of the disaster, and those who were still employed helped the less fortunate members of their own families. Organizations were set up to distribute food and clothing to the needy. There was a revival of farming for the pioneers had proved long before that the mountains of Appalachia will yield a living without a capital investment. The population of Wirt County, as I have noted heretofore, increased during the depression. The census figures indicate that the same thing happened throughout Appalachia.

Though the people adjusted themselves to hard times and many eventually profited thereby, they did not relish the experience. In the campaign of 1928 the newspapers, the magazines, and the radio, the chief moulders of public opinion, had almost unanimously assured their readers and auditors that prosperity was here to stay. The country was entering upon an unparalleled period of development in which poverty would disappear. One of the slogans of the campaign that put Herbert Hoover in the White House was TWO AUTOMOBILES IN EVERY GARAGE AND TWO CHICKENS IN EVERY POT. The attitude of the communications media in 1928 toward Herbert Hoover and the Republican ticket was re-enacted in 1964 by the same media, plus television, in favor of Lyndon B. Johnson and the Democratic ticket. It is one of the prices we pay for the so-called freedom of the press.

The memory of 1928 disenchants me somewhat with the Great Society of Lyndon B. Johnson. It is not that I am opposed to the ideal of a Great Society. Far from it. It is simply that I have heard the refrain before, and I recall that, within a year of Hoover's inauguration, the world was tormented with the most agonizing depression in modern history. "The best laid schemes of mice and men," as Robert Burns noted, "gang aft agley".

When the mines shut down, when the mills and the factories slowed to half time or no time at all, when the stock market crashed and banks and businesses dissolved in bankruptcy, the situation favored a breach in political alignment and tradition. Politics by inheritance crumbled before the hope of a deliverer. In West Virginia for the first time since the Civil War, Republicans deserted their party in droves. In the mining towns, where the light of Republicanism was already dim, defections were practically total. Roosevelt and the Democrat ticket swept the State by a landslide, and right there, in accordance with the predictable defects of human nature, opportunities for corruption arose in a manner and on a scale that Republicans had not even dreamed of.

Roosevelt appeared at a time when the whole country was demoralized and ripe for either a Fascist or a Communist revolution. He and his Braintrusters, who supplied the ideology for the New Deal movement, deserve acclaim for having accomplished their own revolution without bloodshed. Roosevelt's record resembles that of his predecessor, Andrew Jackson, in that his victory of 1932 was a genuine uprising of the people against entrenched wealth and special privilege, and, like Jackson, Roosevelt retained the people's trust and affection to the end. Again, like Jackson, he maintained the outward forms of constitutional government while exercising raw power through the spoils system.

Just as the same war looks entirely different to the commanding general and to the man in the ranks so does a political victory, with its prospects for affluence and power, bear an entirely different aspect to the top strategist and to the lowly worker in the county and in the precinct. Our histories are full of leaders with scarcely a reference to the devoted members of the rank and file who made their leadership possible. Both wars and political campaigns are won by the non-commissioned officers in the battalions. Such men, and nowadays women, win wars and political campaigns precisely because they have no political philosophy of their own, because they are capable of complete loyalty and devotion, and because they understand instinctively that wars and political campaigns demand a total commitment.

A great mass of followers everywhere will, as Hitler proved, follow any leader who has a magnetic personality and promises an opportunity. They will embrace any philosophy, religion, government, or social structure that provides the opportunity, and, once committed, they will by a process of self hypnosis, devote their fortunes, their lives, and their sacred honor to the cause. The triumph of the New Deal in 1932 was a personal accolade to Roosevelt. Most of what has happened since is a tribute to, or a condemnation of, his unsung devotees in the state capitals, the court houses, and the precincts.

When Roosevelt was elected, I had just passed my thirty-third birthday. In that same election the Congressional delegation of the State, the Governorship, the Board of Public Works, the Judiciary, and the Legislature all went Democratic. All have remained Democratic since that time except that Republicans have elected some members of Congress, one United States Senator with whom I was privileged to serve in Washington, and one Governor, Cecil Underwood, who in 1956 was faced with a hostile Board of Public Works and Legislature. Throughout most of my adult life I have been a member of a minority party, often so weak that it seemed about to expire. In 1964 there were nearly two registered Democrats for every registered Republican in the State.

In 1936, when Roosevelt carried every State of the Union except Maine and Vermont, I was approached by a Democratic faction in an overwhelmingly Democratic county in West Virginia with the proposition that the faction would support me for the office of County Prosecuting Attorney if I would move to the county and change my registration from Republican to Democrat. Though I needed both the salary and the public exposure at that time, I politely declined. Since then, I have had ample opportunity to reflect on the curious quirk in human nature that makes human beings carry on in a hopeless cause. The faction that had tapped me won the election and their second choice Prosecuting Attorney later became Governor of West Virginia.

What causes a sovereign State of the Union to switch suddenly from overwhelmingly Republican to overwhelmingly Democratic political control? The answer lies in the ever present political machine. Political machines are founded on patronage and patronage means jobs, contracts, and opportunities for affluence and power. In former times the building and maintenance of roads, the care of the needy, the education of children, the enforcement of law, the encouragement of agriculture and industry, the execution of health measures, the sale of drugs and intoxicating liquors, and public business in general were largely dispensed at the county and magisterial district level. The

Twentieth Century has witnessed a nationwide movement toward centralization of authority, both in the national and in the state capitals. Under the stress of modern living, in a country moving rapidly from an agricultural to an urban economy, such centralization is both desirable and inevitable, but it has created a climate favorable to corruption and dictatorship.

The usurpation of power on the part of the Federal Government and particularly the absence of judicial restraint on the part of the Supreme Court of the United States lies beyond the scope of this discussion. Suffice it to say that the Founding Fathers did not envision a situation in which nine old men, who are appointed for life, could change the character of state legislatures by re-apportionment. Tyranny begets tyranny and the Supreme Court, like the Pope, has no battalions. Some of our intellectuals are too confident that ideas will prevail. Even if that is true, the prevailing ideas may not be their ideas. Ideas did not crush Hitler. What crushed Hitler was his political blunder in turning on his Russian ally, superior technology, and blood and guts. Next time the idea men may not be so fortunate. This discussion deals primarily with local conditions.

In the field of education in West Virginia, the State Board of Education and the State Superintendent of Schools are the real bosses of the school system, though they, in turn, take their cues from the National Education Association and the Federal Department of Health, Education, and Welfare. Even so, school teachers in West Virginia are not required to become a part of the Democrat political machine, possibly because there are not enough Democrat teachers to fill the positions. County law enforcement is now supplemented by the State Police. Farmers claim the services of a County Agricultural Agent and his staff and each county is supplied with representatives of the Soil Conservation Service and lending agencies. These people are supposed to be under Civil Service, but in West Virginia Democrats get the jobs. Welfare needs are dispensed by the Department of Public Assistance, a State Agency operated with Federal help, that is very active in Democrat politics.

The State Department of Health, another offspring of the Federal Government, employs a large number of doctors, nurses, technicians, and lowlier employees in the operation of State Hospitals and in the advancement of health programs. The sale of intoxicating liquors through State liquor stores is a chief source of political power. The State Liquor Commission decides exactly what brands shall be placed on the shelves of its stores. It is an open secret in West Virginia that liquor and wine manufacturers are required to hire salesmen, even though they sell only to the State, before their wares are displayed for public consumption. The men who hold liquor and wine accounts are always persons in a position to wield political influence. They are sometimes newspaper editors, television commentators, labor leaders, and political manipulators. Some, I regret to say, are reputed Republicans.

But the real working force of the Democrat machine in West Virginia is the State Road Commission. Here you have an agency responsible for disbursing more than one hundred million dollars a year. Nowadays, hard surfaced roads are as much a necessity as clothing and shelter. Roads are built and after they are built, they must be maintained. To keep traffic moving three hundred sixty-five days a year, road maintenance crews are based in each county to repair the right of way in summer and to remove snow and ice in winter. Even in Wirt County, with its four to five thousand inhabitants, we have a State Road Building for the employees and a State Road Park for the vehicles. The County Road supervisor is the machine's representative in the county. In these days of television, hard sell advertising, and the greedy hands of the toilers in the ranks, a political machine requires money above all else. While the distillers and the wine manufacturers provide a continuing source of income, their contributions are far surpassed by that mysterious institution known as the Flower Fund.

The Flower Fund, so named because it was originally an assessment for funeral flowers, is one of the most potent and prosperous arms of the State Government. Fundamentally, it is a racket, pure and simple. All State employees, except possibly the Governor, the members of the Board of Public Works, and the Department heads are required to contribute to it, though the contribution is not deducted from the payroll. The levy is, or at least was, the last time I talked to a friendly State employee, two to ten percent of the employee's salary, payable monthly to an enforcer who is not on the public payroll. Like the crime gangs of Chicago the sponsors of the Flower Fund protect the employee, but unlike the gangs, the enforcer is not expected to liquidate recalcitrant contributors. All he does is to report the name of any state employee in any department who balks at paying the protection fee, and the employee is then unobtrusively dismissed. With respect to legalities the Flower Fund has the gangs beaten a mile. It is true, as apologists for the Fund have claimed, that employees are not coerced into contributing, but it is equally true that no one can hold any of the thousands of State positions, except teachers positions, either at the State Capitol or in the counties unless he or she contributes to the Fund.

I first heard of the Flower Fund in 1936 when Alfred Landon ran against Franklin D. Roosevelt for the Presidency. At that time I was practicing law in Grantsville in Calhoun County. The Works Progress Administration, the Federal agency designed to make work for the unemployed, was active, and a number of WPA workers consulted me professionally. They were faced with the dilemma of either contributing five per cent of their earnings to the Democrat campaign fund or of losing their government made employment. WPA employees, as a matter of fact, could not be dismissed at the whim of local politicians, but that fact was not clearly understood by the workers or even by the lawyers. The incident is an illustration of the climate of corruption in West Virginia politics and also of the principle that corruption inevitably follows reform. To advise the unemployed under such circumstances was a ticklish business. A lawyer, after all, owes his first obligation to the interest of his client. These particular clients had no money and no time for court procedure, and they could wind up losing their livelihood. I passed the buck to them saying, "Do whatever you think is right." In the end I think most of them paid.

The man who handles the Flower Fund at the State Capitol and is therefore the Treasurer and the Chief Enforcer of the institution is never a state official at any level. He needs be cut to a special pattern for the bag he carries is worth ninety thousand dollars to one hundred fifty thousand dollars a month, and that adds up to considerably more than one million dollars per year. He must be a man of scrupulous honesty, according to machine standards, and, while his name never appears officially in connection with the administration, he must also be a man of considerable political acumen and influence.

No one outside the inner circle of the machine really knows, or ever will know, exactly how the Flower Fund works. The purpose of the Fund, apparently, is not to enrich the bagman and his cronies, but to establish a campaign fund for future elections. Elections are becoming more expensive all the time, and a machine in power needs more money than a machine out of power simply because more palms require greasing. The machine in power inevitably creates dissension in its own ranks when it supports a slate of candidates in a primary election. To fuse the fragments in a general election costs millions of dollars in jobs and in cash.

The famed Lever Brothers of Logan County is a case in point. Obviously, the Lever Brothers would not be tolerated if Republican election commissioners and clerks performed their sworn duty. So-called Republican officials are present at the polls, as is required by law, but the story of how they get there does not appear in the tally sheets. The Democrat machine, controls a majority of the county Republican Executive Committee. The Executive Committee appoints the Republican commissioners and clerks and these officials, though nominally Republican, are themselves part and parcel of the Democrat machine. The only practical way to reform elections in Logan County is to adopt the methods of the Hatfield family which, in 1924, installed its candidate for sheriff at gunpoint. All this naturally costs money.

The Democrat machine has state-wide power, but no machine anywhere can win consistently without a broad base of public opinion. The Democrats, through liberal platforms and a spate of economic reforms, have generally had broad public support for the past thirty-two years. Nevertheless, public opinion never remains static, and that is why Chapman Revercomb has been elected to the Senate twice and Cecil Underwood to the Governorship once, in the interim, in spite of the machine. Some scientist someday will establish a law of natural opposition in human affairs. Whereas one mass of followers will do anything the leader orders, another group always veers in the opposite direction. Even in Logan County there are many voters, Democrat and Republican, who deplore conditions there, but they constitute a hopeless minority.

Local politics in America cannot be disengaged from the platforms and the organizations of the two dominant political parties. America's unique contribution to the forms of democracy is that, for the past century, either the Republicans or the Democrats have been in power. Numerous attempts to organize successful third parties have failed. Wirt County, though it furnished a considerable number of troops for the Confederacy in the Civil War and has always had a large proportion of registered Democrats, was usually a Republican stronghold from 1864 to 1932. The majority of those hillside farmers, described in an earlier chapter, had fought for, or at least sympathized with, the Federal Union.

Unlike the miners and the timber workers, the farmers were never bossed, and few could be bought at any price. I remember that my Grandfather Reed was highly incensed at one time because a candidate of his own party offered him a bottle of whiskey. Nevertheless, these Republican farmers generally voted the straight Republican ticket and it is only in recent decades that farmers have become selective in voting for candidates of both parties.

The Wirt County voter today goes to the polls in the reasonable belief that his ballot will be counted exactly as he casts it. Election officials are chosen for their fairness and not for their predilection to fraudulent activities. Away from the polling places, there is, of course, a great deal of political infighting far removed from the Jeffersonian ideal of democracy. The Wirt County maintenance crew of the State Road Commission, consisting normally of about twenty-five men, is an integral part of the Democrat political machine. A regular employee of the State Road Commission must be a registered Democrat, though some are former Republicans. In election years the Road Commission customarily adds thousands of temporary employees all over the state, many of whom are college and high school boys working through the summer vacation. In a region where unemployment has been exceptionally high for the past two decades such temporary employment in election years is highly prized and rewarded at the polls. Last summer (the summer of 1964) the Wirt County maintenance crew was augmented by one means or another to approximately one hundred employees, affecting one hundred families including fathers, mothers, brothers, sisters, aunts, uncles, and cousins. The people who hold State jobs or are the recipients of other government favors, added to those who vote Democratic by inheritance, constitute a formidable, though seldom a decisive, voting bloc in sparsely settled Wirt County. The result of the many factors affecting political results in recent years has been an unprecedented growth in ticket splitting.

To illustrate the growing phenomenon of ticket splitting, I am setting down here the Official Results of the General Election of 1964, as applied to Wirt County, in which I was myself the Republican nominee for Secretary of State.

NATIONAL TICKET

Democrats		*Republicans*	
President and Vice-President			
Johnson and Humphrey	1,286	Goldwater and Miller	899
United States Senate			
Robert C. Byrd	1,282	Cooper P. Benedict	876
Congressman, 4th District			
Dr. Ken Hechler	1,220	Jack Miller	953

STATE TICKET

Governor			
Hulett C. Smith	1,112	Cecil H. Underwood	1,118
Secretary of State			
Joe F. Burdett	986	Louis Reed	1,187

Auditor

Denzil L. Gainer	1,194	Donald G. Michels	932

Treasurer

John H. Kelly	1,143	Fred B. Young	971

Attorney General

C. Donald Robertson	1,148	Donald C. Carmen	932

Commissioner of Agriculture

Gus R. Douglas	1,182	Nicholas M. Homes	933

Judges Supreme Court (Two)

Thornton G. Berry	1,141	Herman D. Rollins	953
Frank C. Haymond	1,116	George F. Beneke	926

State Senate, 3rd District

Dr. Earl C. Hahn	1,049	J. Frank Deem	1,083

House of Delegates, 7th District

Paul H. Kidd	1,072	James R. Jones	1,088

COUNTY TICKET

Sheriff

C. D. Powell	1,115	Gay R. Lynch	1,077

Commissioner, County Court

E. W. Allman	1,217	Joe Cheuvront	928

Clerk, Circuit Court

Faustine Huffman	1,052	June Hudson	1,093

Prosecuting Attorney

No candidate		Robert B. Black	1,186

Assessor

Brooks Hardway	1,082	Kendall Amos	1,111

Better Roads Amendment

For	1,108
Against	645

It will be recalled that the voter registration figures for Wirt County in 1964 were 1,435 Democrats, 1,271 Republicans, and 8 Independents, a total of 2,714. Using the combined vote for Governor, 2,230 votes, as a means of comparison, it appears that approximately eighty per cent of the registered voters in the county cast ballots in the 1964 General Election. This is high by national standards, even in Presidential elections, but there is still a sizable number of adults in Wirt County who are not registered to vote as I discovered when I canvassed my own precinct. Actually, there are more registered voters percentage wise in my own precinct than there are in the county. The registration figure of 2,714 includes absentee voters, and I have learned that 15 of the 140 registered voters of my own precinct are absentees. If the population of Wirt County in 1964 is 4,471 and if the number of persons under twenty one is 1,464, there ought to be 3,007 qualified voters in the county apart from absentees. The difference accountable to residence requirements, one year in the state and sixty days in the precinct, is negligible. People are not moving to Wirt County in appreciable numbers. While I have not attempted to hunt up all the unregistered but otherwise qualified voters in the county, I have talked to some of them and have learned that the chief reason for not registering is apathy. Some said that politics is so crooked they wanted nothing to do with it. One woman avowed that woman suffrage is contrary to the teachings of the Bible. All this is news to me, and I am beginning to wonder if I have relied too heavily in this study on voters registration lists. Unfortunately, there are no lists of unregistered voters. While I am convinced that not many family names have been missed, I now believe that perhaps ten per cent of the qualified voters of Wirt County are not registered to vote.

The arresting feature of the vote tabulation for Wirt County is split ticket balloting. If all the voters had voted as they registered, Johnson and Humphrey would have won by 164 votes. Instead, eighty per cent of the voters (2,185 votes) gave Johnson and Humphrey a majority of 388 votes, Byrd a majority of 406 votes, and Hechler a majority of 267 votes on the national ticket. The combined vote for Governor, somewhat surprisingly, is 2,230 votes, which means that 45 voters in Wirt County did not vote for President, 72 did not vote for United States Senator, and 57 did not vote for Congressman. All other combined totals fall short of 2,230, showing that a substantial number of citizens voted for the Governorship and nothing else. The tendency to vote for a favored candidate and then to ignore the remainder of the ticket is a growing pattern of split ticket voting. Except for Underwood and myself the State Ticket in Wirt County went Democratic by lesser majorities than the National Ticket. Gainer won by 264 votes, Kelly by 172 votes, Robertson by 191 votes, and Douglas by 249 votes. Judges of the Supreme Court won by majorities of 188 and

190 respectively. It will be observed that Underwood carried the county by six votes, and that I carried my home county by only 201 votes. Underwood lost the state by approximately 77,000 votes, and the other statewide candidates, including myself, were defeated by even greater majorities.

The split ticket pattern is marked at the county level where the tabulations, in contrast to the National and State tickets, indicate victory and defeat. Powell, a Democrat, was elected Sheriff by 38 votes. Allman, a Democrat, was re-elected Commissioner of the County Court by 289 votes. Hudson, a Republican, was elected Clerk of the Circuit Court by 41 votes. Black, a Republican, was unopposed for Prosecuting Attorney. Amos, a Republican, was re-elected Assessor by a mere 29 votes. Of the five county offices voted for, two went to Democrats and three to Republicans. Even so, the election represented a Republican net loss. In 1956 when Eisenhower was the Republican candidate for the Presidency, the entire Republican county ticket was elected by majorities ranging from 250 votes to 400 votes. In 1964 Republicans who withstood the onslaught squeaked by with bare majorities. The debacle is attributed by the experts to the failure of Goldwater and Miller to attract meaningful popular support.

Irrespective of causes, the campaign of 1964 convinced me that an entirely new attitude toward fiscal responsibility and personal honesty has developed in the electorate. Without repeating campaign charges that are now dead issues, it may be observed that the old Republican machine, at its worst, did not condone stealing or the misuse of public property for private gain. In the famous Teapot Dome case of the 1920's, the Republicans sent a member of the President's Cabinet to prison for misusing the Navy's oil reserves. Shortly afterward, the Auditor of the State of West Virginia, John C. Bond, a Republican, was stripped of his office and sentenced to Moundsville Penitentiary for embezzling state funds. A civilization that lacks private and public morality is declining. History will tell us ultimately what the tattered fabric of morality in the second half of the Twentieth Century really portends.

10. Crime, Divorce, and Juvenile Delinquency

WIRT COUNTY is undoubtedly one of the safest places in the world at the present time. It was not always so. During the Civil War and in the decades immediately following, violent crimes were common. Homicides appeared on nearly every court calendar. There was a mysterious gang of horse thieves and highwaymen, known as the Bughunters, near the oil town of Burning Springs. (Dr. D. F. Stewart of Creston, who died in 1945 at the age of one hundred six, once told me that the Bughunters began as a relay station on the Underground Railway for runaway slaves. He claimed that during and after the War many of the illegal relay stations, with a ready made organization that extended from the Deep South to Canada, turned to horse stealing and highway robbery. If true, that was certainly an inglorious end for the fabled Underground Railway.) The depredations of horse thieves and highwaymen became so flagrant in the decades following the War that a secret society known as the Red Men was organized in retaliation. The Red Men resembled the Ku Klux Klan further South. They retaliated so efficiently that there has been no organized crime in Wirt County since the 1880's. There are dark tales of unsolved murders and of lives spared on condition of instant departure, and the whole clouded episode ended when the Legislature outlawed the Red Men.

The turbulent period following the Civil War ended shortly before the turn of the century at the very time when the County began losing population. When I was a boy, crime consisted largely of misdemeanors such as public intoxication, fighting at square dances, disturbing public worship, carrying concealed revolvers and brass knuckles, and seining for or dynamiting fish, though larceny, burglary, and arson were not unknown. Disturbing public worship, by the way, is thoroughly outdated in 1965. The charge used to arise when the church was a social center because young men under the influence of alcohol would engage in fist fights on the church grounds.

To illustrate how completely Wirt County has been tamed in the Twentieth Century, I need cite only a recent personal experience. My wife and I own two automobiles which are kept, together with many useful household tools, in a double garage on the premises. Last fall, we closed our home and drove my car to Arizona and Mexico, leaving my wife's car in the garage with the doors open. The ignition keys to my wife's car were left hanging openly in a rack on the garage wall. When we returned four weeks later the car was still there and none of the tools were missing. Only the other day when I called at the old twenty-two room house in Elizabeth I noticed a printed sign by the doorbell which read, "If no answer leave messages or parcels inside." The doors of this house are never locked in the daytime. Having lived in New York, Kansas City, and Washington, I know that such carelessness on the part of property owners sounds incredible.

Nevertheless, Wirt County is not wholly free of crime. Most criminal violations these days are misdemeanors. The County Jail is largely a sobering up place for drunks. Physical combat, the plain assault and battery that used to enliven square dances and church services, is out of style. There was a case of assault with a deadly weapon a few years ago, but the old time fist fights in which exuberant youths fought for the pure fun of fighting have gone by the board. During my service as Clerk of the Circuit Court and Prosecuting Attorney, from 1953 to 1961, I cannot recall a single case of simple assault and battery that reached the Circuit Court.

The records reveal that there have been but three murder convictions in the past sixty-five years, though two of the three were gory spectacles indeed. On November 17, 1900, a man named Sam Sheppard was convicted of first degree murder in the slaying of his wife and stepson. He was sentenced to a life term in the State Penitentiary. The crime was one of those senseless, revolting, and utterly inexplicable killings in which the victims were viciously hacked to pieces. The case is still a topic of local conversation because the evidence was circumstantial and also because a man of the same name attracted national notoriety afterward when he was convicted of murdering his wife in Cleveland. Wirt County's Sam Sheppard was paroled after serving about sixteen years in the penitentiary whereupon he is said to have remarried and obtained employment in Pasadena, California, where he lived a secluded life and died in obscurity. Whether there was blood relationship between the two Sam Sheppards has not been established.

In 1911, a man by the name of Jonas Sees was tried for murder, but this proved to be a case of shooting from the hip and Sees was convicted of the lesser crime of voluntary manslaughter. He was sentenced to five years in Moundsville Penitentiary. What happened to him after his release is unknown.

In 1927, Irvin Kidwell was placed on trial for the murder of Bill Grudier. This was another senseless killing for the evidence showed that the killer and his victim were barely acquainted. Kidwell appeared at Grudier's home in the middle of the night pleading that the gasoline tank of his automobile was empty. Upon being admitted, he attacked Grudier with an axe and literally chopped him apart, while the two small sons of the victim, aged seven and five respectively, cowered under a bed. Kidwell was declared insane by a jury and died at Weston State Hospital in 1961. During the period 1927 to 1965, a total of thirty-eight years, there have been no further homicides in Wirt County.

There have been few other crimes of violence. I cannot discover that any Wirt Countian has ever been convicted of rape nor has there been a gunpoint robbery, with one ridiculous exception, in the past fifty years. There have been isolated convictions for the crime of statutory rape which is defined as sexual intercourse on the part of a male with a female under sixteen years of age, with or without her consent. Actually, this crime is often honored in the breach. It is ordinarily undetected until the girl becomes pregnant, and, in that event, the prosecuting witness and her family are usually anxious to avert scandal by a wedding. I know the names of four girls under sixteen who became pregnant during the past fifteen years, and there may have been others. Of the four, three married the putative father, in all instances a boy not much older than the girl. None of the men were prosecuted because no one signed a complaint.

Since the heyday of the Red Men, robbery on the highways or the streets is almost unknown, though a sixteen-year-old boy held up the State Liquor Store employees with a toy pistol a few years ago and walked out with sixty-seven dollars in cash. Whether this was robbery at gunpoint is a moot question. The boy was already on probation from the Industrial Home, and the Judge held him for the Grand Jury as an adult. He was ultimately sentenced to an indeterminate term at Moundsville Penitentiary, and has since been released. His family in the meantime moved to Parkersburg. So far as I know he has not been in any further trouble.

The few felonies that reach the Circuit Court nowadays are nearly all larcenies and burglaries in the nighttime. Most are committed by transients. While I was Prosecuting Attorney the Liquor Store was burglarized twice and other business places were subjected to breaking and entering. During my four-year term of office, Wirt County sent four felons to the penitentiary, all for burglary. Only one is there now, and he would have been released long ago had he not escaped and committed other felonies. Not a single resident of Wirt County has been convicted of a felony in the past four years, though I am advised that within recent months there has been a series of larcenies and burglaries as yet unsolved.

The most serious recent cases have all involved driving a motor vehicle while under the influence of intoxicants. Two of these have terminated in charges of negligent homicide. I have not counted negligent homicide convictions as crimes of violence because they are listed as misdemeanors and because the people who commit them ordinarily have no other criminal record. Nevertheless, the mounting death toll from traffic collisions on our highways has had a hardening effect on juries in prosecutions for negligent homicide. If it is proved that the defendant was intoxicated or even that he was driving in a reckless manner, and that, as a result, someone was killed, that defendant is likely to find himself serving a jail sentence, usually for twelve months.

Despite the local court record, Wirt County has produced some notorious criminals. I have already mentioned Clay Williams, who went unscathed in convictions, but who was, nevertheless, the crime syndicate's payoff man both in Las Vegas and in Miami. The most notorious criminal in Moundsville Penitentiary today is the legendary Holly Griffith, a Wirt County native. What is said here about Holly Griffith has been collected from people who knew him before he turned to violent crime, including his wife. Because he still lives, I have felt that the legend must have some basis in fact and is, therefore, more important than his official record, which I confess I have never seen.

Holly Griffith, according to his neighbors and relatives, was a young man with a growing family shortly before World War I. He first gained local notoriety when he gunned down a constable who was trying to serve him with papers in a civil suit. While he was a fugitive from the charge of murdering the constable, he shot and killed the Chief of Police of Gassaway, West Virginia. Now a double fugitive, he was finally captured while he was asleep by a deputy sheriff and a posse near Cairo, West Virginia. The deputy sheriff, in a flush of triumph, is said to have paraded Griffith through the streets of Cairo tied to the tail of a horse, whereupon Griffith vowed solemnly in the presence of witnesses that he would kill the sheriff.

How Griffith escaped hanging after killing two police officers in succession is merely one of the mysteries in the life of this extraordinary man. He was tried for the murder of the Chief of Police and the jury recommended mercy. Sentenced to life imprisonment in the State Penitentiary at Moundsville, he bided his time and then killed his third law officer, one of his guards, and escaped. Instead of placing distance between himself and the prison, he promptly headed back home with the announced intention of killing the sheriff. There followed a period of tense excitement and terror. Griffith was armed and on foot. He subsisted for weeks simply by calling at farmhouses and asking for food. He committed no crimes except that a man was found shot to death in a boat on the Ohio River and it was theorized that Griffith had killed him because he needed the boat. Instead of leading another posse, the deputy sheriff who had captured him the first time took refuge in a jail cell. Griffith was captured, again asleep, and again a jury recommended mercy. He was returned to Moundsville under an order which provided that he should never be paroled.

Except for the short period when he was an escapee, Griffith has been a prisoner at Moundsville for about fifty years. Ex-convicts who have been there tell me that at the prison he is literally king of the convicts. Some warden discovered long ago that Griffith's word is as good as a bond. He was allowed to open a tailor shop inside the prison walls where he made clothes for the convicts and also carried on a thriving business making uniforms for police officers all over the nation. There was a public outcry when an enterprising reporter discovered that Griffith had savings accounts in various banks amounting to $65,000.00. He lost the tailor shop, but nothing was done about the money because he had earned every cent of it legally. For some years past he has been a trusty. People who know him report that they have seen him walking unmolested through the streets of Moundsville and Wheeling.

Not long ago, I talked to an ex-convict who had served a term at Moundsville for forgery. Speaking of Griffith, he said, "No one outside could possibly understand the power that Griffith wields over the prisoners. While I was there the food was bad, and there was talk of a riot. At Moundsville people do not riot unless and until Griffith says so. A meeting was held in the Yard. When the proposal was explained, Griffith looked at everyone with those killer eyes and he said just five words, 'There will be no riot'. Then, he walked off, and the riot was dead."

It is difficult to explain Holly Griffith for he is the kind of man who, in former times, could have been raised to the nobility. He is a natural leader and, like natural leaders everywhere, he remains lonely and aloof. It is curious and perhaps symptomatic that the Twentieth Century has consigned such men to life terms in the penitentiary. From what I have learned from those who know Holly Griffith best, he has always been a man of the utmost probity and honor. He was too sensitive about his honor. He killed the constable because he warned the constable to stay off his property and the constable disregarded the warning. Having killed once he did not hesitate at killing again. In all the legends that have accumulated about Holly Griffith, there is no hint of remorse.

My own observation of criminals is not extensive, though I once lived in a jail and wrote a series of Jailhouse Stories for the *Atlantic*. Not long ago I was embarrassed when a woman told me at a banquet, "I used to know your father who wrote the Jailhouse Stories." My father did not write the Jailhouse Stories. I wrote them, and I have developed definite opinions on the subject of crime and criminals.

There are three types of criminals in my experience. The first type is weak, irresponsible, and stupid. One of the men I helped send to the penitentiary when I was Prosecuting Attorney is typical. In 1954, I was, among other things, chairman of the Wirt County Chapter of the American Red Cross. A local citizen died and I was asked by the relatives to notify his nephew who was serving in the Armed Forces at Fort Knox, Kentucky. I sent the soldier a routine telegram. The next day, he arrived by taxicab from Louisville, Kentucky, and the taxi driver presented me with a statement in the amount of One Hundred Twenty-Eight Dollars! Since the soldier had not consulted the Red Cross at Fort Knox and the bus fare from Louisville to Elizabeth was about fifteen dollars, I flatly refused to pay the bill. My view was that any reasonable person would have taken a public conveyance. My position was affirmed by the Red Cross and I do not know whether the taxi man ever got his money. A few years later the same man, now a civilian, was indicted for burglary of the State Liquor Store, and I handled the prosecution in court.

Actually, the State had only circumstantial evidence that the defendant had committed the burglary. He became a suspect through a series of blunders. The day after the burglary, he was observed on the Tucker Creek road carrying a heavy burlap bag. A passing motorist offered him a ride. At the conclusion of the ride the defendant opened the bag and presented the motorist with a bottle of whiskey. The motorist, having heard of the burglary, turned the bottle over to a State Policeman, who quickly determined that this was part of the loot. A search warrant of the suspect's home promptly uncovered the bag with twenty-nine unopened bottles and three empty bottles, all of which bore the serial numbers of the missing liquor.

The defendant claimed at the trial that he had found the whiskey under a road culvert, had then hunted up the burlap bag, and was carrying the whiskey home when he was accosted by the motorist. Had he not embroidered this story with a mass of improbabilities, I believe that he would have been acquitted. Only a few people in this world have sufficient memory or imagination to be successful liars. On cross examination, I had him detail just how and when he had found the whiskey. He admitted that approximately two hours had elapsed between the finding and his return with the burlap bag. Queried as to how he happened to look under the culvert in the first place, he stated that he noticed a bottle of whiskey standing upright in the middle of the road and that circumstance caused him to look under the culvert. He then declared that he had left the whiskey bottle standing upright on the highway while he was absent for two hours hunting the bag. In rebuttal, I placed three motorists on the stand who had passed the culvert during the two-hour period and none of them had seen the whiskey bottle.

The jury found him guilty, apparently on the theory that such a clumsy liar was bound to be the culprit. Our penitentiaries are filled with people who are inept, irresponsible, and not smart enough to be good liars.

Again, many crimes are the result of sick minds. These

include all the gruesome murders and most suicides. Suicide, after all, is a crime. Though there are no statistics on suicide in Wirt County, my personal belief is that suicide is increasing. Two suicides of men in their forties have occurred in my neighborhood in the past two years. One was a man who had lost his employment through addiction to alcohol and the other was in ill health. Both were wholly unexpected. I have noticed that suicide is invariably a shock to relatives and friends. During the past ten years three men whom I considered personal friends have taken their own lives.

The tensions that lead up to suicide seem to occur oftener among men than among women. I suspect that statistics on suicide, where they are kept, are often unreliable. Investigating officers and crime reporters are more tender hearted than is commonly supposed. Suicides are often rigged as accidents. Since the deceased has hurt no one but himself and the case may involve life insurance, investigators and reporters often report death by accident when they are convinced in their own minds that the case is death by suicide. Curiously enough, suicide seems to increase in direct proportion to social welfare. I have read that the suicide rate is highest in Denmark and Sweden—countries which furnish security from the cradle to the grave.

Finally, there is a class of criminal that is simply out of touch with modern society. This criminal seems to have been born without ordinary human inhibitions and without a sense of guilt. People who know Holly Griffith well tell me that he has always been thoroughly relaxed. Both times when he was captured, he was sound asleep. He speaks quietly and even gently. No one has ever seen him excited, but, when he is crossed, his eyes flash a deadly fire.

I have met other criminals with the same characteristics. In my very first court case at Winfield in Putnam County, in 1928, I represented a twelve-year-old boy in a juvenile hearing. He had shot a hunting companion through the chest with a 22 caliber rifle, but the wound was not fatal. The victim appeared in court in a wheel chair and testified that the defendant had shot him deliberately following a quarrel.

The very first thing I noted about my youthful client was the piercing stare of his unblinking light blue eyes. He told me without the slightest show of emotion that he was not sorry for what he had done and that he considered the legal proceedings a senseless bore. Let the judge sentence him, he said, and be done with it. His parents were moderately prosperous and I succeeded in having him paroled in their custody. The boy violated the parole by holding up a grocery store at gunpoint. Sentenced to the Boys Industrial Home (the reform school), he served a few years, and then gained local notoriety in a daring escape. After a series of robberies, he was finally killed in the course of a running gun fight with police near Columbus, Ohio, at the age of eighteen.

It is difficult to explain criminals of this type. They are neither inept, irresponsible, mentally sick, nor stupid. As a matter of fact, they are often highly intelligent, and, according to their own warped view of things, are thoroughly responsible. If he had lived, the boy I have just described could have become another Holly Griffith. The only logical explanation for such manifestations of antisocial behavior on the part of obviously intelligent human beings, is, it seems to me, that such people are throwbacks to the original blue-eyed devils who made the white race supreme among the races of men.

I distinctly recall an incident that occurred at Grantsville at the beginning of World War II. A defendant, who pleaded guilty to larceny, was offered the choice of serving his sentence or of enlisting in the army. He chose the latter and lo and behold, when the war ended he was the most decorated war hero in the history of Calhoun County. Verily, the human race still has a lot to learn about crime and criminals.

Crime, like politics, is a controversial subject. There is a widespread belief that crime is an aspect of poverty and that when poverty is abolished crime will disappear. This hope is akin to the old-fashioned theory that woman suffrage was the cure-all for crime and corruption. One theory ignored the nature of women; the other hopefully ignores the nature of criminals. Some communities in the United States, particularly in the larger cities, are favorable to the development of organized crime by reason of their social structure, but even in such communities more children grow up to be honest citizens than grow up to be thieves and murderers. New York's Old East Side is a prime example.

Certainly, the abolition of poverty, if it comes, will reduce crimes against property. At the same time, it will probably increase crimes against the person, crimes against morality, and crimes against public policy simply because people will have more time for pleasure and consequently will get into more trouble. The great law stabilizer in the past has been the necessity to work hard for survival. The American experiment in prohibition in the 1920's proved once again that no government can control appetites by legislation.

Economists and politicians often speak of the great leisure time of the future as a period to be devoted to art and culture. To do so ascribes qualities to human nature that human nature in the raw does not possess. Leisure time for a large segment of the population will be devoted to alcohol, drugs, fornication, and general hell raising as anyone who reads the newspapers and watches television can plainly see. Fortunately, the law of natural opposition will furnish a counterweight. The conflict of these two opposing forces, which approximates the traditional conflict of good and evil, will ultimately decide the fate of western civilization.

It may happen that psychiatry will prove a great boon to mankind. It has already contributed much to our knowledge of human motivations. Psychiatry as applied to criminals, however, at its present stage of development, is more useful in looking backward than it is in looking forward. This truth was brought home to me recently amid all the millions of words that were written and spoken about the assassination of the late President John F. Kennedy.

The assassin of President Kennedy was a young man named Lee Harvey Oswald. Oswald was murdered shortly after the assassination by another eccentric named Jack

Ruby, and both murders, as befitted the theatricality of the occasions, were staged on television before millions of viewers. The new President appointed an investigating commission and the commission produced a book known as the *Warren Report*. The Report delved into every facet of Oswald's life and explained in scientific terms how his background made him a murderer. Though the Report does not say so, there is an implication between the lines that anyone with Oswald's background—no father, an indulgent mother, trouble in school, and other disappointments—is a potential murderer. What made the Report fascinating reading to me personally was the remarkable similarity between Oswald's childhood and my own. According to the report Oswald's potentiality for crime was revealed when he ran afoul of the school authorities at the age of thirteen. Thirteen! At the age of thirteen I was officially expelled from the public school system.

Looking back now I can see that I have always been a non-conformist, but I recognize in myself a broad pattern of caution and common sense that changed me at maturity from a candidate for the barricades into a conservative lawyer and banker. You simply cannot tell about boys, no matter what they do. In any event I can avow truthfully that I have never once considered murdering a president or anyone else. So much for psychiatry.

An aspect of crime in its relation to juvenile delinquency is the growing problem of divorce. For some reason that I do not myself fully understand I have handled in my practice about one hundred divorce cases since 1928. Of these approximately one third have ended in reconciliation. For a country lawyer who spent nearly half of the intervening years outside the general practice of law, that represents a lot of divorces.

The divorce laws of West Virginia are antiquated and encourage hypocrisy and perjury. It is against public policy, for instance, for a husband and wife to agree to a divorce in a civilized manner and evidence of collusion is cause for dismissal. On the other hand, public policy finds it proper that the parties should agree to a division of their property. How it is humanly possible for two married persons to agree to a division of their property without at the same time agreeing to a dissolution of their partnership is one of those legal fictions that only the courts condone and understand.

The edifice of the law, that epitome of logic that Blackstone and other commentators so greatly admired, is full of such fictions. Our whole legal system is based on the common law of England which had its roots in the squirearchy. Take the doctrine of a reasonable and prudent man. Crimes, torts, and many civil actions are decided on what a reasonable and prudent man would do under the circumstances, but if you look carefully you will find that the reasonable and prudent man is always an unemotional English squire surrounded by his property and imbued with the prejudices of his class. Over a century ago Alexis de Tocqueville observed that American lawyers tend toward conservatism. The reasonable and prudent man finds no difficulty in the subtlety that two emotional human beings can agree to divide their property without once mentioning their divorce.

The grounds for divorce in West Virginia are: (1) adultery, (2) desertion for two years, (3) conviction of a felony, (4) addiction to alcohol or drugs, and (5) cruel and inhuman treatment. These are practically the same grounds that are required for a divorce in the State of Nevada, the mecca of divorce seekers, but the difference comes in the residence requirements. In West Virginia the plaintiff must prove that he or she has been a resident of the State for at least one year. In Nevada the residence requirement is six weeks.

The antiquated part of our divorce law is its persistence in the fiction that women have no property rights and are unable to support themselves. Nationwide statistics show that women now own more than one half the wealth of the country and that they can find employment easier than men. Nevertheless, our law says that when a divorce suit is initiated, either by the husband or the wife, the husband must pay his wife's legal fees in addition to his own and besides must pay her alimony pendente lite, which means until the case is heard in court. Both temporary and permanent alimony are payable in one direction only, from the man to the woman. When I was an inexperienced neophyte many years ago, I tried to file an answer in a divorce case for a man seventy-eight years old who had just returned from a hospital and who was penniless. His wife, about the same age, owned and rented twelve dwelling houses. She had sued him for divorce while he was unconscious from an operation and had obtained a routine order for legal fees and alimony pendente lite. The judge, quite properly under the law, refused to let him plead, and, before I could prepare the necessary pauper's affidavit, the wife was granted her divorce on the ground of cruel and inhuman treatment.

All young lawyers have experiences of this nature. Such experiences do not inspire a profound respect for the justice, the impartiality, or the majesty of the law.

The ground for divorce is always a problem for lawyers. The charge set forth in the bill of complaint must be proven by the testimony of at least one corroborating witness. Adultery is the rarest ground of all because people simply do not commit adultery in the presence of witnesses if they know that witnesses are present. Desertion for two years and conviction of a felony are relatively easy to prove when those facts fit the case. Addiction to alcohol or drugs is seldom proffered as a ground for divorce, possibly because women and men often overlook this weakness in a partner if she or he is considerate in other matters. The great catch-all ground in West Virginia divorce cases is cruel and inhuman treatment.

In practice, cruel and inhuman treatment covers about everything. Thirty years ago an uncontested divorce would be granted even on frivolous grounds. In the 1950's the courts for some reason adopted a stricter attitude and held that cruel and inhuman treatment meant exactly what the words implied. They even held that the plaintiff must prove a reasonable apprehension of bodily harm. The divorce rate promptly dropped to near zero and a great howl of protest engulfed the courts. The Legislature intervened, and today the rule is: The conduct of the defendant must be such as to destroy, or tend to destroy, the plaintiff's physical and mental well being, happiness, and welfare, and to render further co-habitation unsafe and unendurable. The new rule is not broad enough to include frivolity, but uncontested divorces are almost always granted.

The question of factors in the increase of divorce in the Twentieth Century is one that is best left to the sociologists and the philosophers. I have read newspaper statements to the effect that in the United States as a whole in the 1950's one marriage in four ended in divorce. That figure is too high for Wirt County. Yet, even here, the divorce rate has climbed steeply.

The Chancery Record Books in the Office of the Clerk of the Circuit Court disclose that prior to the year 1900 divorce was rare and that such divorces as were granted were mostly bed and board divorces. These were decrees of separation in which neither of the parties could remarry. Bed and board divorces were abolished by the Legislature in the 1920's. Nowadays, if both the husband and wife want it and are willing to indulge in the hypocrisy of agreeing to a property settlement without at the same time agreeing to a divorce, permanent divorces are granted almost as a matter of course. Ordinarily, the wife is the plaintiff due to a persistence of a sense of chivalry and also because the husband must pay all lawyers fees and costs. Despite the fiction of the law, men and women do exactly what you would expect them to do under the circumstances. They agree on everything ahead of time, including the divorce. When the case comes up for hearing, the husband does not appear.

For this report I have combed the Chancery Order Books and the Rule Dockets for the period January 1, 1953, to December 31, 1961, a total of eight years, and have checked the marriage licenses issued by the Clerk of the County Court for the same period to determine, if I could, the exact relationship between marriage and divorce in Wirt County. The figures are not definitive because many people who marry in Wirt County move away and the statistics do not show whether any of them have been divorced elsewhere. On the other hand, due to venue and residence requirements, people who have married elsewhere may be divorced in Wirt

County. Admitting that there is no exact relationship between marriages and divorces in the same county, there is obviously a rough approximation in numbers and the numbers of marriage licenses and divorces, by no coincidence, are the only numbers available.

Between January 1, 1953, and December 31, 1961, forty-seven divorce cases were docketed in the Circuit Court of Wirt County. Of these twenty-eight proceeded to a final decree. Some of the nineteen cases that were not decided were dismissed by an order reciting reconciliation, some were dropped under the two year rule, and some were pending at the end of the time period. At least one divorce case, to my certain knowledge, terminated when one of the parties died. About one-fourth of all the cases ended in reconciliation, though the reconciliation was not always permanent. Two cases recited reconciliation only to be followed later by another divorce suit. I know a woman who has started five divorce suits in different counties and states during the past fifteen years. At the moment she and her husband are reconciled.

During the same period the Clerk of the County Court issued three hundred twenty-two marriage licenses. Using this figure as a basis for comparison, with the admonition that the comparison is at best dubious, it appears that one out of every twelve Wirt County marriages ends in divorce while one marriage in nine encounters serious difficulties. These ratios, though far more stable than the reported national averages, indicate nevertheless that, even in Appalachia, the divorce pattern is a growing phenomenon of life in Twentieth Century America.

My own experience has taught me that a divorce lawyer can be an effective marriage counsellor. When I say that I have handled a hundred divorce cases in court, I can add truthfully that I have kept a large number of cases out of court. Many women who consult a lawyer do not really want a divorce. They are hurt and angry at real or fancied wrongs. Whenever I sensed an uncertainty of purpose, I suggested politely that the parties try living together for one more month. Occasionally, I lost a client but more often than not the reconciliation was permanent.

I recall a young man who came to me from a distant county many years ago with a heart rending story. His bride of a few months had deserted him for their landlord and had gone off to Florida. After an interval of some weeks, she had written him from Florida saying that she had made a terrible mistake and asked him to take her back. I had known him from the days when I was his high school football coach, and I asked, "Johnny, what does your family think about it?"

He replied, "Both my mother and my brother tell me I would be a fool to take her back."

I could understand that, so I said, "Tell me how you feel about it. What is it doing to you? How do you feel about your wife now that all this has happened?"

He said, "I'm still crazy about her. I cut up all her dresses when she left, but I can't sleep at night. Sometimes, I think I'm going to end up in the bughouse."

Right there I understood that here was a case calling for infinite wisdom. This boy had driven over a hundred miles to see me because he wanted to take her back. He was going to do whatever I advised, but I was his last chance. I thought that over. A married woman who runs off to Florida with another man is certainly a poor prospect for the title of "Housewife of the Year." What would happen if he did take her back? Would she run off again? Would he blame me if she did?

Finally, I said, "Johnny, the Good Lord did not make me wise enough to decide what any man ought to do about his wife. You will have to decide that yourself. However, it seems to me that if you don't take her back you are going to hurt yourself more than anyone else. Maybe she has learned a lesson, as she says. You decide it. If you take her back, remember this: The surest way to lose her again is to quarrel with her about what she has already done. Forget the whole thing. Wash it out of your mind. Wipe the slate clean and start over."

Fifteen years later, Johnny brought her to see me, and

they had five beautiful children. Looking at them all together, bright and happy, I remembered the many mistakes I have made and how often my judgment has been wrong, but here was proof that on one occasion, at least, I had the good sense to give the right advice.

The chief causes for divorce in Wirt County are:

(1) A couple marries young and neither has sufficient maturity to support responsible marriage and parenthood. The tragedy in these cases is that the grandparents usually bring up the children.

(2) Married couples who have been poor suddenly strike it rich. It is a curious commentary on human nature that marriages often flourish in adversity and flounder in prosperity.

(3) Divorces that occur in middle age are often chargeable to a natural phenomenon that women seem peculiarly unfitted to comprehend. I refer to what is known in literary circles as the dangerous forties in men. The change of life in women has been recognized and understood since prehistoric times, but in recent decades researchers have discovered that men likewise undergo physical and mental changes. A man who has been a model husband for years is suddenly revealed as a philanderer and a cheat. Of all the crosses that woman must bear in relation to their menfolk, this is indeed the most difficult.

I recall a case from my youthful practice that ended tragically. The couple was childless, but the marriage was recognized as an exceptionally happy one. The husband was an able, industrious, and successful oil and gas operator right in the midst of the Great Depression. In their mid-forties, the wife contracted tuberculosis. He promptly installed her in a sanitarium in Arizona. At this critical stage of his life he met a younger woman and soon compromised himself. Someone wrote his wife and she came back home from the sanitarium. He then made a complete fool of himself by hiring an expensive battery of lawyers and suing her for divorce.

The judge appointed me Special Divorce Commissioner in this case and I listened to the evidence for three straight weeks. At the end I ruled that he was not entitled to a divorce. There was no evidence of adultery, desertion, conviction of a felony, addiction to alcohol or drugs, or cruel and inhuman treatment. All that was proved was that she was ill and that he had solaced himself in the meantime with a younger woman.

In the course of the trial, however, she came to me with a proposition that had been submitted to her by her lawyer. Her husband wanted to marry the other woman and he would pay for the privilege. He was willing to give her their house and a Buick automobile. He was also prepared to set up a trust fund that would pay her five hundred dollars a month as long as she lived. Five hundred dollars a month in 1935 was probably equal in purchasing power to one thousand five hundred dollars a month now. In return, she was to accept the property settlement and withdraw her opposition to the divorce. She wanted to know what I thought of it.

I told her, "Mary, the one thing that women never understand is that men also pass through a change of life. That is all that is wrong with him. He thinks he wants to marry this young fool, but he will soon get a bellyful of that. If you take the house, the car, and the trust fund, you will at least save something from the wreckage. One of these days he will come back to you on his hands and knees. I advise you to take it."

That is where I made my mistake. She thought I was on his side. With the deadly fury of a woman scorned, she told me, "I won't do it. So help me God, I'm not going to let that whore have him."

As it turned out, she let her have him, after all. He went to Mexico, got a quickie divorce, and married the other woman. Within a few years he went bankrupt. His second wife divorced him and the last time I heard of him he was in jail in Texas on a bad check charge. Mary lost her home and her financial security. Always an invalid, she was reduced to accepting public charity and was buried in a pauper's grave.

This case confirmed my opinion that a contested divorce is one of the tragic aspects of our civilization. Here were two allegedly intelligent human beings so enmeshed in their own emotions that both lost all sense of perspective and judgment. The experience poisoned both their lives.

Wirt County does not have sufficient juvenile delinquency to correlate that subject meaningfully with divorce. In fact, I am constantly surprised when I meet a group of high school students at their polite and mannerly behavior. They are never boisterous in public, which is a statement I could not truthfully make about my own generation. When I was young, high school and college students often felt impelled to show off in public. Students today do not practice vandalism on an appreciable scale, though I have noticed an occasional overturned school bus shelter. There is so little thievery that householders lock their doors only at night and they do that out of deference to intruders from the highway. The few juvenile offenders that appear in court are likely to be petty thieves, burglars, automobile borrowers, or runaway girls. I recall one runaway girl whose parents were divorced. Another, whose father was deceased, was found upon examination to be suffering from a venereal disease.

The only spectacular juvenile crime of the past decade was that committed by the sixteen-year-old boy who held up the State Liquor Store with a toy pistol. His parents were not divorced, though his father was thirty years older than his mother. He was a younger brother of the man who proved to be such a clumsy liar when he was tried for burglary. Of the four brothers in this family, three have served time in the penitentiary while the fourth has never been charged with any crime to my knowledge. If this circumstance proves anything at all, the proof seems to be completely separated from the problem of divorce.

11. Religion and Changing Morality

THE WHOLE UPWARD HISTORY of the human race is in a sense a history of changing religious beliefs and values intertwined with changing economics. Apart from the instinct for self preservation and the natural ties of family and government, religion is now and always has been a compelling motivation in human affairs. No other area of human endeavor has bred so much dissension, provided so much consolation, or encouraged so much hypocrisy as the practice of religion.

There are some who argue that religion is intuitive among men and others who hold that religion was invented by man to explain the mysteries of the universe. It is true that men with inquiring minds would have been compelled by the circumstances of their primitive lives to invent explanations of natural phenomena observed but not understood. The sum total of knowledge today, which is far superior to the knowledge of the cave men and far inferior to the potentialities of knowledge, is attributable to man's unceasing quest for reliable and unchanging facts, a quest that may be loosely designated by the term, Science.

Some years ago I read a scholarly essay titled "Magic, Science and Religion" by a man theretofore unknown to me named Bronislaw Malinowski. Malinowski, a famed anthropologist, had lived with primitive tribes of savages in the Trobriand Islands off the coast of New Guinea, and his conclusion about the primitive people he lived with was the chief inspiration for this essay. Malinowski observed that there are no people however primitive without religion or magic nor are there any savage races lacking either in the scientific attitude or in science. Assuming that his conclusion is true for all practical purposes, it raises a question as to the degree of difference between the practice of religion and magic among savages and the same practice among representatives of a fringe area of a great civilization. It also poses a comparison in the area of scientific attitude and of science.

When I started to make my own observations in Wirt County, I discovered that Malinowski enjoyed an advantage of detachment among the Trobrianders that I could not hope to equal. He was a white man living among a primitive race of men with a tradition and culture entirely different from his own. Everything he saw and heard was new and interesting, whereas many of the things I saw and heard were so familiar from my childhood that I had difficulty deciding what was and what was not important for the investigation. While Malinowski could observe a garden magician with complete detachment, I became involved, in a prolonged discussion with a water witch, of the exact blood relationship between our grandfathers. That was when I decided that the logical way to handle my subject was to use some autobiography.

Nevertheless, it is astonishing how many primitive superstitions and beliefs persist in the Twentieth Century. Except that the science of agriculture is much further advanced in Wirt County and that no Wirt County farmer would think of hiring a magician to protect his crops, the religious distinctions in liturgy and belief between Trobrianders and my neighbors are more alleged than real. The basic concept of all religions, the concept of a spirit or a group of spirits able and willing to intervene in the affairs of men, has not materially altered these ten thousand years.

Malinowski's essay is helpful to everyone who is confused about modern religion. Before proceeding with my own discourse I think it pertinent to ask again some of his questions: What is the part of society in the establishment of the rules of moral conduct? Why are not only morality but also belief, mythology and all sacred tradition compulsory? Why is there only one body of religious belief in each tribe, and why is no difference of opinion ever tolerated?

Toleration of other religious beliefs is a characteristic of an advanced civilization, though it may well be argued from history that tolerance ultimately succumbs to intolerance and the extinction of the civilization that permits toleration. That, at least, is what happened to ancient Rome. Toleration was established in America when the country was young in political development but old in the warring ideologies of Catholics, Protestants, Moslems, and Jews. Toleration in religion, language, customs, dress, color of skin, or any other foreign attribute is not instinctive in human nature. Indeed, the instinct is just the opposite as Malinowski suggests. Such toleration as exists today is a product of education and is largely confined to specific areas of Europe, of the Americas, and of British and American spheres of influence around the world. If anyone thinks that toleration has gained a foothold outside western civilization, he may disabuse himself by seeking permission to visit Mecca or to open a Sunday School in Tibet.

Toleration and revealed religion are inconsistent and contradictory. If Yahweh is the Only God and the Jews are his chosen people, everyone else is excluded. If Christ is the Messiah who died on the Cross to redeem mankind from its sins, then it behooves Christians everywhere to convert the heathens before it is too late. Indeed, this sense of urgent mission was the central theme of early and medieval Christianity. If there is no God but Allah and Muhammad is his prophet, it follows naturally that both Christians and Jews are infidels. Revealed religion has the advantage of being certain and final, and certainty and finality have been the goals in man's long climb upward from abysmal ignorance. Logic, the fundamental ingredient in science, is lacking in revealed religion, and therefore the two disciplines are incompatible.

Religious toleration was made a part of the Constitution of the United States in the year 1787. The men who framed the Constitution have been acclaimed as the Founding Fathers and one of the things they have been most acclaimed for is the article on religious freedom. The Founding Fathers were indeed generations ahead of their time. They comprised some of the best minds in America. They were men who combined the culture of Europe as expressed in the writings of Newton, Locke, Montesquieu, Voltaire, and Rousseau with practical experience in leading and winning a revolutionary war. They were steeped in the history of the religious wars that had racked Europe for centuries and they hoped to forestall future religious wars by proclaiming complete religious toleration.

How far this type of thinking was ahead of the times may be gauged by what little is known of religion on the Indian frontier at the very time when the Constitution was adopted. Appalachia was still a No-Man's Land, a veritable lawless wilderness. The people who lived there were a violent, turbulent breed, who thought no more of killing an Indian than they did of swatting a fly but who nevertheless represented a long tradition of European Protestant culture. The English, the Scotch-Irish, the Germans, and the French Huguenots were all Protestant in background and religious training. The only Roman Catholics on the frontier were the conquered French and they were promptly overwhelmed. People who kill Indians because they believe that the only good Indian is a dead Indian are not predisposed to Popish foolishness, especially when they have been taught from childhood that the Pope is Anti-Christ himself. If Rousseau had spent even a week on the Appalachian frontier, he would have absorbed much disconcerting information about savages, white and red. (There are still a few old Bibles here and there bound in Indian skin.)

Still and all, the later history of the frontier proves that the frontiersmen were deeply religious and far more susceptible to emotional religious experience than anyone could have reasonably expected. If there is an inconsistency here it is simply the inconsistency of human nature. The great religious revival meetings in Kentucky at the beginning of the Nineteenth Century show that rural settlers travelled hundreds of miles to grovel in the dirt and repent their sins in loud and vociferous lamentations. These penitents were the very same people who had killed Indians without remorse and had snuffed out French Catholicism without qualms of conscience. The phenomenon of the religious revival gives us license perhaps to speculate on the innermost thoughts of the frontiersmen.

That the frontiersmen were introspective and violent, though they seem to have been gentle in family life, is indisputable. Had they been otherwise this country and the English language would not now extend from coast to coast. Though their way of life converted them to near savagery, they retained the rudiments of Anglo-Saxon, Celtic, and Nordic Protestant culture. The arts of reading, writing, and simple arithmetic were cultivated for the purpose of reading the Bible and of conducting commercial transactions, but the frontiersmen knew nothing of the New Enlightenment that was undermining the power structures of Europe. Locke, Voltaire, and Rousseau were not only unread—they were completely unknown. The people of the mountains needed only to watch the stars and to listen to the throbbing, pulsating life of the forest to feel the all-pervading presence of God in their daily lives. Their God was the God of the Christians, Protestant style, and they believed firmly in the pleasures of Heaven and the torments of Hell. They formulated the rules of sportsmanship, which distinguished the later frontiers all the way to the Pacific. An armed man did not shoot an unarmed opponent and he did not shoot another in the back. Frontier formalities required that every contestant be given a chance. If one of the combatants was a poor shot, or was slow on the draw, that was his ill fortune. Murderers were those who failed to observe the rules, and public opinion was against them.

In common with all mankind, the frontiersmen were subject to immoderate self delusion. They could rationalize the most barbaric crimes, such as killing Indians and tanning their hides for household ornaments, by the law of the jungle. The game they were playing was for keeps. When the Indians came to the white settlements or when the white men went to the Indian settlements, in wartime, there was but one alternative, victory or death. Because life was precarious and death mysterious, the frontiersmen were superstitious. They comprehended God vaguely by intuition, but they also preserved vestiges of former pagan cultures in their belief in ghosts and in witchcraft. In short, the frontiersmen were much like the great mass of people everywhere in the Twentieth Century. The veneer of civilization is only skin deep. Remove the veneer and you find a Buchenwald and the specter of genocide.

Side by side with the crimes of man against man, in the vicissitudes of the frontier, was an oppressive sense of guilt. Psychiatrists and psycho-analysts have shown how deeply the sense of guilt affects individuals in their relations with modern society. The sense of guilt may well be an attribute of the undefined law of natural opposition. The sense of guilt was undoubtedly responsible for the historic religious revival on the eastern frontier, though public expiation occurred predictably after the Indians had been permanently dispossessed. Hence, the religious outlook of the frontiersmen was influenced more by the reforming spirit of Methodism than by the philosophers of the Age of Reason. The result of the reforming and Protestantizing process on the frontier, which persisted for generations, was an enormous spread of the more primitive Christian doctrines at the very time when such doctrines were being subjected to criticism and recast in the light of advancing knowledge by the most brilliant minds of the time.

Historically, the first Christian missionaries to obtain permanent results on the frontier were the Methodist and the Baptist circuit riders, of whom the most famous is the Methodist Bishop Asbury. The Methodists and the Baptists, however, were by no means the first missionaries in Appalachia. Father Clifford M. Lewis, a Jesuit at Wheeling College, tells me that the Jesuits were active among the French and the Indians in the days when the French controlled the Ohio Valley. The English element on the frontier was technically Anglican or Puritan; the Scotch-Irish, Presbyterian; and the German, Lutheran. If the Huguenots had a separate denomination of their own, all traces of it have disappeared in Appalachia. The Episcopalians, the Presbyterians, and the Lutherans have survived, though their present day churches are largely found in the cities. The Presbyterians were originally dominant due to the ardor of their Scotch-Irish adherents, but the sect soon fragmented in internecine strife.

The after effects of the Methodist and Baptist circuit riders and of the Protestantizing process in general are evident everywhere in Wirt County at the present time. The little village of Elizabeth with a total population of 727 in 1960 has five Protestant Churches with an enrolled membership as follows:

Methodist	225
Baptist	153
Church of Christ	40
Church of the Nazarene	22
United Presbyterian	21
Total	461

It needs to be remembered that the 461 enrolled church members in Elizabeth are not all residents of the municipality. In fact, in these days of easy travel many of them live in the countryside.

There are no avowed atheists or communists in the county, to my knowledge, but that circumstance does not alter the corollary fact that a majority of the church members of Wirt County do not attend services regularly and that many who are carried on the membership rolls do not attend at all. To find out exactly how many go to church, as distinguished from those who are nominally church members, I made it my business to learn how many worshippers attended the same churches on Palm Sunday, 1965. I chose Palm Sunday for two reasons: (1) Palm Sunday is the Sunday before Easter and is therefore important in the Christian tradition, and (2) Palm Sunday is more representative of regular church attendance than Easter, when many nominal church members make their annual appearance. On Palm Sunday, 1965, attendance at morning church services, by actual count, at the five churches in Elizabeth was as follows:

Methodist	86
Baptist	52
Church of Christ	22

Church of the Nazarene	17
United Presbyterian	12
	189

Allowing for illness and other unavoidable absences, it is apparent that at least one half of the church membership of Elizabeth is a nominal membership. Nominal members appear usually at funerals and at special worship services such as Easter and Christmas. Nominal membership does not mean that the absent member is wavering in his or her faith. It does mean that with the advent of radio and television, people find more entertainment at home and there are fewer motivations for congregating together. Not only the churches but also the fraternal and social organizations are suffering from the stay-at-home habit. The Elizabeth Lions Club has recently been dissolved. The Knights of Pythias, a fraternal organization, has surrendered its charter. The Masons, of which fraternity I am a member, seldom attract more than enough members to fill the official chairs. The local chapter of the American Legion, open to all war veterans and with more than one hundred dues paying members, limps along with a scant half dozen in attendance at regular meetings.

The best figures on church activity in the county come from the Wirt County Council of Churches, Mrs. Evelyn Board, Secretary, and relate to Sunday School enrollment. Sunday School enrollment and attendance is important because the Sunday Schools attract children as well as adults. In fact, the Sunday School is the real indicator of church activity in the county because the Methodist Church in Elizabeth is the only church that has its own exclusive minister. All the other churches, except the Church of the Nazarene whose pastor is a factory worker and the Church of Christ which has no pastor, share their pastors with rural charges. Nearly all the rural churches have preaching services but once a month and some have no church activity other than the Sunday School.

Before setting down the reported figures for Sunday School enrollment, however, I think I ought to point out that enrollment is one thing and attendance at Sunday School is quite a different thing. For instance, I have attended the Sunday School at Elizabeth Presbyterian Church, which my great-grandfather founded, and the Sunday School at the Beulah Presbyterian Church, which my grandfather founded, for the past fifteen years. The enrollment at the Elizabeth Presbyterian Sunday School is listed at 26, but I know from personal observation that 26 people do not attend that Sunday School. The attendance varies from nine to seventeen, an average of thirteen. The Beulah Sunday School lists 63 enrolled members, but this figure also averages to somewhere between 35 and 40. While I have no personal knowledge of the other Sunday Schools, I suspect that all show similar discrepancies.

One would surmise that the churches, of all human institutions, would provide reliable figures on Sunday School attendance. That they fail to do so in Wirt County is not attributable to any calculated dishonesty on the part of the Sunday Schools and their officials but is due rather to the very human desire to place the best foot forward. There are 26 enrollees at the Elizabeth Presbyterian Sunday School and 63 enrollees at the Beulah Presbyterian Sunday School. The difference between enrollment and attendance arises because many persons are carried on the Sunday School rolls, for one reason or another, long after they cease attending Sunday School. Perhaps, they are old and ill. Perhaps, they have moved away but return occasionally. Perhaps, they are negligent and the Sunday School does not wish to offend by a public declaration. After all, when you have only a few adherents in a community that is losing population, you avoid chances of ill feeling. You keep negligent people on the rolls in the hope that they will eventually perceive their errors and return.

Following is the reported Sunday School enrollment for the thirty active Sunday Schools in Wirt County in 1964. Of the six listed as not reporting I have ascertained that four suspended operations in 1964, though one resumed its roll in 1965. The figures for the other two active Sunday Schools have been obtained from responsible officials of the Sunday Schools involved.

WIRT COUNTY CHURCHES

Sunday School Enrollment as Reported to The Wirt County Council of Churches, 1964.

Church		Enrollment
Burning Springs District		
Guthrie Methodist	)	
Straight Creek Baptist	) These six reported	
Owl Hill Methodist	) together	
Burning Springs Methodist	)	
Standing Stone Baptist	)	
Bell Chapel E.U.B.	)	201
Shiloh Baptist		34
Clay District		
Big Island Run Baptist, (inactive)		
Big Island Run Methodist		30
Elizabeth District		
Bethesda Baptist		21
Palestine Methodist		62
Two Ripple Baptist		70
Wesleyan Chapel Methodist		25
Elizabeth Methodist		201
Elizabeth Baptist		101
Elizabeth Presbyterian		26
Elizabeth Church of the Nazarene, (Did not report. Av. Attdn.)		28
Elizabeth Church of Christ, (Did not report. Av. Attdn.)		42
Newark District		
Newark Baptist		60
Newark Methodist		20
Merrill Chapel Methodist		44
Beulah-Humble Memorial Presbyterian		63
Reedy District		
Union Chapel Methodist		20
Two Runs Baptist		40
New Home Methodist		37
Pisgah Methodist		64
Center Valley Methodist		70

Spring Creek District	
Hill Grove Baptist	70
McCutcheon Chapel Methodist	30
Mount William Baptist, (inactive)	
Creston Methodist, (inactive)	
Tucker District	
Mount Hope E.U.B., (inactive)	
Rose Hill Methodist	38
Bethel E.U.B.	82
	1,479

The arresting feature of this report is that, inflated though the figures undoubtedly are, it still shows that approximately two thirds of the inhabitants of Wirt County are not identified by name with a Sunday School. I can scarcely believe the figures myself. Wirt County is not a refuge of the intelligentsia. It is an obscure farm community on the fringe of the Bible Belt. Wirt County has a long tradition of Protestant theology and Protestant ideology. This two thirds of the population that does not associate itself publicly with the church community is directly descended from the frontiersmen who, whatever their shortcomings as Christians, were unmistakably fighting Protestants.

The difference between now and former times seems to lie in the sphere of religious toleration. There is no longer anything worth fighting for. The sole exceptions in Wirt County are the Church of Christ, with its dogged insistence that its way is the only way, and the Church of the Nazarene which holds somewhat similar views. In practice, there are no recognizable distinctions between Methodists, Baptists, and Presbyterians. They hold revivals together and their pastors appear in each others pulpits. If the Baptists continue to use immersion in the baptismal ceremony and the Presbyterians use both sprinkling and immersion, according to the candidate's choice, what of it? Baptism, after all, is a ceremony, and the form of the ceremony is unimportant. It is of no more consequence, really, than an individual choice of clothing or haircuts.

I am myself a Presbyterian for the same reason that I

am a Republican. My people were Presbyterians. But I differ from nominal Presbyterians in that I do attend church and Sunday School, though irregularly, and I do contribute within the bounds of reason and my own capability to the financial needs of the parish and the church. My reasons for doing so are wholly divorced from Presbyterian theology. Once upon a time I laid out a course of reading on John Calvin and John Knox, but I gave it up for two reasons: (1) the reading was excessively dull, and (2) both these leaders of the Reformation were fanatical on subjects that are no longer controversial. Anyone who reads this essay will understand that I am no doctrinnaire Presbyterian.

My conversion was thoroughly illogical. Logically, I should have become a Communist. (One of my short stories was republished in O'Brien's *Best Short Stories of 1933*. Years later when there was a great to-do in Hollywood about Communist writers in moving pictures, I noticed that a number of the proscribed writers had also appeared in O'Brien's 1933 selections.) Actually, I tried to find out what the Communists stood for and I soon discovered that the Communists wanted to destroy all religions and that meant destroying the concepts of mercy and brotherly love that constitute the very heart of the teachings of Jesus of Nazareth. Admitting that the Christian tautology has been abused and that many crimes have been committed in its name, what kind of world would we have if love and mercy were disavowed? Admitting further that the Presbyterian Church is a bundle of contradictions wherein tolerance has replaced faith, that church is still one of the institutions by which the teachings of Jesus are transmitted to the modern secular world. If my conversion was more of the head than of the heart, it was nevertheless a genuine conversion. Perhaps, the development was merely a facet of my growing conservatism, though I have never been so conservative as to think that the status quo is possible or even desirable. The true conservative believes that inevitable change ought to be orderly instead of chaotic.

The phenomenon of disinterest in religion in Wirt County is traceable to two main sources: (1) the principle of religious toleration incorporated in the Constitution, and (2) the unparalleled advance in scientific knowledge since the beginning of the Industrial Revolution. Toleration is indeed a beneficial prescription for religious strife, but toleration also creates doubts concerning the authenticity of particular revelations. Once you admit that another revelation is as good as your own, you undermine certainty and finality, the very cornerstones of revelation. Again, magic and religion have traditionally flourished in the areas of human existence where knowledge was weakest and least comprehensible. With advancing knowledge it is now clear, even to the uneducated, that nature operates under predictable laws of cause and effect. This circumstance casts a shadow of doubt on the image of God as the Traffic Officer of the skies. Religion today is not dying, but it is certainly shedding its skin. I think it probable that a new religion, geared to present knowledge and capable of absorbing unsuspected scientific discoveries of the future, will ultimately replace the old. This new religion, it is hoped, will retain the best of the old religion, particularly in the domain of morals.

A curious feature of Church and Sunday School attendance in Wirt County is the disparity in numbers between the sexes. While I was counting attendance at Palm Sunday services in Elizabeth, I took advantage of the opportunity to count the congregations according to sexes. This is what I found.

ATTENDANCE AT PALM SUNDAY SERVICES

	Women	Men	Total
Methodist	58	28	86
Baptist	35	17	52
Church of Christ	16	6	22
Church of the Nazarene	12	5	17
United Presbyterian	8	4	12
Total	129	60	189

Though these figures are obviously deficient because of their miniature scale, I am convinced from other non-arithmetical observations that they represent roughly a cross section of church attendance not only in Wirt County but also elsewhere in the United States. Go to any church service anywhere, Protestant or Roman Catholic, and you will find that women worshippers outnumber men.

Why men are apparently less religious minded than women is a problem in psychology upon which I do not care to hazard an opinion. Strangely enough, though many Protestant denominations now ordain female candidates for the ministry, women pastors are even scarcer than women doctors or lawyers. All the pastors in Wirt County are men and the same thing is true, to the best of my knowledge, of the State of West Virginia. Some women are employed as denominational missionaries in the southern mountains, but I have not yet learned of a woman anywhere who holds down a regular pastorate. (There must be one somewhere. The Congregational Church of Belpre, Ohio, used to have a pastor who was the wife of the pastor of the First Presbyterian Church of Parkersburg, Mrs. Gill A. Wilson.)

The preponderance of women in the congregation and the exclusive role of men in the ministry is a pattern of modern religion. The pattern holds, I am told, for Roman Catholics as well as Protestants, though it may be that the disparity in numbers between the sexes is less with the Catholics. A Protestant minister, in some respects, resembles a candidate for public office. To become successful in his parish, the minister must first of all acquire the confidence and support of his parishioners, the majority of whom are women. He is the confession hearer and the handholder in ill health in a society that is rapidly becoming feminized. While the Victorian myth that women exist on a higher moral plane has been exploded, it does seem that women are peculiarly fitted by nature to transmit culture and tradition from one generation to the next. In a world that is rapidly changing, either for better or worse, the role of women is a weakness of the churches and of modern society.

Side by side with religious traditions and practices, Wirt County retains a few odd superstitions and rituals that are vestiges of ancient pagan cults. These persist in spite of education and religious training and their observance is by no means confined to the ignorant. A common manifestation is the frequency with which people knock on wood when they speak of another's ill fortune. I do it myself without thinking, though reason tells me that the magical formula is useless. All superstitions relate in some way to the elusive quality of fortune. Finding a coin or a pin is a good luck omen. Having a black cat cross your path is a sure sign of bad luck. So is walking under a ladder. Two but not three persons may safely light cigarettes from the same match. Seven and eleven are lucky numbers but thirteen is extremely unlucky. I know a distinguished judge who was once a football player. As an athlete he expressed his contempt for superstition by wearing the number 13 on his football jersey. Today, his telephone number which he requested, ends in thirteen. This man is so obviously unsuperstitious that he believes thirteen is *his* lucky number. There is a whole compendium of superstition in gambling which ranges from dice conversation to performing a sequence of physical exercises to propitiate Old Lady Luck in card games. The evil eye, while not unknown, receives scant attention in Wirt County, possibly because the evil eye is in better repute among Latins than among Nordics.

Exactly where these various superstitions originated is not known, and their persistence in the face of nearly two thousand years of revealed Christianity is preposterous. Certainly, Christian mothers have consistently taught their children to pray and not to knock on wood as a substitute. I recall that I learned about knocking on wood, black cats, and lucky and unlucky numbers in that greatest of all educational institutions, the boys gang. Is it possible that men pass on pagan heresies while women transmit traditional religion? Are any of the current superstitions traceable to the American Indian?

The only magician, who still commands a fee, in Wirt County, is the water witch. Water witches, incongruously enough, are always males, which indicates that there has been a slip in terminology somewhere. When I made my first notes for this thesis, I listed the water witch as a product of Appalachian culture. Then, I learned, to my chagrin, that the services of water witches may be obtained in New

England, in the South, in the Midwest, and in the Far West. Clearly, the water witch is no regional phenomenon, and, strange as it seems, thousands of intelligent and highly educated people believe in them implicitly. Inasmuch as I employed a water witch myself on one occasion, not wholly without misgivings, I am giving my testimony, without embellishment, for the record.

Ten years ago I built a new house in the country and the first thing I did, after the site was marked off and prepared, was to engage a contractor to drill a water well. All my neighbors had fine wells, and I did not anticipate any trouble. The well proved to be insufficient in quantity, and upon the advice of friends, I then employed a water witch to locate the second well. The witch was a part time Methodist preacher. I showed him where I wanted the well drilled and he explored the site with his forked stick. The trick in water witching is that the stick is supposed to turn downward of its own accord when the witch walks over an underground water stream. The witch did indeed locate a water well but it, too, proved inadequate for the needs of a ten-room house, a utility room, a kitchen, and two bathrooms. When that happened I picked a location for the third well about one hundred yards distant from the other two wells, and this time the drillers found a well that produced thirty-five gallons of water a minute, enough to supply the needs of a small village! Prior to this time I had not learned that drilling for water in the countryside often produces erratic results.

In fairness to the witch who located an insufficient underground stream, I must state that he did not explore the ground where I drilled the good well. I was trying at that time to locate a well nearer the house. Actually, I was desperate. I knew that many good wells had already been drilled in the neighborhood and I could not understand why I had drilled two poor ones on my own property. At last, I had a hunch and the hunch paid off. The hunch itself is one of the mysteries of human existence. Gamblers believe in it fervently and some scientific research has been done in extrasensory perception. My own conclusions about the whole episode are these: (1) If water witches can indeed locate underground streams, their art tells them nothing about the size and the strength of the streams, and (2) the hunch in this instance would have been more beneficial to me had it manifested itself before and not after I had experienced two costly failures.

It will be recalled that Malinowski asked, "What is the part of society in the establishment of moral conduct?" If Malinowski had been given the opportunity, as I have, of growing up with the natives under investigation and then of conducting his investigation fifty years later among a new generation, he might have phrased his question a trifle differently. What is the part of society in the establishment *and in the gradual changing* of the rules of moral conduct?

Religion in America, has been interpreted in individual terms and has been influenced by numerous dissenting sects. Proliferation of sects has flourished among the Protestants, but toleration has taken its toll among Catholics also. It is obvious from the excommunication of a Catholic political leader in Louisiana that there is no general agreement among Catholics on the subject of civil rights for Negroes just as there is no general agreement among Protestants on the same subject. Catholics have proved time and again that they vote as they please no matter what their priests say or think. While statistics show that there are fewer divorces among Catholics than among the population as a whole, I think it significant that I have myself handled two divorce cases for Catholic couples in the past five years. Since these couples were the only married Catholics in the county, the divorce rate among the Catholics in Wirt County stands at one hundred percent.

To attempt to describe the current attitude of Wirt County citizens toward religion would be an unending task. One's attitude toward religion is influenced by inheritance, by education, and by the possession or lack of possession of worldly goods. But, despite individual differences of opinion, tradition has established certain fundamentals of religious belief, such as (1) there is one supreme God, (2) Christ is his only begotten son, and (3) the Bible is God's word.

The Fundamentalist view of the universe dominated the thinking of the early Methodists, Baptists, Presbyterians, and Lutherans on the frontier and its moral precepts became a part of Appalachian culture. The moral code was based on the Ten Commandments. Vestiges of that code are visible everywhere today even among the two-thirds of the population that is not associated by name with any church.

Since the advent of the automobile and the increasing migration of young persons to the cities, the residents of Wirt County have been subjected to successive social and economic strains. We are in the unenviable position of educating our youth for export. Technology and industrialization have changed our way of life and at the same time have changed the way we used to look at life. Though the Ten Commandments still serve as a moral code, the temptations and opportunities for evasion of the rules have multiplied. The Sabbath is still a day of rest. Even today no self-respecting farmer would till his fields on Sunday, but he needs only to turn on his television set to watch a big league baseball, football, or basketball game. Persons and property are relatively safe, partly because the people have been educated to law observance and personal honesty and partly because there is no real grinding poverty. At the same time, there has been a slackening in the standards of public honesty and fiscal responsibility. The fabled independence of the frontiersmen has degenerated into too much dependence on the government dole. Sexual taboos are still prevalent, but there has been a striking change in attitude toward sexual delinquencies. In all this, our people are simply following the trends of the nation. Indeed, the most significant moral changes that have occurred since my own boyhood lie in two main areas of social behavior: (1) in the area of partisan politics, which I have already discussed, and (2) in the area of sexual attitudes and behavior.

The rules by which sexual conduct are regulated are clear enough. Adultery is indefensible and I am convinced that, on the whole, very little adultery is indulged in. Women form the backbone of the churches and most of them try to lead decent lives. Fornication is frowned upon, but the unforgivable offense, both in adultery and fornication, is to be brazen about them. If you give them half a chance, people are usually willing to look the other way. If you flaunt an illicit sexual enterprise in such a way that others cannot help noticing it, you have forfeited both your own self respect and the good will of your fellow men, which ought properly to be written fellow women.

In actual fact, I have no statistical information on premarital sexual intercourse and related topics which seem nowadays to be in such literary demand. Prudence and an understanding of my neighbors' tempers have warned me that Wirt County is a hostile testing ground in the pursuit of such information. Descendants of the frontiersmen may have been tamed to live within the law, but the surest way to arouse their latent streak of violence would be, in my opinion, to go snooping into the sexual aspect of their private lives. In this, I agree with them thoroughly. There is so little personal privacy in modern society that what remains ought to be jealously guarded. Sexual behavior *is* jealously guarded, and for that reason I have less than complete faith in the scientific value of that best-selling book called, *Sexual Behavior of the American Female.* Women are naturally adept at fooling men and sometimes other women and I have no reason for supposing that they made an exception of Doctor Kinsey. After all, illicit sexual enterprises on the part of a male always require the cooperation of a female partner, with the single exception of homosexuality. (It is a curious circumstance that homosexual relationships, both male and female, are almost wholly confined to the cities.)

In the area of sexual conduct, all I can discuss with confidence is what appears on the surface and what I have learned in my legal practice. In modern society, doctors and lawyers are often made confidantes in matters that never become public knowledge. It may be stated confidently that there are no recognizable prostitutes in Wirt County in the sense that bodies are publicly offered for sale, though I shall never forget an experience I had once in a neighboring county. A young woman with a black book consulted me professionally. She had recently taken up prostitution for reasons that social workers never understand. She liked it. But she was so incredibly naive concerning the nature of men that she had been rendering services on a credit basis. The book was revealing. She had kept a meticulous record of her customers—their appearance, their length of stay on the premises, whether or not they had provided whiskey, and finally the service charge, Paid or Unpaid. The book could have been blackmail except that no human being in her right mind will ever commit blackmail for two dollars. She wanted me, as a lawyer, to collect what was due her from defaulters!

There were formidable legal barriers here, as any lawyer will appreciate. Prostitution was and still is under our law illegal. I am not a reformer by natural inclination, but I do retain a strong Presbyterian sense of right and wrong. Some of the men whose names were listed were known to me—a few were my friends. While listening to the utterly incredible story of this poor but misguided creature, I became aware of one of the world's injustices. Any man who buys a woman's body ought to have the decency to pay for the privilege. These chiselers, I decided, ought to be taught a lesson. I did not make the mistake of instituting suits nor did I ever divulge to anyone else who the culprits were. All I did was to write a letter to each delinquent telling him that I had the claim of Miss So-and-so for collection and suggesting that he pay her at once. Never in my life have I witnessed a more prompt and vigorous response.

Let it be noted here and now that the case I have just described was a far-out and non-typical experience. In a small community, such as the Beulah Hill Community in which I live, there are rigid standards for sexual conduct. Even in the age of the automobile and the airplane, it is difficult to conceal prolonged extramarital enterprises. Such liasons are not unknown but they are exceedingly rare. Women are the protectors and often the victims of moral vigilance. The married woman who becomes involved with another woman's husband will discover that women can close ranks, in this situation, with a unanimity rare among men.

The same vigilance is less apparent in the ranks of unmarried women, but it is there, nevertheless.

Still and all, there is a different attitude toward sexual irregularities now than there was in my childhood and in my mother's childhood. For instance, on a recent trip to Arizona I noticed that vending machines for contraceptive devices were installed in gasoline filling station rest rooms clear across the country. These vending machines seem to be confined to men's rest rooms. My wife tells me that similar machines are not installed in women's rest rooms. Ironically, the machines often bear the inscription, "Not for Sale to Minors" though it is not clear how the machine, which responds to a coin, calculates the age of its customers. Recently, I made a special trip to a filling station in Elizabeth to determine exactly what these machines dispensed. There were three machines on the wall. One dispensed two latex contraceptives for a quarter. Another, claiming better quality and a guarantee of safety, dispensed one contraceptive for a quarter. The third offering a package deal dispensed three contraceptives for a half dollar. All the machines bore the legend "Sold Only for the Prevention of Disease."

Having examined the machines and their advertisements individually and in absolute privacy, I concluded that any young man who gets a girl pregnant these days ought to have his head examined. He is thoroughly irresponsible and reckless. But here again the fact remains that, that in spite of the ease with which contraceptives may be obtained, girls still get pregnant.

I have already mentioned the cases of four girls under sixteen who, to my certain knowledge, became pregnant. Three of the girls married the putative fathers while the fourth was content to withhold the father's name and to draw public assistance. Of the three who married, two have been divorced. The third is still following her husband from job to job and from jail to jail because he is so irresponsible that he is frequently in trouble with the law. Certainly, there is no aspect of human relationship more complicated by emotion and less subject to reason than the compact of marriage.

It was my privilege to be the counsel for the defendant in the only paternity suit tried in Wirt County in the past twenty years. The trial took place in 1963. My client was a clean looking young boy, who had recently married, and whose nineteen-year-old bride was pregnant. The complainant was also nineteen years old and she had a fatherless baby.

Actually, I did not want to take this case at all. The trouble with free love in practice is that someone always gets hurt. When the young man first consulted me, I advised him to settle the case out of court. My experience with juries was that in paternity suits the jury takes the position that the mother knows who the father is, no matter what the defendant proves about promiscuity. It was only after attempts at compromise had failed and the pregnant bride appealed to me personally that I consented to defend the case in court. Having taken the case against my better judgment I was bound by the ethics of the profession to put up the best defense I could for him.

In the course of the trial I was surprised twice. The first surprise came when the special prosecuting attorney, employed by the complainant's parents, asked the defendant, my client, if he had written a letter to the complainant from the State of Texas. To my dismay, my client examined the letter, then threw it on the floor, and announced, "So you've got that letter. I plead guilty."

Nothing in this world is more calculated to throw a defense lawyer off his stride than to have his client plead guilty in the presence of a jury without prior consultation. Without really knowing what it was all about, I promptly objected on the ground that my client could not plead guilty at this point because he had already pleaded "Not Guilty." That happens to be good procedural law and the judge upheld me. The trial continued. The letter was offered in evidence, and I then had an opportunity to examine it. One point was clear immediately. The letter contained terms of endearment and the defendant did not want his wife, who was sitting at the counsel table, to know that he had written such a letter from Texas. She had already testified that she had accompanied him to the railroad station and that they were engaged to be married at that time. On the other hand the letter itself proved a vital point in controversy. The date of the defendant's departure had already been established and the defendant had testified that he had not seen the complainant for two months before he left. Conception could only have occurred, according to the calendar, immediately preceding his departure for Texas. The letter began, "I am sorry I did not see you before I left West Virginia."

Thereafter, in the course of the trial, I concentrated on the letter as the best evidence of my client's innocence. It was fortunate, from the point of view of the defense, that the opposing side had introduced the letter in evidence. When the jury returned its verdict, I was surprised again. The verdict was "Not Guilty." This is the only case in my experience as a trial lawyer in which the jury returned a verdict of not guilty after the defendant himself had pleaded guilty.

The trial of this case established a pattern of sexual behavior. The defendant admitted that he had dated the complainant for about a year and that they had often had sexual intercourse, usually in automobiles and in the company of other teen-age couples. He insisted that he had never had intercourse with her after he had started dating his wife. The jury, fortified by the evidence of his letter, obviously believed him. The result of the trial showed that verdicts are often won by the perspicacity or the negligence of lawyers.

Still, who can say that justice ultimately triumphed? Here was a case in which someone obviously had to be hurt. On one side was a mother with a nameless child, on the other a pregnant wife. There are excellent reasons even today for the rules against adultery and fornication. If all the parties had observed those rules, there would have been no occasion for this trial, which, regardless of the outcome, must be thought of as a personal tragedy.

How widely attitudes toward sexual irregularities have changed in the past seventy years is illustrated from two examples, one of which comes from my mother. Seventy years ago my mother was a school teacher attending Institute in Elizabeth. Among the teachers attending that Institute was a young girl who was pregnant and had recently married after her pregnancy became apparent. My mother tells me that under the moral code in force at that time none of the other girls would associate with the outcast, despite the fact that the girl was married. She occupied a bench by herself throughout the proceedings of the Institute.

Admitting that the conduct of the teachers on this occasion was barbaric, I offer, by way of contrast the case of a young girl which came to my attention in the 1950's. This girl likewise had become pregnant and later married. She happened to be the organist of one of the churches. Had she actually borne an illegitimate child, I presume that her position as organist would have been jeopardized, but she was legally married and no one questioned her fitness for the position. Unfortunately, this girl was divorced three times before she was twenty-two years of age and she left the church and her position as organist of her own accord.

No discussion of religion is complete without reference to the consoling aspect of religious faith and doctrine. In Wirt County, as elsewhere, the Christian religion offers a sanctuary of hope in times of grief and adversity. There is comfort in the recollection that the injustices of this world will be corrected in the world to come. I have sometimes attended friends in their final illnesses and I have noted how frequently they speak of the assurance of eternal salvation. Such is the power of human rationalization. Not once have I found a dying person who was conscious of the fate of the damned.

The concepts of the immortality of the soul and of the Day of Judgment are indeed the opiate of the masses, but the opiate itself, or some logical substitute, is necessary to communal life and stable government. On this point the Communists have undoubtedly erred. Man does not live by bread alone.

12. Trends of the Times

WE LIVE in a world of changing social patterns, headlong technological advances, and unbounded confidence in man and his works. Due to changing social, economic, and religious influences, the present generation of white men and to a lesser extent the present generation of all the races of men differ from the generations that preceded them. How far we have come, either for better or worse, may be illustrated by a brief glance at the generation of Americans that fought the great Civil War only a century ago.

By the 1860's there had likewise been far-reaching technological advances. The new nation that began with the revolt of thirteen English colonies, scattered along the eastern seaboard, had spread all the way to the Pacific Ocean. The Indian frontier, which hovered near the Alleghenies for nearly two hundred years, had hedgehopped to the West Coast, with unconquered areas between, in a mere fifty years. Americans had every reason to be proud of their accomplishments as men, but they differed from Americans today in that doubt had not yet arisen to plague their daily thinking.

There was no widespread religious doubt. The New Enlightenment of the Eighteenth Century and the far more disturbing enlightenment of the schools of Darwin and of Marx had reached the public forums and touched the public conscience only in the struggle for freedom and equality. There was no doubt about the superiority of democracy or the virtues of capitalism. So long as there was free land ahead only a few worried about those who piled up fortunes behind. Indeed, Americans of all classes were proud of their millionaires, perhaps because the mere existence of millionaires showed that even the humblest could aspire to the same pinnacle of worldly success.

Today, if I read my glass correctly, some of the old optimism remains but there is a growing cloud of doubt and even downright pessimism. There is doubt about religion, doubt about capitalism, doubt about democracy, doubt about patriotism, doubt about the bomb, and doubt about the future of mankind. Is it true or do I merely imagine that the prolonged Cold War and the mounting sense of insecurity in a world of fabulous weapons have made all of us edgy and irritable? To ascertain the truth, I spent a noon hour on a busy Washington Street looking for a face that expressed a sense of inner serenity and happiness. Except for some children and two Catholic nuns each face bore a harried and troubled look. Of course, the weather was hot. It was lunchtime and many of the people on the street were probably hurrying out to lunch or else were hurrying back to work, but, even so, one hoped to find at least a spark of contentment. Not a single passerby looked ill-dressed or ill-fed.

If you doubt my powers of observation in this matter, I suggest that you try it yourself. I have repeated the experiment in other cities, and so has my wife, with similar results. All it proves is that Americans, who are supposed to have everything, do not look happy on the street during work hours.

These lines were written in the spring of 1965 with Lyndon B. Johnson as President of the United States. Whatever may happen hereafter, Johnson at the moment is the strongest president, in the sense that he has been able to impose his will on the Congress, on the courts, and on the country, since Franklin D. Roosevelt. Whether or not the emergence of an all-powerful chief executive is a good thing for the country and for the future of mankind is a question that will be decided ultimately by historians. Strong leaders, dictators, and tyrants do not achieve power by ambition alone. They always fill a power vacuum or a social need. In my lifetime, I have lived under four strong-willed chief executives namely, Theodore Roosevelt, Woodrow Wilson, Franklin D. Roosevelt, and Lyndon B. Johnson.

During that same lifetime, I have witnessed undreamed of changes in the social and political life of the country. The steam locomotive, the telegraph, the electric light bulb, the telephone, the automobile, the phonograph, the moving picture and many other modern conveniences were all invented before I was born. All contributed to what has been aptly named the Industrial Revolution. The social benefits of the Industrial Revolution, however, were spotty and sporadic until Henry Ford produced an automobile so cheap that all could aspire to own one. Prior to the manufacture and distribution of the Model T Ford automobile, there were great disparities between the inhabitants of cities and the inhabitants of rural areas, which comprised most of America. The latter were called rubes and country jakes, both of which were terms of opprobrium. Long after city dwellers became accustomed to running water, electric lights, and telephones, rural people continued to live in the style of their ancestors with wood fires, outside privies, and horse locomotion providing the fundamentals of daily existence.

In the span of my lifetime there have been revolutionary discoveries and inventions and innumerable refinements of previous discoveries and inventions for the benefit of home living. It seems incredible now, when men have already orbited the earth in flying machines and are reaching out for the moon and the planets, that I was four years old when the first airplane flight in the history of mankind was made by the Wright brothers at Kitty Hawk, North Carolina. The accomplishment was not universally acclaimed. I remember hearing a sermon during my childhood in which the preacher declared that "if God had intended man to fly, God would have placed wings on him." I was twenty-four years old and a resident of New York City when I heard my first radio broadcast. The occasion was the Democratic National Convention of 1924 when neither Al Smith nor William G. McAdoo could obtain the required majority for the nomination. In the final outcome the nomination went to my fellow West Virginian, John W. Davis. (One of my most cherished souvenirs today is a ticket of admission to the 1924 Democratic National Convention in New York City.) In 1945, when I was Administrative Assistant to a United States Senator in Washington, the first nuclear bombs were dropped on Hiroshima and Nagasaki, thereby terminating the Second World War. These bombs were one result of the discovery of the principle of nuclear fission.

Famous contemporaries known to me by repute but not personally include Bell, Edison, Burroughs, Einstein, Fermi, Hitler, Groves, Oppenheimer, Lenin, Stalin, Heller, Salk, Hemingway, Faulkner, and Martin Luther King. Other contemporaries whom I have met formally are the two Roosevelts, Churchill, Halifax, Hoover, Robert A. Taft, Eisenhower, Truman, Kennedy, Johnson, Sloan, Reuther, and Henry A. duPont. Let me emphasize that I do not claim friendship with any of these people except Colonel duPont. I met them at public functions, exchanged banalities, and passed out of their lives. Colonel duPont, however, was my kinsman, benefactor, and friend. (Henry Algernon duPont, 1838-1927, was a soldier, businessman, and politician. He won the Congressional Medal of Honor in the Civil War and later in life served eighteen years as United States Senator from Delaware. I used to visit him when I was a student at Cornell University. He was then an aged man, but I have not forgotten the wisdom he tried to pass on to me during our evening talks in the great hall at Winterthur.)

The greatest social change that has occurred during my lifetime is the urbanization of the countryside. This began with the distribution of the Model T Ford automobile and the subsequent construction of all-weather roads. Roads terminated the isolation that was formerly an inescapable part of rural living. The introduction of electric power brought heat, light, air conditioning, radio, television, electric water pumps, and other electrical appliances to people who were barely aware of their existence. I happen to live within sight of the spot where I was born and where I spent my early boyhood. When I turn on the television set, I sometimes reflect that such a fantastic mode of communication was not even dreamed of when I was a boy.

Machinery and power have transformed the countryside (1) by relieving the harshness imposed by nature, (2) by minimizing regional distinctions in dress, speech, and customs, (3) by spreading the preventive and curative advances in medicine, and (4) by intensifying the feminizing of society and the consequent search for security, no matter what the cost.

Nevertheless, it is difficult, for all the displacement of hand labor, to hire and keep household help. This problem is not confined to the countryside. In our new society practically no one wants to be a servant. My wife cooks and keeps house and I tend the lawn. We are fortunate in having a once-a-week cleaning maid and a laundress, though the latter is above seventy years of age. For some years past we have maintained a separate home in Elizabeth for my mother and keeping someone with her has proved to be a continuing headache. She does not require a nurse, but housekeepers come and go, often on short notice. I have learned from experience that the only available ditch diggers in the county are the alcoholics. Alcoholics are thoroughly undependable for sustained effort, but if you have a frozen water line or some other household disaster and you happen to catch them sober, alcoholics are indispensable. This comment leads naturally to the query, "Who will ever do the dirty work in this world if the doctors find a cure for alcoholics?"

One aspect of our assembly line civilization is that people are looking and talking more and more like carbon copies of each other. The trend is world-wide. At the beginning of this century the Chinese often wore pigtails and the Japanese kimonos. Nowadays representatives of both nations, and of all nations, are likely to be barbered and clad in western style.

In the United States the urbanization of the countryside is rapidly dissipating regional differences in speech, dress, and customs. A native of Alabama still speaks the English language with an accent that distinguishes him from a native of Massachusetts, but even the difference in accent is lessening. With broadened travel horizons, higher standards of education, and the all-pervading presence of radio and television broadcasters our speech is becoming standardized, both in enunciation and in content. Old English words in common usage only fifty years ago are absent from the vocabulary of the present generation. Offhand, I recall the use of clever for hospitable, "streenious" for opinionated, and the pronoun hit for it. There have been noticeable changes in manners and forms of address. Gentlemen are not required to lift their hats when greeting a lady, possibly because so few of them wear hats. The dictum that children should be seen and not heard is largely disregarded. Children often address their parents and other adults by their first names, assuming a familiarity that was utterly unpardonable when I was a child.

Except for the cowboy, including the drugstore cowboy, and certain religious sects such as the Amish, the apparel with which both men and women adorn themselves is more a matter of individual preference and economic status than a regional characteristic. Men's work clothes in Wirt County are usually blue denims exactly like those worn by workmen in Maine and in California. Denim levis are popular among high school students and the younger generation generally for informal wear. Business suits are standardized throughout the nation. Prior to World War I, the well-dressed male had his suits made to order by custom tailors but now the tailors are employed almost exclusively to make alterations on ready-made suits at men's clothing stores. If there is a single custom tailor left in the State of West Virginia I have not found him in the classified sections of the telephone directories.

Women's fashions are always changing and to the baffled male the changes are an expression of unreasoning feminine logic. All that a male can safely say about them is that the choice is unquestionably dictated by economics. The latest styles are worn by women with access to the largest bank accounts. The styles, however, are quickly copied for general distribution. I am convinced that the average girl student at Wirt County High School could walk the streets of New York, London, or Paris without attracting attention to herself by her clothes. My wife tells me that the one really great difference she has noted in women's fashions is that nearly all women today acquire permanent hair waves and that many of them frequent public beauty shops.

The customs that once set Appalachia and rural America apart from the cities have all but disappeared. Literary societies and Institutes are dead. So are play parties and square dances. There is a recreation club in Elizabeth where young people congregate nightly for dancing. When I asked a high school girl if the club taught square dancing, she replied, "Square dancing? That's for squares." These youngsters dance to the latest records and they speak a language that is unintelligible to me.

Even the old enthusiasms have waned. The Fourth of July used to be a roaring holiday devoted to oratory, ox roasts, marching bands, fireworks, and veterans' parades. Nowadays, the Fourth of July is still a holiday, but everyone goes away to a beach, a swimming pool, or a baseball game. There are more than three hundred veterans of World War I, World War II, and the Korean War in Wirt County. From that abundance the local Commander of the American Legion has difficulty in obtaining four riflemen for a firing squad at veterans' funerals.

The increased span of life is traceable to advances in knowledge and in skills in the areas of preventive and curative medicine. On the whole, more deaths are probably postponed by preventive than by curative medicine. In my boyhood, the plagues which used to decimate Medieval Europe, including smallpox, had been largely brought under control. (Nevertheless, millions perished in the great influenza epidemic of 1918.) I still bear a scar on my right arm that represents a smallpox vaccination placed there when I was an infant. No identifiable case of smallpox has appeared in Wirt County during my lifetime. Typhoid, diphtheria, pneumonia, appendicitis, and tuberculosis were common in my boyhood and often fatal. Nowadays, when typhoid appears the health authorities seek out the source of polluted water or milk. Inoculation gives added protection. I have not heard of a local death from diphtheria for fifty years. Pneumonia is still prevalent but it is usually cured promptly by injections of sulfa drugs. Appendicitis, one of the greatest killers of all time, now demands only a brief but highly skilled surgical operation and a few days' rest in a hospital.

The simple remedy for appendicitis reminds me that the disease was one of the scourges of my ancestors. My son, in preparing a genealogical chart, encountered a number of death records which recited, "Cause of death: locked bowels." Locked bowels was the medical term for appendicitis before researchers discovered what caused locked bowels. I have two brothers and two sisters, all of whom are now past fifty years of age. Of the five children in our family, four have undergone appendectomies. I had my own appendectomy when I was eighteen years old. What these facts add up to is that without the knowledge and skills of physicians and surgeons, all but one member of my immediate family would probably have succumbed, to appendicitis alone, before reaching the age of thirty.

Tuberculosis, likewise, has been a great killer of mankind. Two of my grandparents, two aunts, and my first wife all died of tuberculosis. Today, thanks largely to preventive health measures, tuberculosis has been contained and largely conquered.

The great disease killers today are various forms of heart disease, cancer, and mental illness. The doctors have learned a great deal about heart disease with the result that, if a first attack is not fatal, the victim has a good chance of recovering and living a normal life thereafter. Two of our presidents, Eisenhower and Johnson, have suffered severe heart attacks in recent years. After a period of prescribed rest and treatment, both were able to resume normal living and an extremely burdensome work routine. Cancer so far has proved unconquerable.

Mental illness is a growing phenomenon of the times and the phenomenon is exaggerated by the increasing number of aged people who became senile from natural causes. Whether or not senility is a disease is a problem best left to the medical men, but I know from having practiced law in a community with a disproportionate number of senior citizens that aging is accompanied by its own peculiar set of economic and social problems. I would guess that I have spent at least one-eighth of my working hours in the past fifteen years trying to console old people whose chief problem was that they could not adjust themselves to the Twentieth Century. They live in the past and the mere suggestion that the present or the future ought to be different is anathema. They are not only unsympathetic toward modern industrial progress, they utterly despise the whole theory of progress. These people want to be left alone with their memories. They are incapable of absorbing a new concept of any kind, and they embody, as a class, one of the portents of failure. Of this, more later.

Senility, of course, is only one facet of mental illness. To discuss the subject in depth requires more knowledge than I possess. However, I do think that mental illness is a relative condition. A person is sane or insane only with reference to the accepted sanity of the society in which he or she lives. As a one-fourth American Indian, and for that very reason a more devoted partisan of the white man than the white man himself, I am becoming more convinced every day that the modern breed of white men is showing signs of physical and moral deterioration.

The increased use of machinery, the lengthened span of life, and the phenomenal skill of physicians, surgeons and dentists, have all contributed to the feminization of our society. I use the word feminization to denote a state of mind rather than a sexual aberration. In modern society every effort has been made to assure that women have equal rights with men in citizenship and in property. The theory of equality between the sexes, which is justified on the principle of universal liberty and equality, conveniently overlooks the physiological fact that every atom of a woman's body is different from the same atom in a man's body. The natural function of women is to carry on the species by reproduction. To perform that function, the female requires protection during pregnancy. Women naturally seek security from the hazards and disasters of a dangerous environment. When you establish a republic in which women have the same voting rights as men and actually own more than one half of the nation's wealth, you are heading for serious trouble.

The increasing span of life appears to have increased the span of women's lives on the whole, more than the span of men's lives. At least, I can discover in Wirt County a large group of widows and a corresponding scarcity of widowers. Sometime ago I read in a newspaper column that an assessment of the general census of 1960 showed that the average married woman today will outlive her spouse by eleven years. Ordinarily, I am not impressed by columnists' figures, but my own observations have convinced me that in this instance the columnist was close to the mark. In the Beulah Hill precinct in 1962 there were nine widows and no widowers. (Eleven widows appeared on the voter's registration list for 1962, but two of these, including my own mother, actually lived outside the precinct during part of that year.) In the same precinct there were two bachelors, and no old maids. In the residential block in the village of Elizabeth to which my mother moved, there were twenty-one households in 1962. These households were occupied by ten widows, one widower, and ten married couples.

Wirt County today has less than one half the population that it had in the year 1900. During the same period the population of the United States as a whole tripled. This is migration on an excessive scale, though there is nothing new or startling about migration itself. The whole human race has been migrating one way or another since prehistoric times. What makes this migration different from any previous migration is that the increasing span of life in the Twentieth Century is creating whole communities of stay-at-homes who are already past the normal life expectancy of the year 1900. One person in four in Wirt County is above sixty years of age. Spot checks indicate that one person in twenty is above eighty years of age. The oldest male resident of Wirt County to my knowledge is ninety-six years old, the oldest female is ninety-five years old. It is a curious local manifestation, though I do not know whether the observation is supported by statistics, that men above the age of ninety tend to live longer than women. Centenarians are not unknown in Wirt County, but I know of none who live here at the present time.

The mortality tables show that persons who live to be sixty-five have an excellent chance of dying in their eighties.

Only a few reach ninety, though I have compiled a list of nine nonagenarians in Wirt County. There may be more for aged people are often immured in distant nursing homes. One of the greatest misfortunes of a hazardous lifetime is to live beyond one's allotted span. I know the case history of a woman who has outlived all her children, lost her reason, and now lives as a vegetable among strangers.

Wirt County is not yet a community of senior citizens but it is rapidly approaching that status. If the majority of those above sixty-five actually live to their eighties, if those who are in their forties and fifties continue to live here, and if the migration of young people follows the pattern of the past sixty-five years, it is easy to see what Wirt County will be thirty years from now.

Frankly, I doubt if all the factors will remain stable. Because we are so close to the expanding industrial City of Parkersburg and cities throughout the nation are expanding toward the suburbs, I think it probable that Wirt County will attract a new generation of suburbanites and resume a population growth that turned downward sixty-five years ago. This, of course, is pure conjecture, but I am fortifying my judgment by investments in real estate. The important point here is not the immediate time element but the ultimate composition by age classification. The percentage of senior citizens is increasing throughout the social fabric of the nation. With earlier retirements, with the span of life increasing each decade, one of the vital problems of today and tomorrow is: What are we going to do with the old people? The problem is exactly that because the old people, unfortunately, are not going to do anything for themselves.

That aging is a national and not a local problem was brought home to my wife and me last fall in Arizona. Both of us, technically are members of the rocking chair brigade ourselves, though we have retained sufficient energy to surmount a statewide political campaign and to make this investigation and report. We went to Arizona where we learned that whole city subdivisions are being built for the exclusive occupancy of senior citizens.

Under the guise of prospective participants, we made a

tour of one of these subdivisions, and this is what we learned. Living in the desert with the combined advantages of running water, refrigeration, and air conditioning is the easiest and most comfortable life in the world. The sun shines almost every day but the uncomfortable heat and glare are softened by air conditioning and refrigeration in living quarters and places of public congregation. The one-story houses are constructed largely of small cement blocks, of a type that I have not seen in the East, which are painted on the outside to resemble brick. The houses we inspected ranged in price from fifteen thousand dollars to thirty thousand dollars, and financing was geared to retirement income.

These subdivisions are really little cities within other cities. The one we inspected had its own shopping center, an enormous clubhouse, and a nine-hole golf course conveniently devoid of traps. Only a cripple could fail to shoot par on that course. The clubhouse was designed for all kinds of recreation. There was a swimming pool in the yard. Inside, was a theater both for movies and stage plays, a restaurant and bar, dancing rooms, card rooms, and reading rooms. There was a book, newspaper, and magazine library, though the book titles were mostly western novels, mystery novels, and love stories. There was no school, which was understandable, and no church within the community. Through questioning, I learned that some of the inmates attended church in nearby unsegregated communities. If you wished to withdraw from the world and live among people who could not digest a new idea if it was handed them on a platter, here indeed was paradise.

Withdrawal was the main attraction of the place, and, at the same time, its most repellent aspect. These houses were for sale, but, according to the prospectus, you could not buy one unless you proved that you were at least fifty years old. Children were not permitted to live on the premises, though certain visiting hours were provided. You could buy one of these houses in the belief that squalling brats, feuding in-laws, and importunate chiselers had been banned to the outer pale. You could circumscribe your circle of friends and acquaintances to people of your own age and economic attainments, confident that your check would arrive on the first day of the next month, and for the first time in your life you could indulge your whimsical fancy of saying to hell with responsibility, to hell with family, to hell with government, to hell with progress, and to hell with everything.

The truth is that thousands of retirees each year are doing exactly that. The ones who buy homes in the senior cities of Florida and the Southwest belong to the minority able to afford such extravagances. Most retirees stay at home. Of the seventy houses in the Beulah Hill precinct today forty-three have no children under twenty-one years of age, though this condition is not solely attributable to the increased life span. Here we come face to face with another product of liberal thinking, the sponsorship and practice of birth control. The percentages applicable to childless homes hold, I am confident, for Wirt County, and perhaps for rural West Virginia. A spot check of a rural community in upper New York State suggests that the same percentages may even apply to rural America as a whole.

Birth control, like chastity, is a subject that is not widely discussed in polite conversation. What is said here in that regard is based on circumstantial evidence, which, though not the best evidence, is recognized in court throughout the English speaking world. One item of circumstance is that contraceptives may be obtained cheaply and in complete privacy from vending machines. Again, there were eight more houses in the Beulah Hill precinct in 1964 than there were in 1910, yet the number of minors living in those houses had decreased by an estimated two thirds. Of course, more than fifty percent of the population of the precinct is now above forty years of age and that means that, in addition to birth control, barrenness is a factor in the declining birth rate. The circumstantial evidence of birth control practices must be gleaned from the twenty-seven families, out of seventy, who have children living in their homes. A breakdown of these families with children according to the number of children at home reads as follows:

Families and Numbers of Children

Families with one child 9

Families with two children	5
Families with three children	10
Families with four children	1
Families with five children	2
Families with more than five children	0
Total	27

Though I cannot furnish exact figures for all the families in the precinct for the year 1910, I remember our neighbors distinctly because the children played together and attended the same school. There were five children in my family. Our five nearest neighbors had 7, 6, 9, 6 and 8 children respectively, a total of 41 for the six households. Some of the families grew even larger later on. I have no children at home now and my five nearest neighbors have a total of 4 children between them. Birth control, obviously, is no longer a prerogative of the cities or of any class or classes of our society. It must be practiced widely in the very rural communities that in former times contributed so greatly to the natural increase in our population.

The foreseeable consequences of these trends are frightening. Residents of cities have long raised small families, possibly for lack of living space. City dwellers have always been more sophisticated than country people in birth control procedures. In the countryside, with the whole wide outdoors to turn them loose in, children have traditionally multiplied. The Anglo-Saxon, Scotch-Irish, French and German elements on the eastern frontier reared enormous families. Their descendants who pushed west and those who stayed behind did the same. The decimating migration of farm hands to industrial cities that has taken place in my lifetime occurred because there was too much population and too little productive land. Now, through the combination of an increasing life span and the widespread practice of birth control, the traditional sources of white population increase are drying up.

Epilogue

THIS BOOK was written at odd intervals over a period of nearly two years from February, 1964, to December 1965. In the interim, I was busily occupied with other pursuits, that is to say with winding up my own law practice, and, during 1964, with a ten months long political campaign. The materials were assembled over a period of fifteen years, though in a larger sense I have been assembling the materials all my life. My character and accomplishments, such as they are, have been molded in the culture and traditions of Wirt County and of Appalachia.

Nevertheless, since I wrote the first chapter nearly two years ago I find that some of the material is already obsolete. The following corrections are necessary.

(1) Three of the householders listed in the Beulah Hill Precinct, Arthur Nutter, Okey Turner, and Lizzie Gibson, are now deceased.

(2) In 1965 the Legislature of West Virginia passed a law increasing the salaries of school teachers. To the salaries of School Teachers set forth in the chapter on Education, it is now necessary to add approximately four hundred dollars a year to the salaries of teachers and one thousand dollars a year to the salaries of principals.

(3) Congress has superseded the Kerr-Mills Act, which provides hospital and medical care to a limited number of aged persons, by a general provision for aged persons who become ill, known as Medicare.

(4) There is a new footnote to crime. In the fall of 1965, a former Wirt County superintendent of schools was convicted of embezzlement of public funds and a former assistant high school principal was convicted of falsifying records. Both were sentenced to the penitentiary and both are now on bond pending an appeal. It is a curious commentary on

the moral climate of our times that law-abiding Wirt County should find its criminals among the class of people best qualified by intelligence and education for community leaders.

(5) West Virginia now has a birth control law, an ironic development for the only State in the Union that is losing population in 1965. If this study has knowledge value for the future, I think the value will lie in identification of the twin follies of aging and birth control. The generation that proclaims publicly that God is dead and that relies more and more on what men can do for themselves is possibly ill advised. God may be dead only in the sense that this generation has rejected him. The historical process, as it is imperfectly understood, seems to show that neglect of religion is a prelude to calamity and disaster, which in turn lead to a new interest in religion. Religion aside, the combination of a steadily increasing span of life with the widespread practice of birth control would seem to constitute, if unchecked, a sure prescription for mass suicide.

Appendix

Data on Counties

DATA ON COUNTIES

County	County Seat	Formed	Area (Sq. Mi.)	Magisterial Districts	Voting Precincts	*Congressional District	Senatorial District	Judicial Circuit
Barbour	Philippi	1843	345.41	8	33	2	15	19
Berkeley	Martinsburg	1772	324.78	7	45	2	16	23
Boone	Madison	1847	506	5	40	3	7	25
Braxton	Sutton	1836	519.70	4	37	1	12	14
Brooke	Wellsburg	1797	92.50	3	32	1	1	1
Cabell	Huntington	1809	285.95	7	115	4	5	6
Calhoun	Grantsville	1856	280.20	5	17	1	3	5
Clay	Clay	1858	346.61	5	25	3	4	14
Doddridge	West Union	1845	321.61	8	17	1	2	3
Fayette	Fayetteville	1831	666.50	7	100	5	11	12
Gilmer	Glenville	1845	342.40	4	16	1	13	14
Grant	Petersburg	1866	478	3	16	2	15	21
Greenbrier	Lewisburg	1778	1,022.80	10	59	2	11	11
Hampshire	Romney	1753	641.44	7	28	2	16	22
Hancock	New Cumberland	1848	88.55	3	36	1	1	1
Hardy	Moorefield	1786	575.52	4	16	2	16	22
Harrison	Clarksburg	1784	417.85	10	123	1	13	15

County	County Seat	Formed	Area (Sq. Mi.)	Magisterial Districts	Voting Precincts	*Congressional District	Senatorial District	Judicial Circuit
Jackson	Ripley	1831	471.98	5	35	4	4	5
Jefferson	Charles Town	1801	212.41	5	25	2	16	23
Kanawha	Charleston	1788	913.38	10	285	3	8	13
Lewis	Weston	1816	391.35	5	42	1	13	26
Lincoln	Hamlin	1867	437.04	8	33	4	7	25
Logan	Logan	1824	455.82	3	82	4	7	7
Marion	Fairmont	1842	313.55	7	95	1	14	16
Marshall	Moundsville	1835	315.26	9	58	1	2	2
Mason	Point Pleasant	1804	445.75	10	41	4	4	29
McDowell	Welch	1858	538.40	6	103	5	6	8
Mercer	Princeton	1837	423.91	5	87	5	10	9
Mineral	Keyser	1866	330	6	29	2	16	21
Mingo	Williamson	1895	423.50	8	44	5	6	24
Monongalia	Morgantown	1776	368.82	7	71	2	14	17
Monroe	Union	1799	473.80	6	25	5	10	11
Morgan	Berkeley Springs	1820	231.26	6	18	2	16	23
Nicholas	Summersville	1818	656.77	7	30	3	12	28
Ohio	Wheeling	1776	100	10	131	1	1	1
Pendleton	Franklin	1788	696.88	6	14	2	12	22
Pleasants	St. Marys	1851	134.65	6	14	4	3	3

County	County Seat	Formed	Area (Sq. Mi.)	Magisterial Districts	Voting Precincts	*Congressional District	Senatorial District	Judicial Circuit
Pocahontas	Marlinton	1821	942.61	4	21	2	12	11
Preston	Kingwood	1818	653.88	8	55	2	15	18
Putnam	Winfield	1848	350.57	6	35	4	4	29
Raleigh	Beckley	1850	610.15	7	113	3	9	10
Randolph	Elkins	1787	1,046.34	9	44	2	12	20
Ritchie	Harrisville	1843	455.27	4	28	4	3	3
Roane	Spencer	1856	486.20	7	32	4	4	5
Summers	Hinton	1871	367.76	6	30	5	10	11
Taylor	Grafton	1844	177.19	6	31	1	15	19
Tucker	Parsons	1856	421.67	7	19	2	15	21
Tyler	Middlebourne	1814	260.12	6	19	4	2	2
Upshur	Buckhannon	1851	354.86	6	25	2	15	26
Wayne	Wayne	1842	517.88	7	48	4	5	24
Webster	Webster Springs	1860	558.60	4	24	2	12	14
Wetzel	New Martinsville	1846	360.47	7	37	1	2	2
Wirt	Elizabeth	1848	234.41	7	16	4	3	4
Wood	Parkersburg	1798	377.82	10	95	4	3	4
Wyoming	Pineville	1850	507.30	7	42	5	9	27
TOTALS			24,282.45	353	2,731	5	16	29

*Effective January 1, 1963, under apportionment 1961.

Wirt County Court Levy Estimate
1964-1965

1964-65:

WIRT COUNTY COURT LEVY ESTIMATE

State of West Virginia,
County of Wirt, to-wit:

At a regular session of the County Court of Wirt County, held on the 16th day of March, 1964, Present E. W. Allman, President, and Hubert Full and Donald Lockhart, Commissioners.

In accordance with Section 10, Article 8, Chapter 67, Acts 1933, Second Extraordinary Session, the Court proceeded to make an estimate of the amounts necessary to be raised by a levy of taxes for the current fiscal year, and doth determine and estimate the several amounts to be as follows:

GENERAL COUNTY PURPOSES ESTIMATE

Estimate Form No. 1

ESTIMATED RECEIPTS:

The amount due, and the amount that will become due and collectible from every source during the current fiscal year, EXCEPT FROM THE LEVY OF TAXES to be made for the current year upon the county as a whole and upon any district of the county for which the levies are laid by the County Court.

Balance due fund from Sheriff (Estimated)	$ 4,560.00
Delinquent Taxes, Redemptions and Sales	350.00
Earnings, Sheriff	50.00
Earnings, Clerk County Court	2,500.00
Earnings, Clerk Circuit Court	300.00
Miscellaneous Receipts	450.00
Total Estimated Receipts	$ 8,210.00

ESTIMATED CURRENT EXPENSES:

Clerk of the County Court	$ 2,400.00
Deputy Clerk County Court, 1 in Number, Assistants and Employees	1,900.00
Clerk of the Circuit Court	1,800.00
Sheriff and Treasurer	3,050.00
Deputy Sheriffs, 2 in Number, Assistants and Employees	1,925.00
Expense Serving Processes and Making Arrests	400.00
Prosecuting Attorney	1,500.00
Assessor	2,400.00
Deputy Assessors, 2 in Number, Assistants and Employees	2,330.00
Assessor's Mileage	150.00
Assessor's Agricultural Report	110.00
County Commissioners	1,920.00

County Agricultural Agents, Clerk, 1 in Number		1,200.00
Audits by Tax Commissioner		1,000.00
Expense of Circuit Court		2,600.00
Expense of Justices' Courts		50.00
Jail Expense		100.00
Feeding Prisoners		475.00
Court House Expense		200.00
Janitor Court House and Jail, 1 in Number		1,200.00
Furniture and Fixtures		100.00
Repairs		500.00
Water, Light, Fuel and Ice		1,200.00
Record Books		700.00
Stationery and Office Supplies		500.00
Postage		200.00
Freight and Drayage		10.00
Advertising		500.00
Insurance		100.00
Premiums on Official Bonds		370.00
Telephones and Telegraphs		750.00
Expenses—General Election		2,000.00
General Relief Fund		2,100.00
Lunacy		200.00
Inquests		100.00
Transportation and Support of Inmates: Penal and Other Institutions		2,400.00
Vital Statistics		50.00
Fire Department (Contribution)		500.00
Social Security		800.00
Contingencies (Mandatory Only)		547.00
A—Total Current Expenses		$ 40,337.00
Estimated Outstanding Obligations:		
Orders	$ 1,580.00	
Bills	158.00	
Estimated total amount outstanding June 30, 1964	$ 1,738.00	
B—Amount of above obligations proposed to be paid from Current Levy		$ 1,738.00
Total estimated disbursements (A + B)		$ 42,075.00
Less estimated receipts	$ 8,210.00	
Net amount to be raised by levy	33,865.00	
Total Receipts		$ 42,075.00

CLASS	Assessed Valuation	Rate of Levy Proposed
Number I		
Personal Property	$ 965,445.00	14.3¢
Public Utility Property	61,100.00	14.3¢
Total Class No. I	$1,026,545.00	
Number II		
Real Estate	$4,534,040.00	28.6¢
Number III		
Real Estate	$1,250,240.00	57.2¢
Personal Property	677,485.00	57.2¢
Public Utility Property	1,023,000.00	57.2¢
Total Class No. III	$2,950,725.00	
Number IV		
Real Estate	$ 364,540.00	57.2¢
Personal Property	282,015.00	57.2¢
Public Utility Property	111,300.00	57.2¢
Total Class No. IV	$ 757,855.00	
Total Valuation	$9,269,165.00	

STATE OF WEST VIRGINIA,
COUNTY OF WIRT, to-wit:

I, Lella Ingram, Clerk of the County Court of said County, do hereby certify that the foregoing are true copies from the record of orders made and entered by said Court on the 16th day of March, 1964.

Given under my hand this 24th day of March, 1964.

LELLA INGRAM, Clerk
County Court, Wirt County

Wirt County
Board of Education
Levy Estimate
1964-1965

WIRT COUNTY BOARD OF EDUCATION LEVY ESTIMATE

STATE OF WEST VIRGINIA,
COUNTY OF WIRT, to-wit:

At a Regular Session of the Board of Education of Wirt County, held at the regular meeting place thereof on the 19th day of March, 1964, Present: George Robinson, President of said Board of Education, and John Hale, Clyde Cale, Donald Hickman, and Preston Andrick, Members.

In accordance with Section 12, Article 8, Chapter 67, Acts, 1933, Second Extraordinary Session, as amended by Section 12, Article 8, Chapter 142, Acts, 1961, Regular Session, the Board proceeded to make an estimate of the amounts necessary to be raised by a levy of taxes for the current fiscal year, and doth determine and estimate the several amounts to be as follows:

SCHOOL CURRENT—ESTIMATED RECEIPTS

(1) The amount due and the amount that will become due and collectible during the current fiscal year EXCEPT FROM THE LEVY OF TAXES to be made for the year:

Amount Due from Sheriff	$ 3,000.00
Taxation and Appropriations Received (Other than net tax collections)	300.00
Other Revenue from Local Sources	2,000.00
State Funds	219,150.00
Federal Funds Received Through State	5,842.00
Non-Revenue Receipts	700.00
Total Estimated Receipts	$230,992.00

(2) The total of all other expenditures to be paid out of the receipts for the current fiscal year with proper allowance for delinquent taxes, exonerations and contingencies:

SCHOOL CURRENT—ESTIMATED DISBURSEMENTS

ADMINISTRATION:

Salaries	$ 14,470.00
Contracted Services	1,500.00
Other Current Expense	1,900.00
Total Administration	$ 17,870.00

INSTRUCTION:

Salaries:

Principals	$ 31,562.00
Teachers	159,900.00
Other Instructional Staff	4,855.00
Secretarial and Clerical Assts.	2,558.00
Teachers Sick Leave	1,000.00
Total Salaries	$199,875.00

Other Current Expense:	
Textbooks	$ 2,850.00
School Libraries and Audiovisual Materials	1,200.00
Teaching Supplies	2,000.00
Other Expenses	1,000.00
Total Other Current Expenses	$ 7,050.00
Total Instruction	$206,925.00
PUPIL TRANSPORTATION SERVICES:	
Salaries	$ 35,687.00
Replacement of Vehicles	9,000.00
Pupil Transportation Insurance	975.00
Expenditures in Lieu of Transportation	450.00
Other Expenses for Operation and Maintenance	10,436.00
Total Transportation	$ 56,548.00
OPERATION OF PLANT:	
Salaries	$ 7,500.00
Heat for Buildings	4,000.00
Utilities (Except Heat for Buildings)	6,200.00
Supplies	1,300.00
Other Expenses	100.00
Total Operation of Plant	$ 19,100.00
MAINTENANCE OF PLANT:	
Salaries	$ 4,300.00
Contracted Services	75.00
Other Expenses	2,400.00
Total Maintenance of Plant	$ 6,775.00
FIXED CHARGES:	
School District Contributions to Employee Retirement	$ 9,000.00
Insurance and Judgments	6,703.00
Total Fixed Charges	$ 15,703.00
COMMUNITY SERVICES:	
4-H Club:	
Salaries	$ 500.00

Other Expenses		175.00
Total 4-H Club		$ 675.00
Adult Education:		
Salaries		$ 588.00
Total Adult Education		$ 588.00
Total Community Services		$ 1,263.00
CAPITAL OUTLAY:		
Sites	$ 2,500.00	
Buildings	8,000.00	
Equipment	2,000.00	
Total Capital Outlay		$ 12,500.00

SCHOOL CURRENT EXPENSES—RECAPITULATION

1. Administration	$ 17,870.00
2. Instruction	206,925.00
3.	.00
4.	.00
5. Pupil Transportation Services	56,548.00
6. Operation of Plant	19,100.00
7. Maintenance of Plant	6,775.00
8. Fixed Charges	15,703.00
9.	.00
10. Community Services	1,263.00
11. Capital Outlay	12,500.00
12.	.00
13.	.00
14. Total School Current Expenditures	$336,694.00
Estimated Outstanding Obligations June 30, 1964	
15. Former Years Orders	$ .00
16. Current Year Orders	3,000.00
17. Encumbrances and Bills Unpaid	.00
18. Total Orders Outstanding, Encumbrances and Bills Unpaid	$ 3,000.00
19. Amount of Above Obligations Proposed to be Paid from Current Levy	$ 3,000.00
20. Total Estimated Disbursements Lines 14 and 19	$339,694.00
21. Estimated Receipts	$230,992.00

22. Net Amount to be Raised by a Levy of Taxes		$108,702.00
23. Total Lines 21 and 22 (Must agree with Line 20)		$339,694.00

SCHOOL CURRENT—EXPENDITURES ESTIMATE

	Assessed Valuation	Rate of Levy Proposed
CLASS NUMBER I		
Personal Property	$ 965,445.00	22.95¢
Public Utility Property	61,100.00	
Total Class No. I	$1,026,545.00	
CLASS NUMBER II		
Real Estate	$4,534,040.00	45.90¢
CLASS NUMBER III		
Real Estate	$1,250,240.00	91.80¢
Personal Property	677,485.00	
Public Utility Property	1,023,000.00	
Total Class No. III	$2,950,725.00	
CLASS NUMBER IV		
Real Estate	$ 364,540.00	91.80¢
Personal Property	282,015.00	
Public Utility Property	111,300.00	
Total Class No. IV	$ 757,855.00	
Total Valuation	$9,269,165.00	

SCHOOL BOND PURPOSES ESTIMATE

	Assessed Valuation	Rate of Levy Proposed
CLASS NUMBER I		
Personal Property	$ 965,445.00	16.31¢
Public Utility Property	61,100.00	
Total Class No. I	$1,026,545.00	
CLASS NUMBER II		
Real Estate	$4,534,040.00	32.62¢
CLASS NUMBER III		
Real Estate	$1,250,240.00	65.24¢
Personal Property	677,485.00	
Public Utility Property	1,023,000.00	
Total Class No. III	$2,950,725.00	
CLASS NUMBER IV		
Real Estate	$ 364,540.00	65.24¢

	Assessed Valuation	Rate of Levy Proposed
Personal Property	282,015.00	
Public Utility Property	111,300.00	
Total Class No. IV	$ 757,855.00	
Total Valuation	$9,269,165.00	

EXCESS LEVY ESTIMATE

	Assessed Valuation	Rate of Levy Proposed
CLASS NUMBER I		
Personal Property	$ 965,445.00	22.95¢
Public Utility Property	61,100.00	
Total Class No. I	$1,026,545.00	
CLASS NUMBER II		
Real Estate	$4,534,040.00	45.90¢
CLASS NUMBER III		
Real Estate	$1,250,240.00	91.80¢
Personal Property	677,485.00	
Public Utility Property	1,023,000.00	
Total Class No. III	$2,950,725.00	
CLASS NUMBER IV		
Real Estate	$ 364,540.00	91.80¢
Personal Property	282,015.00	
Public Utility Property	111,300.00	
Total Class No. IV	$ 757,855.00	
Total Valuation	$9,269,165.00	

STATE OF WEST VIRGINIA,
COUNTY OF WIRT, TO-WIT:

I, Charles A. Cline, Secretary of the Board of Education of said County do hereby certify that the foregoing are true copies from the record of orders made and entered by said Board on the 19th day of March, 1964.

Given under my hand this 19th day of March, 1964.

CHARLES A. CLINE
Secretary, Board of Education
Wirt County

Municipality of Elizabeth
Levy Estimate
1964-1965

STATE OF WEST VIRGINIA,
COUNTY OF WIRT,
MUNICIPALITY OF ELIZABETH, TO-WIT:

At a special session of the council of the municipality of Elizabeth held in the council chambers thereof, in the Town building on the 27th day of March, 1964, there were present Charles A. Cline, Mayor, Eloise Cline, Recording Officer, and Harley Lee, Albert Cain, Foster McClung, Walter Dailey, Earl Villers and Frank Munday of the council of said municipality.

In accordance with Section 14, Article 8, Chapter 67, Acts 1933, Second Extraordinary Session, the Council proceeded to make an estimate of the amounts necessary to be raised by levy of taxes for the current fiscal year, and doth determine and estimate the several amounts to be as follows:

CURRENT REGULAR MUNICIPAL PURPOSES ESTIMATE

Estimate Form No. 1

ESTIMATED RECEIPTS:

(1) The amount due and the amount that will become due and collectible from every source during the fiscal year, EXCEPT FROM THE LEVY OF TAXES to be made for the year.

Balance in Hands of City Treasurer (Estimated)	$ 3,500.00
Balance in Hands of Sheriff (Estimated)	1,350.00
Redemption and Sale of Delinquent Lands	.00
Police Fines and Costs	350.00
Permits—Building, Street, Sewer and Other	.00
Parking Meters	3,600.00
Paving and Sewer Assessments (Advanced from General Fund)	5,000.00
Federal Housing	.00
Rents, Buildings and Concessions	.00
Sale of Cemetery Lots	.00
Taxes: Gross Sales	.00
Capitation and Dog	100.00
Franchise	.00
Consumers' Sales (Liquor)	2,500.00
Amusement	.00
Fees: Electrical, Plumbing and Other	.00
Crematory and Garbage	.00
Airport	.00
Parking Lot	.00
Library	.00
Market House	.00

Licenses:	
Electricians and Plumbers	.00
Drivers	.00
General	100.00
Miscellaneous	240.00
Total Estimated Receipts to Page E-6	$ 16,740.00
ESTIMATED CURRENT EXPENDITURES:	
Salary of Mayor	$ 50.00
Salary of Recorder or Clerk	50.00
Salary of Treasurer	.00
Salary of Police Judge	.00
Salary of City Attorney	100.00
Salary of City Auditor	.00
Salary of Councilmen or Commissioners	108.00
Salaries of Assistants and Clerks	.00
Salaries of Chief of Police	1,200.00
New Equipment Police Department	.00
General Expenses Police Department	100.00
Policemen's Pension Fund	.00
Salaries and Expense Feeding Prisoners	100.00
Salaries of Chief and —— Firemen	.00
General Expense Fire Department	1,500.00
Firemen's Pension Fund	.00
Salaries Health Commissioner and Employees	.00
New Equipment Health Department	.00
General Expenses Health Department	.00
Salaries, Crematory and Garbage Employees	.00
New Equipment Crematory and Garbage Department	.00
General Expenses Crematory and Garbage Department	.00
Janitors' Salaries and Supplies	25.00
Repairs to Jail and City Buildings	100.00
Furniture, Fixtures and Office Machines	.00
Stationery, Office Supplies and Equipment	100.00
Postage	40.00
Water—Fire Protection, Streets and Sewers	.00
Water—City Building and Other Purposes	.00
Light for Street Lighting	1,920.00
Light—City Building, Traffic Lights, Etc.	30.00

Repairs, Street and Traffic Lights	.00
Fuel—Heating City Building	190.00
Telephone and Telegraph (All Departments)	25.00
Rents—City Hall and Other Buildings	.00
Legal Publications	130.00
Insurance on City Building and Other Property	600.00
Premiums on Policemen's and Official Bonds	40.00
Election Expenses	.00
Attorneys' Fees, Court Costs and Damages	.00
Salaries, Engineering Department	.00
General Expense, Engineering Department	.00
Salaries and Wages all Street Employees	.00
New Equipment Street Department	.00
Materials, Supplies and Expenses, Street Department	1,000.00
Maintenance of Sewers, Salaries and Supplies	.00
Construction of New Streets, Sidewalks and Sewers	10,000.00
Workmen's Compensation Premiums	25.00
Audit by Tax Commissioner	100.00
Refunding Erroneous Payments	.00
Parking Meters, Salaries, Supplies and Expenses	1,975.00
Parks and Playgrounds, Salaries, Supplies and Expenses	.00
Cemetery—Salaries, Supplies and Expenses	.00
Traveling and Car Expenses of City Officials	.00
Parking Lot, Salaries, Supplies and Expenses	.00
Market House, Salaries, Supplies and Expenses	.00
Airport, Salaries, Supplies and Expenses	.00
Library, Salaries, Supplies and Expenses	.00
Social Security	250.00
Public Employees Retirement	75.00
Contingent Expenses (Mandatory Only)	1,430.00
A—Total Current Expenses	$ 22,063.00

Estimated Former Year's Obligations:		
Orders Outstanding	$ .00	
Unpaid Bills	300.00	
Estimated total former year's obligations	$ 300.00	
B—Amount of unpaid obligations to be paid from current levy		$ 300.00
Total estimated disbursements (A + B)		$ 22,363.00
Less estimated receipts brought forward from page E-4	$ 16,740.00	
Net amount to be raised by levy (page E-7)	5,623.00	
Total Receipts		$ 22,363.00

CLASS	Assessed Valuation	Rate of Levy Proposed
Number I		
Personal Property	$ 322,735.00	12.5¢
Public Utility Property	14,800.00	12.5¢
Total Class No. I	$ 337,535.00	
Number II		
Real Estate	$ 683,950.00	25.0¢
Number IV		
Real Estate	$ 364,540.00	50.0¢
Personal Property	282,015.00	50.0¢
Public Utility Property	111,300.00	50.0¢
Total Class No. IV	$ 757,855.00	
Total Valuation	$1,779,340.00	

STATE OF WEST VIRGINIA,
COUNTY OF WIRT,
MUNICIPALITY OF ELIZABETH, TO-WIT:

I, Eloise Cline, Recording Officer of said municipality, do hereby certify that the foregoing are true copies from the Record of orders made and entered by the council of said municipality on the 27th day of March, 1964.

ELOISE CLINE, Clerk

An Automobile Trip West
1963

On December 1, 1963, my wife and I began a month's vacation and started by automobile for my son's residence in Mesa, Arizona. I drove my 1961 Falcon stationwagon and we carried a large number of presents for my son and his wife.

We left our home in Wirt County about ten o'clock a.m. on December 1st, which was a Sunday. There had been a light snow the night before which covered the hills and the fields, but the roads were clear and the sun was shining. We had made up our minds to make the trip by easy stages and to visit interesting points along the way which we had never seen. We drove first to Elizabeth then took a back road through the country to Ripley. Thence we followed State Route No. 2 to Point Pleasant and Huntington, West Virginia. We did not have lunch until late in the afternoon when we reached Ashland, Kentucky, on U. S. Route 60. After lunch we drove on Route 60 to Winchester, Kentucky, and then turned South to Richmond, Kentucky, where we arrived about dark and where we spent the night at the Glendon Hotel in Richmond.

Richmond, Kentucky, is a college town and we found an interesting eating place there. It was in an old brick residence with extremely high ceilings and doors and they served a smorgasbord meal for $1.00. When we learned that the place customarily served college students all they could eat for $1.00 we wondered how they could stay in business. The next morning, December 2nd, we lunched at a drug store in the Glendon Hotel building and set forth for Hodgenville, Kentucky, which is near the birthplace of Abraham Lincoln. We arrived at Lincoln's birthplace in the midmorning and I was astonished to discover that the log cabin in which Lincoln is supposed to have been born is enclosed in a granite building with fifty-six steps leading to the entrance, each step representing a year of Lincoln's life. The morning was cold and there were only a few visitors about. This is a national monument under the jurisdiction of the National Park Service, and we found a solitary girl behind the desk in the large room where the cabin is enclosed. She told us that only four visitors had been there the day before and that we were the first that morning.

The cabin itself is a genuine frontier cabin with a stick chimney. It is very small and one wonders how the frontiersmen reared families under such conditions. The thought occurred to me that the American people have made a God of Lincoln and in doing so have followed the myth making religious instinct of the human race. Without detracting in any way from Lincoln's accomplishments, it seems absurd that the government would preserve a frontier cabin under such luxurious conditions solely because Lincoln is supposed to have been born in it.

From Lincoln's birthplace we travelled to Mammoth Cave near Bowling Green, Kentucky, and took the short tour. This short tour is strenuous enough in Mammoth Cave as one must clamber up and down narrow and steep stairways. We were duly impressed by the stalactites and stalagmites, but I think that the really impressive thing about Mammoth Cave is the presence of small fish there which have no eyes. These fish are no larger than what we would call minnows, about one and one-half to two inches long and are white in color. Since the cave is in complete darkness except for artificial lighting, and eyes therefore are useless, the presence of these blind fish is one more confirmation of the principle of adaptation as the same was expressed in the Darwinian theory of evolution. Another curious circumstance in this cave is that where electric lights have been installed, as they have been for the benefit of tourists, the walls of the caves are covered with algae. I never knew before that algae would grow in artificial light. The circumstance must have some bearing on the mystery of life itself.

From Mammoth Cave, where we spent perhaps three hours we drove on to Russellville, Kentucky, and spent the night at a motel.

The next day, December 3rd, we drove to Fairview, Kentucky, to see the monument erected in honor of Jefferson Davis, President of the Confederate States of America, at his birthplace. Having visited Lincoln's birthplace we thought it was only fair to visit the birthplace of his adversary during the Civil War. We found there a little village with an enormous monument perhaps three hundred feet high. The weather being very cold, the monument was closed, but the caretaker who lived nearby saw us and took us inside. The first thing we noted was the difference between the management of National Historical Sites by the Federal Government and the management of this historical site which is operated by the State of Kentucky. The caretaker is obviously a political appointee with no historical knowledge of the Civil War nor much of anything else. We bought some post cards in the souvenir room operated at the base of the monument and took the elevator to the top. From there we could see all over the surrounding countryside. In this room we found a number of pictures of Confederate Generals, some of which were improperly labeled. To my astonishment I found that the picture of General Stonewall Jackson bore the label of General Imboden and General Imboden's picture bore the label of some general I never heard of. When we explained this to the guide he seemed surprised that the labels were wrong, and I believe he thought we were wrong.

From Fairview we struck South across Tennessee on a road which led us eventually to the Shiloh Battlefield in Southern Tennessee. This again is a National Historical Site and we found it one of the best marked battlefields in the country. The people at the Visitors Center asked us to go to a darkened room where a moving picture was shown which was a re-enactment of the battle. At the same time we were furnished with maps of the surrounding countryside which showed where all the important fighting had taken place. The battlefield contains roads for an eleven mile automobile drive with markers to show where the action took place. When the drive was finished we felt that we knew more about the Battle of Shiloh then than we had ever learned from the history books. That night we drove on to Corinth, Mississippi, where we spent the night at a motel, the name of which escapes me.

The next day, December 4th, we drove South from Corinth, Mississippi, to Oxford, Mississippi, where we took pictures of the buildings of the University of Mississippi which has been so much in the news during the past year because of the riots which took place there over integration. All was quiet at the University.

Before leaving Oxford we stopped at a filling station and I asked the attendant where William Faulkner was buried. The attendant consulted another attendant and both of them said they had never heard of him. I then asked the man who appeared to be the owner of the filling station and he gave me the information that William Faulkner was buried in a cemetery nearby and also told me how to reach the Faulkner home. We drove to the home first and had a great deal of trouble finding it as it is located in a wooded area off the highway. We finally had to get a fellow motorist to guide us there.

The first thing we noticed was a sign at the gate which said "No Trespassing." The woman who had guided us there told us that the building was now occupied by William Faulkner's wife and her sister, but that she thought the notice was put there to keep people from going to the house. She thought there would be no objection to going inside the gate and taking a picture, which we did and were not molested in any way. The house is a very large old-fashioned house with double chimneys, and we saw no one whatever about the place.

Returning to Oxford we sought out the cemetery and I drove through it without finding William Faulkner's grave. I recalled seeing a photograph in Life magazine which showed that the grave was dug at the foot of a hill. There was a sign in the cemetery which said a new section was at the foot of the hill, so I drove to the new section. The only people in sight were a white man who was sitting in a truck and two Negroes who were using shovels to fill a grave. I stopped my car and walked over to the white man who was sitting behind the wheel of the truck. To my surprise he did not roll down the window and when I motioned for him to roll down the window so that I could talk to him I found that his hand was shaking. He seemed to be scared about something. When I asked him where Faulkner was buried he pointed right behind the truck and said "There".

A new marble slab was erected there and a monument. We took a picture of the monument and the slab. The monument itself simply had the name Faulkner on it and the slab had the name William Cuthbert Faulkner with the date of his birth and the date of his death. The only inscription as I recall it from memory was "Beloved, Go With God." Nothing was said about his being a world famous author or the winner of the Nobel Prize for literature.

Leaving Oxford we proceeded to Jackson, Mississippi, where Dr. Curtis P. Artz, who used to be at Grantsville, West Virginia, is a professor at the University of Mississippi Medical School. I looked up his telephone number in the telephone directory and called his home from a telephone booth at a gasoline filling station. His wife, Lucy Artz, answered. When I told her who we were she said that Dr. Artz had gone to Galveston, Texas, where he had just taken a new position with the University of Texas, that the children were all gone, and that she was staying behind to sell the house. She invited us out for a cup of coffee and gave us directions how to get there. We spent possibly a half hour talking to Lucy about old times and about Curt's new job in Texas. It seems that in addition to being a professor of surgery at the University of Texas Medical School he will also be the head of a new Shriner's Children's Hospital in Galveston. She said that they had been in Italy, Yugoslavia, Czechoslovakia, Poland, and Germany during the summer and that Curt had become a recognized authority on burns, including atomic burns. He has written a book on the subject which seems to be authoritative among doctors and is writing another book which will come out soon. They have three children. The oldest daughter is taking journalism at the University of Iowa, the son is in some preparatory school in Connecticut, and the youngest daughter has been attending parochial school in Jackson.

This parochial school was a surprise to me as Lucy used to be a Protestant. Later in talking to my son in Arizona, I learned that Lucy had been converted to Catholicism and that she and Curt had had a great deal of trouble about it. My son said they almost got divorced. The two older children have been reared as Protestants, but the youngest child is being reared as a Catholic. After leaving their home we drove through Jackson again on Route 80 toward Vicksburg. As night was approaching we stopped at the Bill Will Motel between Jackson and Vicksburg.

The next morning, December 5th, we stopped briefly at the Vicksburg Battlefield which is also a National Historical Site and is very well run. We did not attempt to go over this battlefield as we had been there on a previous occasion, but we did pick up some literature. We crossed the Mississippi River at Vicksburg and drove West on U. S. Route 80 to Bossier City, Louisiana, which is a suburb of Shreveport. We spent the night at the Airview Motel at Bossier City.

During all of the trip through Kentucky, Tennessee, Mississippi and Louisiana we found that the weather was unseasonably cold. At Jackson and Shreveport the temperature was about twenty-two degrees (Fahrenheit) above zero, but there was no snow and there was plenty of sunshine all the way.

Throughout the trip we had an opportunity to observe the great social change that has come over American motorists in the past generation. Only thirty years ago every small town in the country had at least one hotel and often three or four hotels to accommodate the travelling public. Nowadays the smaller villages often have no hotel at all and a place like Richmond, Kentucky, with a population of perhaps fifteen thousand will have only one hotel and a number of motels. On this trip we stopped at only two hotels and the rest of the time we used motels. One great advantage of a hotel is that it usually has additional service available such as barber shops, shoe shine parlors, and tailor shops where pressing and cleaning can be obtained quickly. It also has a lobby and a dining room where guests can congregate and, if they wish to do so, can get acquainted with each other. Motels, on the other hand, are much less hospitable and at the same time much more efficient. Both hotels and motels generally have a television set in the room, though we found one motel in Graham, Texas, without a television set. Prices for rooms vary with the hotels in general being cheaper than motels. A double room for myself and my wife at the Glendon Hotel in Richmond, Kentucky, cost $6.00 with tax of $.24. We found both hotels and motels charging a consumers sales tax wherever we went. In fact I am inclined to believe that the consumers sales tax is now general throughout the United States. Motel prices on the other hand varied from $3.00 per night in Graham, Texas, to $10.00 per night in Pasadena, California. The Graham, Texas, motel was the worst we saw. It was clean, but it lacked a television set and the place was cheaply furnished. Generally speaking, motel rooms with a single double bed, a bath, telephone, and a television set run seven to eight dollars per night. We always tried to find a motel which had a gasoline filling station nearby and also a place to eat. The motels lacking these accessories were much cheaper as was the case in Graham, Texas.

From Bossier City, Louisiana, on December 6, 1963, we followed U. S. Route No. 80 into the State of Texas. We were tempted to drive through Dallas and Fort Worth in order to see the place where President Kennedy was recently assassinated, but upon consideration thought that such a journey would be motivated only by morbid curosity. Besides, we had been through Dallas and Fort Worth before and the traffic there is something to think about. We decided therefore to skirt Dallas and Fort Worth and bore north to Greenville, Decatur and Jacksboro, Texas, with the thought of reaching U. S. Route No. 180 at Breckenridge, Texas. This was a part of Texas that neither of us had seen before and we were much impressed by it. There are many oil fields, cotton farms, and cattle ranches along the way.

Texas is an amazing state with such a diversity of climate, business enterprise, and even people that in passing from one part of Texas to another you often feel that you have entered into a different part of the country. The northern part of Texas is well watered and has timber. It also has hills and valleys. The great central plains nowadays are often flourishing agricultural domains with oil fields scattered all over them, while the southwestern part of Texas is desert. They have some fine roads and the gentle climate of middle and southern Texas permits them to build roads all the year round.

We stopped at Graham, Texas, on that day and spent the night at Moody's Hotel. The place was clean, but the only advantage was the price which was $3.00 per night. The next morning, December 7th, we got up early and drove to Breckenridge on U. S. Route 180 where we had breakfast. We had already decided, after visiting Mammoth Cave in Kentucky, that we would like to see the Carlsbad Caverns in New Mexico and the map showed us that U. S. Route No. 180 was the nearest way. We made good time on this day as the weather was sunny and the roads straight. We arrived at Hobbs, New Mexico, about two o'clock according to our watch, but we soon learned that we had crossed a time zone and it was only one o'clock. There is a large oil field around Hobbs, New Mexico, which extends for miles. This part of New Mexico is very much like neighboring Texas, in that the desert is being subdued and the flat land is being turned to agricultural purposes. However, great stretches of so called desert still remain. We arrived at Carlsbad, New Mexico, about three p.m. Mountain Standard Time and obtained a room at the La Caverna Hotel. This was the second hotel we had used on the trip. This hotel has a motel next to it and I was interested to learn that a room at the hotel cost $8.00 per night whereas a room at the motel run by the same people next door cost $10.00 per night. Actually, the service is superior at the hotel, but these differences in the prices of hotel rooms and motel rooms reflect the growing preference of the American tourists for motels.

We remembered in the course of the afternoon while approaching Carlsbad, New Mexico, that December 7, 1963, was the twenty-second anniversary of the Japanese attack on Pearl Harbor in 1941, and we regaled each other with our own reactions to the news of that momentous event. In talking to people throughout the years I have never found anyone who could not recall distinctly where he was and what he was doing when he learned that the Japanese had attacked Pearl Harbor.

Our purpose in going to Carlsbad was to visit the world

famed Carlsbad Caverns, but we soon discovered that distances in New Mexico are deceiving. The Carlsbad Caverns are not at Carlsbad, but are twenty some miles distant near a tourist town called White City. I will not go into a description of the Caverns as there is an abundance of literature about them, but will only mention certain incidents of our tour. The Caverns are located in a National Park and the Visitors Center to the park is located on the top of a mountain. My recollection is that they called this range the Guadulupe Mountains. It was extremely cold when we arrived there, probably between fifteen to twenty degrees above zero and there was considerable wind. Unlike Mammoth Cave there are elevators directly from the Visitors Center to the cave itself so that one is spared the effort of travelling up and down stairways and steep inclines. We took a tour of what they call the Big Room which is indeed impressive. Unlike Mammoth Cave there is apparently no underground river in the Carlsbad Caverns, but they have one feature at Carlsbad Caverns which is unique in my experience. There is a restaurant, or rather a sort of cafeteria, seven hundred fifty feet underground and we found here, in addition to the sale of prepared food, a number of stalls for the sale of various souvenirs. At one place I picked up a booklet about Jim White, a cowboy who first explored the caverns, and I did not know until later that the man who sold me the book was Jim White's son. White City nearby is named for Jim White.

We made the tour of the Big Room at the caverns on Sunday and at this time of the year not many tourists were present. There were only eleven in our party which was presided over by a uniformed guide, an employee of the National Park Service. He made a fine lecture on the geology of the caverns, a lecture no doubt that all guides have to learn by heart. Among other things he explained to us that water for the use of the Visitors Center and the employees of the park is piped in from Rattlesnake Springs, several miles distant. He also said that Rattlesnake Springs was a natural water hole once owned by the Apache Indians and that it had been the cause of a number of Indian wars in the past.

Leaving the caverns we returned to White City and then struck due South on U. S. Route No. 180 for El Paso, Texas. This is desert country and is very sparsely inhabited. At Pine Bluff, Texas, we stopped at a filling station and got a sandwich where the proprietor told us that he had been reared in an orphans home in Ohio and that he had run his desolate filling station and restaurant seven years, living by himself. He said that the railroad company many years ago had drilled a well for water nearby and that the water was used for washing and all other purposes except drinking and cooking. The water was brackish. The water that he used for drinking and cooking was brought in by truck from El Paso more than one hundred miles away.

Late that afternoon we reached the outskirts of El Paso. We had intended to spend the night there and go over to Juarez, Mexico, for a Mexican dinner, but we found that a new interstate road has been built between El Paso and Las Cruces, New Mexico, and we could save considerable time by going direct to this interstate road without passing through El Paso. We did so and reached Las Cruces, New Mexico, about forty miles North of El Paso about 5:30 p.m. where we spent the night at the Mission Inn, a very good motel which has a restaurant called the Pancake House. On this night for the first time we decided to see a movie. I do not recall the name of the moving picture, but it starred Debbie Reynolds. Again the night was cold, but I noticed that you do not see frozen ice on the ground in New Mexico and Arizona as you do in the East when the temperature is low. This is true no doubt because the earth is dry and there is no water in the soil to freeze.

We had been somewhat concerned throughout the trip about the possibility of running into December snows in the Rocky Mountains, and that is why we had taken the southern route through El Paso. I am told that it is only rarely that snow has ever fallen at El Paso. However, from Las Cruces to Tucson, Arizona, we passed through Lordsburg, New Mexico, Benson, Arizona, and Wilcox, Arizona over mountains of considerable height. I was told at Lordsburg that they usually have snow this time of year, but had had none so far this year. Throughout our entire trip with the exception of one morning in Richmond, Kentucky, we had beautiful sunshiny days and no hint of rain or snow although the nights were quite cold. Arriving at Tucson, Arizona, on December 9th we first hunted up a motel and were very comfortably lodged at a motel called the Aireview. One reason for going to Tucson was to visit my brother, Henry, and I called him soon after I got there. He came over with his daughter Carolyn and we had a Mexican dinner in a place called County Fair in Tucson. Later we saw his daughter Linda and spent a very pleasant evening.

The next day we drove on to Mesa, Arizona, arriving shortly after noon. My son Bill is the half owner of a mercantile business in Mesa called Lane's Market. He and his wife, Mabel, have a house, with a mortgage on it, at 1036 East 6th Place, Mesa. This is only a few blocks from Lane's Market, which is located at 1431 East Main Street, Mesa. U. S. Routes 60, 70, and 80 go by Lane's Market.

We had brought from Elizabeth some Christmas trimmings for Bob Davis and his daughter, Mary, sent by his mother, Mrs. Minnie Fought, who lives only two doors from my mother in Elizabeth. Bob lives in a trailer directly back of Lane's Market. One of the first things we did was to deliver the Christmas trimmings to Bob and his daughter.

This was the first Christmas that I had spent with my son for many years, so Mildred and I had taken along a good many presents. Since both Bill and Mabel work in the store, Mildred trimmed their house and installed a Christmas tree. They told us how unseasonably cold it was in Mesa, but the sun shone every day while we were there and the temperature at night was about 40 degrees Fahrenheit. In the day time it was 65 to 70 degrees, which they considered cold. Bill has a house with two palm trees in his yard and all the houses on his street have irrigation pipes to keep the grass green. Most of the grass was rather brown at this time of year. We met many of Bill's and Mabel's friends and spent most of our days loafing and sight-seeing. There is a beautiful Mormon Temple in Mesa, and Bill tells me that Mesa is a Mormon Town. The town council members there are all Mormons. He has a license to sell in his store packaged beer, wine and liquors and he said for a long time the Mormons would not permit such articles to be sold in Mesa as their religion forbids the use of intoxicants. Nevertheless, he said that a number of Mormons are his liquor customers. He knows them personally and when they come in the store he waits until a good opportunity presents itself before serving them. This is an interesting sidelight on the practice of Mormonism.

Since we had a full month's vacation we decided to make a little trip of our own and therefore on December 15th we left Mesa, passing through the City of Phoenix and travelled to Yuma, Arizona. Yuma is on the border between California and Arizona and is also near the Mexican border. To our surprise, the weather was cold in Yuma so we needed to turn up the heater in our room at the Thunderbird Motel. Yuma is supposed to be the hottest place in the United States, but the temperature got down to about 35 degrees that night. Having missed going over into Mexico at El Paso we decided to go to San Luiz which is about twenty miles from Yuma. There is a parking lot on the American side of the border, and the Town of San Luiz is partly in the United States and partly in Mexico. We parked and walked over, though I saw many American cars going through. Most of these cars were from California, and I learned a bit of interesting information on the liquor import laws. It appears that one is not allowed to carry liquor across the line from Mexico to California, but one can carry one gallon for each person from Mexico to Arizona. Those many California automobiles were bringing liquor back from Mexico to Arizona and then carrying the liquor into California because there is no law against transporting liquor between these states.

We had dinner at a Mexican place which was quite clean. The contrast between the United States and Mexico is obvious all along the border. There are fine irrigated farms, many of them cotton farms, on the United States side and you never see any beggars on the streets. As soon as you get into Mexico you realize that you are looking at poverty. The people in the stores are often shifty types and you see many old and decrepit automobiles. We bought a fifth of vodka and a fifth of Mexican gin at the recommendation of the proprietor of the Thunderbird Motel in Yuma. He said that Mexican vodka and gin were just as good as the Russian's manufacture and they are very cheap.

The next morning, December 16th, we visited the Territorial Prison at Yuma, part of which was hollowed out of solid rock and which had a reputation in the early days of being a veritable hell on earth. Part of the old prison is standing and they have an interesting museum there. We took some pictures. We then took Route 90 out of Yuma toward San Diego and this road runs practically along the Mexican border for a considerable distance. Not far from Yuma we came to a real sand desert without vegetation of any kind. This was listed on the maps as the Sand Hills, and we were told that when they have sand storms there the sand particles will ruin the paint finish of an automobile. Fortunately, there was no wind and all was peaceful. I should judge that this desert was only ten to fifteen miles wide where we crossed it. We thought originally of going to San Diego and to Tia Juana, Mexico, to see a horse race, but, when we found that we could follow the Imperial Valley into Los Angeles, we changed our itinerary and struck north for the Salton Sea. The Imperial Valley, which was once desert is one of the most fertile farming lands in the world. It is incredible what they have done to that country. The Salton Sea is a body of salt water 238 feet below sea level. The road we were on skirted a part of the sea on the eastern side and we stopped at one place to take pictures and to talk to some fishermen. From the information we received the fish that day were not biting.

Our route led us to Indio, California, and from thence we took the road toward Palm Desert and Palm Springs, the famous playground resort in the desert. This is date country and we bought some dates and tangerines at a roadside market. We passed through Palm Desert where ex-President Eisenhower has recently bought a home, but he was expected there momentarily and we found that we could not drive past his home. A good many movie stars have homes at Palm Desert and Palm Springs. We stayed that night at the St. Christopher Motel in Palm Springs, a clean little motel with the unexpected price of $6.00 per night for a double room.

The next morning we drove through Palm Springs itself and were properly impressed with the big name stores we saw in the business section. I do not know how big Palm Springs is, but I soon learned that in California pedestrians always have the right of way. If you happen to see someone crossing the street you must stop your automobile. They do not seem to have pedestrian traffic lights such as we have in the East.

An additional thing about Palm Springs was that it was very warm there in the valley, but we could look ahead and see a snow-capped mountain in front of us. One of the attractions at Palm Springs is a ski lift and many lovers of skiing go there. We soon got on Route 60 which in California is what is called a freeway. The most amazing thing about the California freeways is that they are all six or eight lanes wide and no one would think of driving at less than sixty miles per hour on the outside lane. As a matter of fact I found myself driving seventy and seventy-five miles an hour while other cars passed me up easily. They must have been making at least a hundred miles an hour. In spite of all the speed, we did not see a wreck anywhere.

We had determined to call on a cousin of Mildred's in Pasadena and left Route 60 at Arcadia, California, which is a suburb of Los Angeles. It was only a few miles from the turnoff to the city limits of Pasadena where we soon found a motel called the Pasadia Motel. This was the fanciest motel that we stayed in during the trip. It was built in the Spanish style with an inside court and a swimming pool, which we did not use. The rate was $10.00 per night.

As soon as we bathed and made ourselves presentable, Mildred called her cousin, Homer Johnston, and we made arrangements to call on them. It so happened that we were not far from his home and he gave us explicit directions how to get there. We spent most of the afternoon and evening with them and found them to be fine hospitable people. It seems that Homer Johnston is now a retired insurance man from Fort Wayne, Indiana. Their only daughter is an employee of one of the large department stores in Los Angeles, and, upon his retirement, the daughter persuaded him and his wife to move to California. They had a very nice small home on a residential street and I took the occasion to find out what real estate was worth there. He told me that he had bought the house and lot seven years ago for $14,500.00 cash, that he had been offered $22,000.00 for it only recently and that a real estate firm had appraised its value at $40,000.00. All this convinced me that they have a terrific real estate boom on in southern California and in Arizona and that the bubble will burst one of these days. Homer Johnston, his wife and his daughter took us out to dinner at Eatons, a famous restaurant near the Santa Anita race track. The food was fine and the walls of the dining room were covered with pictures of race horses. We also saw the famous Rose Bowl.

Leaving Pasadena the next morning we returned by the freeway to Indio, California, but, instead of going south through the Imperial Valley to Yuma, we now struck directly eastward on U. S. Route 60 for Blythe, California. On this leg of the trip we passed through a vast desert, much of which was covered with cactus and Joshua trees, but we saw no shifting sands here such as we had seen near Yuma. There are only two or three filling stations in a stretch of more than one hundred miles but we did note that an oil or gas pipeline runs across this desert near the road and every now and then we found compressing stations belonging to the pipeline company. Apparently, the employees of the company live in the desert because we saw one place which seemed to have a number of dwellings around it. We stopped at a filling station about half way across this desert and the woman there told us that she and her husband had run this place for seventeen years and had to haul their water from Indio. However, they had finally struck a water well at about seven hundred feet beneath the surface and now had their own water for the first time. She seemed to think that this would be a great boon to populating the desert since they now know that water can be found beneath the surface. Possibly, all this desert country will be transformed through irrigation if sufficient underground water can be obtained.

That night we stayed at the Sunset Motel in Blythe, California, near the Arizona border. Aside from Graham, Texas, this was the worst accommodation we had on the trip. There was a television set but there were no bed lamps and both my wife and I like to read in bed. We found that the only electric lamp in the place had a twenty five watt bulb in it, so my wife went out and bought a sixty-watt bulb and we used that.

The next day, December 18th, we followed Route 60 back to Mesa through a part of Arizona that we had not seen before. I remember in particular the towns of Salome and Wickenburg. Near Salome we saw a sign which said "Visit the Camel driver's grave". We found a monument to Hi Jolly who was, it appears, a Syrian camel driver who was brought to Arizona in 1856 in charge of a herd of camels to be used by the Army. His real name was Haidja Ali. The camels went wild in the desert, but Hi Jolly appears to have lived out the rest of his life there, dying, I think in 1910.

It was near Salome also that I saw a sign reading "540 acre ranch for sale". The ranch was all desert, the only vegetation being cactus and desert trees. To my surprise I found that it was being offered for sale at $250.00 an acre. That amounts to $135,040.00. I was told that they were preparing to irrigate that section and, that after the brush and cactus were bulldozed off, the land would be worth $1,000.00 an acre as they can raise four crops a year in Arizona. I did not wish to become an Arizona farmer and passed on. This is another example, in my opinion of inflated real estate prices. I am going to venture the prediction that one of these days that same property can be bought for one-tenth of what it is selling for now. We arrived back in Mesa about 3 o'clock in the afternoon of December 18th. On this occasion we passed another time zone, as the time changes at the California-Arizona border.

We had gone to Arizona originally in order to spend Christmas with Bill and Mabel and we now spent a week preparing for Christmas and enjoying ourselves. Unfortunately, Bill and Mabel were both extremely busy in the store. They were having difficulty about clerks and we tried not to make them any extra trouble. We found that Mabel gets up about 5 o'clock every morning and opens the store about 6 o'clock. Bill usually got up about 8:30 and had breakfast with us. He then went down to the store, and since they were short of help he stayed there until about one o'clock the next morning, while Mabel tried to leave about 7 o'clock in the evening. They have the system devised for efficiency as Mabel likes to get up early and Bill likes to sleep late.

We were surprised at the business they do in the small store they have. They sell groceries, soft drinks, beer, and packaged wine and liquors. They sell for cash and ordinarily take in from seven hundred to one thousand dollars per day. Since many of the sales are small items this means waiting on a lot of customers. The day before Christmas they took in nearly $1,500.00.

On Christmas Eve we had the tree ready and all the presents spread out beneath it. Because they were so busy at the store Mabel had remained there until one o'clock even though she had been working since six o'clock the previous morning. We thought they both should go to bed, but they insisted on opening the presents and we had a very delightful family party. The next morning Mabel got up at 5 o'clock and opened the store. I sometimes wonder how she and Bill stand the pace.

Bibliography

BIBLIOGRAPHY

Books

Notes on the Settlement and Indian Wars by Joseph Doddridge, published 1824.

Chronicles of Border Warfare, by Alexander Scott Withers, published 1831.

The Tithables (tax lists) of Harrison County, Virginia, 1784-1810, unpublished.

Memoirs of William Wirt, by John P. Kennedy, published 1849.

Law and Chancery Records, Wirt County Circuit Court, 1848-1965, unpublished.

Deeds, Estate, Land Books, and Marriage Records, Wirt County Court, 1848-1965, unpublished.

Voters Registration Records, Wirt County Court, 1960-1964, unpublished.

Constitution and Statutes, Restored Government of Virginia, 1861-1863, and same for State of West Virginia, 1863-1866, published by the State of West Virginia in 1866.

Memoirs of Hiram Pribble, 1884, (unpublished).

The Lees of Virginia, by Burton J. Hendrick, published by Little, Brown and Company, 1944.

The Randolphs, by H. J. Eckenrode, published by the Bobbs-Merrill Company, 1946.

George Washington in the Ohio Valley, containing parts of Washington's Journals and the Journal of Christopher Gist, edited by Hugh Cleland, University of Pittsburgh Press, 1955.

A History of Education in West Virginia, by Charles H. Ambler, published by Standard Publishing Company, 1951.

The Appalachian Frontier, by John Anthony Caruso, published by Bobbs-Merrill Company, 1959.

The West Virginia Blue Book, 1964.

History of Wood County, by Donald F. Black, unpublished.

Manuscripts

"The History of the County Unit in West Virginia," by Roy C. Woods, *West Virginia History,* October, 1957.

"General George Washington's Last Trip Across the Allegheny Tableland, 1784," by C. W. Beerbower, *West Virginia History,* April, 1958.

"George Washington in West Virginia," by Leona Given Brown, *West Virginia History,* October, 1958.

"The Evolution of the Common School in West Virginia," by Roy C. Woods, *West Virginia History,* July, 1959.

"Slavery in Present West Virginia in 1860," by Barbara Louise Emmerth, *West Virginia History,* July, 1960.

"Conflict and Error in the History of Oil," by Louis Reed, *West Virginia History,* October, 1963.

"First Oil Lease South of the Mason-Dixon Line," by Louis Reed, *West Virginia History*, January, 1964.

"Footnote to Judge Gideon Draper Camden," by Louis Reed, *West Virginia History*, April, 1965.

INDEX

Allman, E. W. (Jake), 73, 158
Altech Division of Financial Development and Research Corporation, 95
Ambler, Dr. Charles H., 121
American Indian Ancestry, 16
Amos, Kendall, 104, 108, 158
Andrick, E. C., 94
Andrick, Preston, 105
Archer, Lewis D., 98

Baldwin, Ruth, Introduction, xiv
Batten, William M., 69
Bethany College, 126
Beauchamp, Elizabeth, Introduction, xii
Beulah Hill Community, 71
Bill's Tavern, 98
Bing, Dr. Lois, 70
Birth Control, 217, 218
Black, Dr. Amos H., 69
Black, Amos Eckert, 42
Black, Donald F., Judge, 65, 69, 70, 104
Black, Edward V., Introduction, xii
Black, Mary, 96
Black, Paul E., 96
Black, Robert B., 98, 109, 158
Blair, Denzil, 97
Boggs, Chester, 97
Bond, John C., 160
Buck, Pearl S., 65
Bughunters, The, 161
Burning Springs, 2, 4
Busch, Noble, 99

Cabot Corporation, 99
Cain, Albert, 105, 118
Cale, Clyde, 105
Callison, W. H., 108
Caltrider, Ralph, 97
Camden, Gideon Draper, 144
Campbell, Alexander, 125
Carter, Mary Roberts, 69
Caruso, John Anthony—*The Appalachian Frontier*, 17
Casual Post, The, 96
Chambers, E. C., 94, 96
Chambers Furniture Store, 96
Chancery Record Books, 175
Chesapeake and Potomac Telephone Co., 99
Cheuvront, Joe, 97, 158
China Store, The, 96
Chronicles of Border Warfare by Alexander Withers, Introduction, xiii, 17
Cline, Charles A., Sr., 105, 117, 118
Cline, Charles A., Jr., 97
Cline, Eloise, 118
Cline, Heraldy, 98
Clinton, Carl, 97
Common Schools, 127
Cook, Lloyd C., 95
Coplin, R. W., 94, 98
Costly, Ronald, 51
Counties, Data on West Virginia, 225-227
County Superintendent of Schools, 135, 136
Cunningham, Mrs. Thomas (Phoebe), Introduction, xiii
Curry, C. D., 95
Curry Lumber Company, 95

Dailey, Walter, 105, 117
Dairy Queen, The, 96
Daugherty, Duncan, 69
Davis, Emory N., 108
Davisson, Sue, 96,
Davisson, William Gene, 94
Deem, J. Frank, 158
Department of Public Assistance, 82
Dick's Market, 96
Disciples of Christ, 125
Divorce Laws, 173
Dovener, Blackburn, 68

Eberhart, Ethel, 96
Eisenhower, Dwight D., 160
Elizabeth Pharmacy, The, 96
Elizabeth, Town of, Introduction, xii, 3, 115, 243-248
Elizabeth Town Council, 100, 114-119
Ellison, Ruth, 139
Elson Readers, 2, 129

Families, Beulah Hill Community, 73-77
Family Names, 17-30
Farmhouses and farms, 4-8
Farm Implements, 5
Farm Social Life, 8-9
Finch, Rev. K. D., 98
Flesher, Charles, 96
Flower fund, 153-155
Foley, Rev. Harry C., 98

Fought, A. F., 99
Fought, Gordon, 69
Founding Fathers, 183
French Creek Community, 68
Frontiersmen, English, 17-30
Frontiersmen, French, 17-30
Frontiersmen, German, 17-30
Frontiersmen, Scotch-Irish, 17-30
Full, Hubert, 105

George, Carl, 95, 96
Goodwin, Maggie, 97
Goodwin's Store, 96
Grand Army of the Republic, Major Joe Steele Post, 3
Griffith, Holly, 165-166
Grudier, Bill, 163

Hale, John, 105
Hamrick, John, 98
Hardway, Brooks, 158
Hatfield family, 155
Henthorne, Earl, 97
Hickman, Donald, 105
High School Principals, 135
Horse and Buggy Era, 8
Hudson, June, 97, 104, 109, 158
Huffman, Faustine, 94, 98, 158
Huffman Transport Company, 98
Hutchinson, John, 105

Jackson, Andrew, 150
Jackson, General T. J. (Stonewall), 65
Jailhouse Stories, 167
Johnston, Mildred B., Introduction, xv, 43
Jones, James R., 158

Kidd, Paul H., 158
Kidwell, Charley, 98
Kidwell, Irvin, 163
Kreider, Rev. Maynard, 98
Ku Klux Klan, 161

LaDeaux, Mae, 99
Lee, Harley H., 105, 117
Lee, Howard B., 68
Lee, J. Frank, 97
Lee, Richard, 36, 37
Lewis, Father Clifford M., 186
Lever Brothers, 155
Literary Societies, 9
Litton Electronics Company, 96
Lockhart, Donald F., 105
Lockhart, Doral, 98
Lockhart, Harry, 98
Lowe, Bernard, 97
Lynch, Gay R., 158

Magic, Science and Religion, 181
Malinowski, Bronislaw, 181
Marcum, Glen, 97
Marshall University, 125
McClung, Foster, 105
McCray, Harry, 97
McFee, Elmer, 97
McFee, William, 97
McGuffey Readers, 2, 129
Meredith, Phil, 64
Milhoan, Robert, 64
Model T Ford Automobiles, 9
Monongahela West Penn Power Company, 99
Morehead, Florence, 108
Morgan, Beverly, 96
Morgan, Melva, 96
Morgan, Lowell, 95
Munday, Frank, 105, 118
Myths, Indian Ancestry, 16
Myths, Three Brothers, 15

Oswald, Lee Harvey, 171, 172

Patton, General George S., 65
Pierpont, Francis H., 145
Plantation Schools, 121, 122
Play Parties, 57, 62
Pomroy, Don, 97
Poor Schools, 122
Powell, C. D., 104, 158
Pribble, Hiram, 47, 122
Prominent Contemporaries, 206, 208

Rathbone, M. J., 69
Ravensmetal, Inc., 95
Red Men, 161
Reed, Amaziah, Introduction, xiii, 43, 125
Reed, George William, 43
Reed, Joel, 44
Reed, John, 43
Reed, Malinda Jane Keck, 43, 125
Reed, William, 98
Reed, William Baldwin, Introduction, xv, 42
Reed, William Peter, 43
Religions, Toleration, 182-183
Rendezvous at Fifty, a novel, 13
Revercomb, Chapman, Introduction, xv, 99
Revival Meetings, 8-9
Reynolds Bus Company, 99
Rice, A. A., 96
Righter, Harry L., 94
Roberts, Denver, 94

Roberts, Dorothy, 69
Roberts, George W., 89
Roberts, Glen W., 70, 95
Roberts, Dr. Hazel, 70
Roberts, Herbert, 89
Roberts Hereford Farms, 70, 95
Roberts, James H., 95
Roberts, Leslie V., 95
Roberts, Louise, 130-131
Roberts Oil and Gas Company, 95
Roberts, Roger E., 94, 95
Roberts Store, 95
Roberts, Walter M., 95
Robinson, French, 69
Robinson, George, 105
Robinson's Trucking Company, 96, 97
Roosevelt, Franklin D., 148
Ruby, Jack, 172
Rule Dockets, 175
Russ, John, 9

Salt wells, 127
Scites, Mr. and Mrs. O. F., 99
Scott, R. M., 96
Sees, Jonas, 163
Senior Citizens, 211-218
Shears, Larry, 96
Sheppard, June, 96
Sheppard, Sam, 163
Shimer, Harley, 99
Simonton, Zelma, 96
Sims, B. B., 94
Sims, B. B., Jr., 95
Sims, Edgar B., 68
Sims and George Store, 95
Smith, Edna, 97
Smith, Howard, 95
Smith, Olive Hays, 105
Snider, Virgil, 105, 114
Snyder, Dr. Stark W., 98
Stanley, Ruth, 109
Stanley, W. A., 96
State Liquor Store, 96
State Road Commission, 153
Steed, Henry, 122
Steele, Major Joe, 3
Steele, Reverend Jonathan, 3
Stewart, Dr. D. F., 161
Sturm, Eloise, 94, 95
Sturm, Fred, 95
Sturm Insurance Agency, 95
Subscription Schools, 123
Summers, George W., 102
Sydenstricker family, 65

Thorn, Richard, 96
Thorne, A. W. and Company Store, 96
Thorne, J. Cecil, 96
Tithables, Tax lists of Harrison County, Virginia, 17
Trobrianders, 182

Underground Railway, 161

Van Horn, Rev. Gaylord, 98
Villers, Earl, 105, 117
Villers Nursing Home, 97
Virtue, Reverend Andrew, 42
Virtue, John, 1
Virtue, Mary, 42, 126
Voters Registration, 158

Warren Report, 172
Washington, George, Journal of, 17
Water witches, 195
Watson, Rex, 97
Welch, Mary Jane, 65
West, Howard, 69
West Liberty Seminary, 126
West Virginia University, 125, 130
Western Auto Sales, 96
Williams, Clay, 70, 165
Wilson, Woodrow, 96
Wirt, William, Introduction, xi
Wirt County Bank, 89, 94
Wirt County Board of Education, 100, 110-114, 237-241
Wirt County Churches, 187-194
Wirt County Court, 100, 105-110, 231-233
Wirt County Industries, Inc., 94
Wirt County Journal, The, 96
Wirt County,
  population, 1
  economics, 81-100
  County budget, 101 ff
  well known sons and daughters of, 68-70
Wiseman, Russell, 109
Woodyard, Dora Bee, Library, 130-131
Woodyard, Ronald B., 69, 131
Woofter, Dr. Cary, 62
World War I, 10